MIGHTY

vision for the supernatural normal Christian life

MIGHTY

Vision for the supernatural normal Christian life

First edition: September 12, 2021

Editor: Dan Worley
Consultants: Cynthia Leal Massey, John David Ramirez,
Darda Burkhart, Stephanie C. Del Bosco

Cover Design: God & Dan Worley
Layout: Dan Worley

Front cover image credit: NASA, ESA, and the Hubble Heritage
(STScI/AURA)-ESA/Hubble Collaboration

Deepest thanks to all who contributed to this book
in story and in prayer.

ISBN
978-1-887400-63-3 (paperback)
978-1-887400-64-0 (kindle)

Earthen Vessel Productions
www.earthen.com

Contents

for Tina
and Hedy

1

The Love Bomb

Darren was nervous as he followed the young Indian man on the narrow dirt path. He focused his video camera on the back of the one he called Ravi and confessed softly that he really didn't want to be there. In fact, he was so frightened he thought he might throw up. Why? They were going to the house of the most powerful witch doctor in India. Recently a TV news program had aired a report about him. He had cursed a Christian pastor and, two or three days later, the pastor and his wife were found dead on the ground.

Darren really didn't want to be anywhere near the witch doctor's house. When he informed his prayer community about the proposed visit, those back home and in Ravi's church immediately began praying. They advised against it, but when Ravi called to say the Lord had told him that morning to go there, Darren knew not to refuse. He was making a documentary on the power of God, and God sent him to record what He would do in that remote, demon-infested place.

Ravi was only seventeen when he decided life was just too difficult and began making plans to kill himself. He had purchased the rat poison and was getting ready to do the deed when Jesus spoke to him in an audible voice and revealed Himself to him. Since then, every morning at 4:00 a.m., the God of the Universe whom Ravi calls Daddy, wakes him up and gives him his marching orders for the day. More than ten years after that first surprising encounter, Ravi was well-practiced in hearing the voice of God. Now he stood before the door of the witch doctor's house and asked to talk with him. This was not unusual. People came from all over India to ask the witch doctor questions, giving him handsome offerings in exchange for his wisdom and the power he would dispatch against their enemies on their behalf. He usually came out and met with them in his front yard, but not this time. The door was shut tight. Inside the house a man's voice told Ravi to go away. Ravi said he wanted to come in. The man said no. The door was locked, and the man whom hundreds came to see refused to come out. "He's scared to death," Ravi said. "He's obviously afraid of us now." Ravi tried to tell him about Jesus, but the man refused to listen. Finally Ravi stepped to the side and prayed, "Father, I come to You in Jesus' name. I come to Your place, Daddy. And this is Your place. We take over. We take over this place, Daddy, and ask this would be a famous place for You. Release Your Holy Spirit right now."

From inside the house, the witch doctor was saying, "I cannot see. Go." Then the witch doctor's wife came out and said, "This is the time we go into the forest and do sacrifices there. We sacrifice animals and do other sacrifices there." She said the police do not allow other people to go into the forest. "Even the animals listen to us," she said. "We are very powerful people. More powerful than anyone here. No one has come against us until today. So we're very confused now." She was bragging even in this confusion, a half-smile on her face. Ravi knew about those sacrifices. Some of them were human babies. He said everybody knew that was why the witch doctor had so much power.

When the witch doctor's wife went back into the house, Ravi prayed, "Father, release Your Spirit right now and fill this place with Your completeness. And I thank You for who You are in this place, Daddy."

Six months later, Ravi happened to be in the states and gave Darren an update.

Right after their visit, the witch doctor disappeared and nobody knew where he was. His wife tried to continue his work, but without demonic presence, nothing happened.

People stopped showing up with questions and offerings, and eventually the witch doctor's wife also disappeared.

We were stunned. Wow! Who would have guessed? "He love bombed him," Debra said. "Ravi prayed, Jesus love bombed the witch doctor, and the whole house was so full of the presence of God that all the demons fled, never to return."

Debra, Carol, and I were watching Darren Wilson's documentary, *Father of Light.* Carol had lots of inspiring documentaries and we three gals met as often as we could to watch them, revel in the wonders of our miracle-working God, and pray together for whatever was on our hearts. Often there was something we had not known before—something others did that showed us different ways to pray. Some people get together and trade recipes in combinations of flavors new to them. For Carol, Debra, and me, it is sort of like that with prayer. Love bomb. What a concept! It never occurred to us we could do that. And then, of course, we had to try it out. But first, a word from our Sponsor: "The LORD thy God in the midst of thee is mighty; he will save, he will rejoice over thee with joy; he will rest in his love, he will joy over thee with singing." (Zeph 3:17 KJV)

First we have to know our God is mighty. Then we harmonize our hearts with His song.

Jesus said if we ask in His name it will be done that the Father will be glorified. What does it mean to "ask in His name"? For the Hebrews, a name represented the essence of the character of the person. It's praying in harmony with His character, will, and ways. Here's how it looks in the Amplified Bible: "And I will do [I Myself will grant] whatever you ask in My Name [as presenting all that I AM], so that the Father may be glorified and extolled in (through) the Son." (John 14:13 AMPC) When we pray in the name "Jesus," we are operating on His behalf, asking what He would ask. If we are in full alignment with His character, we have His permission to request that action be taken in the power and authority of the One who defeated the devil, death, hell, and the grave. Jesus told His disciples, "All authority has been given to Me in heaven and on earth." (Matt 28:18) That authority inhabits those prayers, which the Holy Spirit then empowers. With this in mind, when we get ready to pray, it's helpful to ask ourselves, "Would Jesus agree to this prayer? Is this harmonious with His character? Is it something He wants to happen? Is this something that will bring glory to Father God?" If it is, He said He'll do it.

Next we need to know we're not helpless. We're not confined to what we can reason with our puny human minds. We are citizens of the Kingdom of God, and we operate from a different reality, one that is, by nature, supernatural. Webster's Dictionary says, "supernatural" means "of a manifestation or event attributed to some force beyond scientific understanding or the laws of nature." For that kind of provision, try this on for size: "The weapons of our warfare are not flesh and blood (carnal) but mighty through God for the pulling down of strongholds, casting down imaginations and every high and lofty thing that exalts itself against the knowledge of God." (2 Corinthians 10:4, 5)

Let's take a look at this truth. We have weapons for the war. God did not leave His Bride helpless, victimized and harassed by emotionally toxic environments, hostile humans, demons, and scary unknowns—a weak, worried, wimpy presence in the world. We have weapons and they're mighty. What are those weapons? Ephesians 6 mentions seven pieces of the armor of God, but I felt, for this book, God wanted me to focus on just two. One is the Word of God. Talk about mighty! When the devil tempted Jesus in the wilderness, our Lord used the sword-Word to defeat him every time. The sword of the Spirit, which is the Word of God, has the power and authority that backs up those written words spoken by His children to release His will on Earth.

A word about our words. I really don't think we take this seriously enough. Scripture says, "Bless those who curse you." "Bless and curse not." It says, "Overcome evil with good." Jesus said we have the power and authority to do what He did and more. He stilled storms. He cast out demons. He healed the sick and raised the dead. He gave new understanding of the heart of Father God. He gave comfort, encouragement, hope, peace, and love in many words and forms. He has charged us to do the same. But here's the part I don't think we take seriously enough. We can't bless and curse, spewing bad water and then expecting living water to flow from the same fountain. When 1 John says to purify ourselves just as He is pure, this is one of the main ways. Why? Because words are so powerful. Proverbs says they can be like swords or arrows. They can even break bones. And they can heal. We have to decide where we're going to stand. Do we want to be on the Lord's side or be contributing to the poisonous atmosphere of the enemy?

While I was praying this morning, I realized how terrible it would be not to have these weapons. The Lord reminded me the only reason we have them is the cross. As a young Christian, I got tired of songs about the cross, the blood, the focus on that terrible sacrifice that had to be done because we were so wretched and bad. I wanted to sing about the good stuff. This morning the Lord said the cross *is* the good stuff. It enables us to keep our bearings and something more. He reminded me, when their computer system was shut down, the Apollo 13 astronauts needed to set their course using one fixed point in space. As they did their burn, they kept Earth in their window, their chosen fixed point, so they could get back on course and make it home. When we keep our eyes on the cross, we keep the Main Thing the main thing. Everything we have is because of what Jesus did for us on the cross. That's not so we must always feel indebted and humiliated. Jesus told me, "I didn't do it so you'd owe Me; I did it because I love you." When the cross is always before us, everything we encounter in the day is seated in the context of our salvation. It's our fixed point in space. It shows us where we are and where we're going. We remember we are loved and nothing can separate us from Him, neither things present nor things to come.

The other weapon is prayer. Prayer tends to be ignored, underrated, or misunderstood by a whole bunch of Christians. What is it, and why do we need to do it? Since God already knows our needs, why should we say anything? Since He knows our needs before we ask, why should we ask? Why would Jesus say to keep on asking, knocking, seeking? I'll be talking a lot about prayer later, but the first purpose for prayer is the most important one. It's about connecting with God. That was the first relationship between human and God mentioned in the Bible. God wanted a partnership with loving people expanding the Paradise of Earth in their own creative ways. Walking with the Lord in the cool of the day, there would be sharing of the most amazing things Creator would reveal to beings who, having been made in His image, were capable of comprehending the deep things of God.

The first and most special purpose of prayer is communication with Father God. When I was a Taoist, I didn't know there even *was* a God, much less a personal one who would hear me and respond to me. Prayer is supernatural. It's communication with the Lord of the Universe, Almighty God, Creator of everything, and then it's partnering with Him to bring His will to Earth. He gave us the privilege of asking Him to intervene in human affairs, changing lives, shifting spiritual terrain, affecting history and even the course of the celestial war.

Why Don't We Pray?

Prayer is one of our most powerful weapons. So why don't we use it? Things keep getting stranger and more distorted, yet I find so many of the Christians I know complaining, having fits of fury in their frustrations, and berating whoever seems to be creating the chaos. Like the children of Israel in the Wilderness, they complain to humans, blaming them for their lacks and limitations. Even with the visual evidence of the presence of God in a pillar of cloud before them every day and the pillar of fire guarding and warming them at night, it didn't occur to the Israelites to cry out to God. And often we don't think of it either.

When I asked my friend Dan why he thought people don't pray, he said, "They feel too dirty. They think they have to clean up first. Or they think they'll be told what to do, or will have to answer for things they've done. Or they don't want to be told life-changing things. Let's face it, we're pretty comfortable in our sin. If I hear anything too radical, I go, 'No, that's not You.'"

Here are a few others I want to add to Dan's list. First, there are so many enticements in the world. It's easier to play a video game or watch TV than read a book, and the less you read, the less you want to. Those exciting, entertaining attractions reduce our appetite for both prayer and Bible reading. Too much like work.

Another has to do with comfort level. Reminds me of when I'd be left at my grandma's house for the summer. She didn't speak English and I knew only a few words in our dialect. In fact, when I tried my halting *Sam Yup*, I always managed to offend her. And she was violent. She murdered chickens and left them bleeding in the sink. I really didn't want to commune with her. I think God scares people. What if they say something offensive? He's God Almighty. How can they speak His language?

Another reason is it's easier to talk to a human being than a spirit one. When the trouble comes, we run to a human—a spouse or a friend or a spiritual leader. They get the multitudes of details and they'd give counsel and consolation. When we finally take it to God, He gets the short version. There's a principle in the Bible of First Fruits. Whoever gets the honor of receiving the First Fruits is the one we bond with most. Don't get me wrong. I love my human friends and family, and the spiritually mature Christians in my life, but when the horror is upon me and urgency is great, that's when I need to take it to my Savior God, pour out my heart, and then listen and receive His counsel. It's always better than what a human can supply. It strengthens my relationship with Him. Later, the humans get the short version, which is probably a good thing.

Sometimes we simply don't know what to say. That's when we can let the Holy Spirit help us out. Scripture says when we don't know what to pray, He will do it for us. "Likewise the Spirit also helps in our weaknesses. For we do not know what we should pray for as we ought, but the Spirit Himself makes intercession for us with groanings which cannot be uttered. Now He who searches the hearts knows what the mind of the Spirit is, because He makes intercession for the saints according to the will of God." (Romans 8:26, 27 NKJV) We have a hotline to heaven, and the prayers will always be answered with action from on high because the Holy Spirit knows what to ask, and it's always in perfect alignment with the will of God for the situation.

A few days ago, I heard the family of a friend was struck with an unspeakable tragedy. I felt moved to pray but the horror was so immense I didn't know what to say. I waited before the Lord and He breathed into my voice groanings and sobbings. It was Spirit prayer—tearless weeping that I knew was Him coming alongside and taking some of the load off them so they could make it through the catastrophe.

Sadly, prayer tends to be the last resort in times of trouble—what people do when all else fails. My son John and his wife Shelly have been going through one of the worst times in their lives. A few months ago he told me, "I've always thought of prayer as good wishes. It's something Christians say to each other. 'I'll pray for you.' It's like 'Have a nice day.' It's a nice, polite thing to say but it doesn't mean a great deal. Are you actually planning to pray for me? Nah. Just being polite.

"During this incredibly difficult season of my life, I have seen God's faithful and loving answers to prayer over and over. I now believe that praying is actually the most powerful thing you can do for someone. If I tell someone 'I'll pray for you,' I actually will pray for them."

One day early in the first weeks of John's hard times, he called me. "Mom, remember that Scripture about renewing your strength? You know, the one with eagle's wings?"

"Yes," I said. "'They that wait upon the Lord shall renew their strength.' Is that the one you mean?"

"That's the one," he said brightly. He paused, then added with tears in his voice. "It works."

John grew up in the church, attended a Christian school, and then Bethany Bible College. He has heard a thousand sermons, memorized Scripture and read the whole Bible more than once. He was a nice Christian man who didn't think of prayer as anything particularly special or powerful. But in his time of greatest need he cried out to God with His Word, and God poured upon His grieving son a wealth of strength that was undoubtedly supernatural. It was the start of a journey discovering the power of prayer in dealing with the difficulties of life, connecting with the One who knows what to do about it all. It was a Romans 8:28 moment, God working all those troubling, distressing things together for John's good, because John loves Him and now wants, more and more, to live for Him. God knows how to transform the worst to the best, and it often starts with prayer, a supernatural connection extending from Earth into the heavenlies where the Father of Eternities waits to hear what His child will say.

Working on this section, I sent the story to John to check for accuracy. He's busy right now packing to move because his landlords sent him an eviction notice six weeks ago. It's illegal because of the COVID-19 restrictions, but John asked the Lord and felt he was not to contend for his rights. He, and we who pray for him, all felt God wanted him to be in a different place, one not an hour and fifteen minutes from work. Trouble is, because of the housing shortage, it's hard to find an available place. We're getting down to the wire, but God understands John's needs and knows all about deadlines. God's timing is perfect. He's never late. He's never early either. Anyway, I sent the piece to John to check and he emailed back right away.

"This sounds good to me. I don't know if you want to mention the odd joy that I felt after waiting on God that morning. I was just so worn out. God met me while I waited on Him and bore me up on wings like eagles. I have prayed that same prayer other times and God always meets me. That first time was special though. I think He did it in a way that even I couldn't miss.

"Funny, I ran into a friend at Fred Meyer today. She's very nice and always asks about Shelly and tells me she's praying for us. Talking about my upcoming move she said all she can do is pray which is a little something. I said, 'It's not little at all. It's the best thing you can do.' She said, 'Well, it gives you a little hope anyway.' I was stunned speechless. She belittled prayer like it was an insignificant act that we only do to make people feel better. The thing is, I was right there 8 months ago. I certainly have learned about the power of prayer."

If I look at my son's troubles with my mom-eyes, I would be in despair. We're in a COVID-19 crisis with housing availability at one percent and people hunkering down, trying to hang onto what they have. It looks like the children of Israel hemmed in by mountains on one side, chariots of Pharaoh on the other, and the Red Sea before them. Do I say, "All I can do is pray"? Or do I say, "I get to pray! God, glorify Yourself. People are watching. Let them see there is one true God, and You are never at a loss no matter how impossible things look. Show Yourself mighty on John's behalf!! You are Yahweh, the I AM God. Nothing is too difficult for You. Miracles are Your specialty!"

As John is discovering, prayer is one of the best things we can do—for ourselves and for one another. It's a weapon designated very specifically for the spiritual war. It can be dispatched in a multitude of astonishing ways, one of which is the love bomb. Carol, Debra, and I pondered that for a moment. Might as well try it out. Doesn't hurt to experiment. Debra had a neighbor who was hostile if anyone asked him to turn down the very loud music late at night when he had his friends over for parties. Talking to him face to face only made things worse, so we decided to love bomb him. We asked the Lord to fill his house with the peace of Jesus, and to help him feel how deeply and completely he is loved by the One who created him for wonderful and significant destiny. Not many days after, the neighbor's friends gathered for another party, but this time the music did not disturb the neighborhood. Wow! We were surprised, but pleased. It works!

Since then, we have love bombed other places. Most recently we asked the Lord to drop one on the troubled community where another of our dear friends lives. When I asked her if she noticed anything she sent this email: "Yes, we can definitely tell that you are praying! Today I got up feeling so tired but as the day wore on, I started to feel lighter and more energetic, and more hopeful."

We have been love bombing cranky workplaces, hospitals where friends are sick or having surgeries, a minimum-security prison where a friend is incarcerated, and our neighborhoods and counties. We ask Jesus to fill the places with His presence, the blessing of His peace, the awareness that there is a transcendent reality ruled by Almighty God, Creator of heaven and earth, the God today's sophisticated modern society has declared non-existent, cruel, or inconsequential.

When I told my son, John, I felt a tiny bit guilty for asking God to release blessing on unsuspecting people, he replied that Wiccans don't have any problem cursing and releasing bad things on others. They do it because they don't like them or they have been offended by them and they do their things to make the person uncomfortable or worse. But we're not doing witchcraft. We don't do it out of malice or to control them; we do it to free them.

I will always be grateful to the Gideons who prayed for "the little Chinese girl—that she might see what she's dealing with." At the time, I was in training to be a psychic healer, a road that would have led me to hell. I am so glad they prayed for me, even though God answered by letting me be attacked by the demons I was unaware were behind the new knowledge and power I was cultivating with their help. At the time, I didn't believe in demons, but for two nights in a row, I got a clear view of what the dark side is really like, and how they flee in a hurry when Jesus shows up. So I love praying for people in the occult because I was one of them and I'm so glad somebody prayed for me. I'm so grateful to belong to Jesus instead. I pray they will see what they're dealing with, who Jesus really is, and feel His call to a wondrous loving relationship with Him, the Lord of the Universe.

Jesus said to do to others what you want them to do to you. Who wouldn't want a sudden explosion of the lavish love of God, an overwhelming embrace of acceptance and belonging? What a relief to feel the peace of God that passes all understanding that guards their hearts and minds from chaos and confusion! How wonderful to be bathed in the perfect love that destroys all torment and casts out all fear!

Wherever we are, we can ask Jesus to love bomb the place and everyone in it—irritated customers, overworked clerks, jaded prison guards, hostile neighbors, and schools where bullies and spiritual darkness dominate places that are meant to encourage children to learn and interact in security and safety. It's so much fun! Does this sound frivolous? It's not. The presence of God always changes things. Psalm 16 says in His presence is fullness of joy. Wherever we are, God is there, mighty in our midst, rejoicing and singing over us with joy. Jesus said He is the Light and we are the light of the world. We are His representatives on Earth. Personally, I think Earth could use some joy. Some peace. Some love. Hence, the requests to Jesus to love bomb any place I see in need of an explosion of the wondrous love of God.

We have no idea how much power we have in Jesus. Ravi, Darren, and the community of faith prayed and the witch doctor and his wife left. No more babies murdered in the woods. No more curses giving demons legal access to harass and incapacitate others. No more terror, worry, or dread. Defilement and dark power was gone from the area because Jesus filled it up with His Divine presence and Father God was glorified.

The eyes of the Lord go to and fro looking over all the earth seeking those whose hearts are completely His to show Himself strong on their behalf. (2 Chronicles 16:9)

2

The Supernatural

Supernatural. What does that mean? The Dashboard dictionary on my Mac says it's beyond or above what is natural, and includes ghosts. To many people today, "supernatural" means weird, creepy, spooky, childhood fears—the Boogieman hiding in your closet. Supernatural is nothing friendly or transcendent; it's typical of the terrifying unknown realms, some real and some imagined—ghosts, ghouls, zombies, vampires, werewolves… Then again, there are those traditionally attractive peeks into the mysterious unknown realms—ouija boards, tarot cards, fortune tellers, astrology, magic ("white" or "black"). I know some very decent, respectable women who dabble in all of those things and have gone to seances as well. They think it's fun, a titillating flirtation with secret things hidden in the dark. Make no mistake. There's power in the dark side and it's very seductive. I know some smart people, intellectual, educated professionals who have gone whole-heartedly into witchcraft or Satanism. They have no problem believing they can curse their enemies and put spells on them, all through the powers of demons. They see nothing special in Christianity. Not much supernatural going on here. Certainly nothing powerful or miraculous.

Two centuries ago, David Hume said miracles are impossible because they violate natural laws. In his day, and ever since, there has been an emphasis on empirical evidence. If it can't be measured or understood by logic and human reasoning, it doesn't exist. Mathematician John Lennox said this assumes we live in a closed system. A billiard ball rolling across the table doesn't suddenly begin to fly. That would violate natural laws. But if you pick up the ball, that doesn't violate any laws; it simply introduces a different energy, one from outside. We do not live in a closed universe, but one open to different dimensions and energies. We are not confined to survival of the fittest, life with no meaning, purpose, or significance, futile, finite—existence limited to the ephemeral, temporal world. There's More. A LOT More.

Still, most people don't believe there's anything outside of this present life. This kind of worldview results from scientific materialism based on the tenets of Darwinian evolution. Life exists in its complexity because of random mutation and natural selection, with no divine intelligence, causality, purpose, or design behind it. When you die, you cease to exist. There is no spirit or invisible realm beyond the tangible domain of matter and energy. There's no final judgment, no accountability to your Creator for the life He gave to you, or eternal destination. Problem is, you can believe that with every neuron in your brain and it still doesn't make it true. I had a patient who lived a wild lifestyle and, to his shock, after he died he found himself not only alive, he was also in hell. I won't repeat what he described to me, just that he thought to cry out to God, came back into his body, and is living a very different life, one he likes much better than the one before.

Sadly, there are Christians who also don't believe in the supernatural. A survey showed that 58% of Americans who regularly attend a Christian church say there is no such thing as the Holy Spirit. That's just a symbol of the Lord's presence. And 57% say there's no such thing as the devil. That's just a symbol of evil. Really? Not believing in demons is like not believing in viruses. You may not see them, but their effects can be deadly. Worse yet, not believing in the Holy Spirit is a terrible loss of what Jesus came to provide for you. We need to know what we're really dealing with in our lifetime on Earth. Scripture says we live in the middle of a war between supernatural powers, and we play a role in the final outcome, surprising as that may be.

In this book, my intention is not to prove the invisible realm exists, but to show you different expressions of it in the experiences of normal human beings. They show how very supernatural the Christian life truly is, and what wonders God has provided for us. But just to make a case for the reality of the realm of the spirit, I remind you of all the incidences of people toodling around while their body lies dead for a while, reporting things they couldn't possibly have heard or seen. After decades of this happening with hundreds of documented cases, it's pretty obvious that the physical body is not all there is to a human being. Along those lines, I want to share two more accounts, different from these Near Death Experiences (NDEs).

There are times when normal human beings encounter something that can't be explained by scientific materialism. My agnostic friend Hal had them. He doesn't believe in the supernatural, the spiritual, eternal realms where our software goes on without our usual hardware. Yet, this rationally-minded friend of mine has had vivid supernatural experiences he can't explain. Here's one of them.

Hal is an avid cyclist. He has ridden across the United States three times. Once was mostly by himself after his riding buddy became ill and had to go home. Hal decided to continue the ride. The following account is from his journal on the trip he was making all alone.

"In the South the only cool part of the day is in the early morning. I stopped to see this battle site. It was still early. There were no cars in the parking lot. It was quiet. Being a history major in college it was fun to see the Civil War sites (it appears that it was far from civil) in Virginia with numerous historical signs telling about famous battles. I was leaning up against my bike when I began to hear the sounds. This did not come from a loud speaker system because there was no one there. I'm not much on ghost stories or other world experiences but as I passed the sites of the Seven Days Battle (Malvern Hill, White Oak Swamp) which occurred the end of June 1862, I could hear the sounds of the guns and the screaming of the living, injured and the dying. Even the screaming horses. It was truly eerie. It felt real but it wasn't, It was just me and I was in the midst of it. It slowly faded away. I was stunned. As I started to ride off I noticed that this battle had taken place almost exactly 150 years prior to today."

I included this account because it shows the existence of something beyond the material world, reported by a rationalist who doesn't believe in such things. This next story happened to my friend Denis when he was a child.

"My first memory of anything is becoming aware of a sort of grainy light, and a sound like static, like a TV station at 3 AM that has gone off the air. Then I see a floor and there is dust on the floor and I am sort of floating and tumbling with the dust. Above me is the bottom of something, it is a bed. Suddenly I am floating above the room, looking down on a little boy jumping on this bed. Then I became that boy called Denis. I don't know what to make of it; I have no idea whether it was the result of a blow to the head or my near-death experiences with asthma before that, or something deeper. I have no idea."

Denis can't wear a regular wristwatch. If he puts one on, it soon starts running backwards. That shows me something happened to him during his time Beyond—something electromagnetic or dimensional perhaps. I don't know. It makes me think of when Jesus suddenly appeared among His disciples the evening of His resurrection, somehow entering the room whose doors were shut. He could still be felt, but He was…different. What happens to people who leave their bodies for a time? Where do they go? Apparently they take on other properties that aren't reversed after they come back. Many people who have an NDE have symptoms like Denis'. There's even a list of phenomena most of them have in common. Something definitely changes in their physical bodies, something that can be observed and verified.

Why does this matter? It means the material world doesn't always stay the same. We miss out on a whole spectrum of possibilities when we don't expect anything except what we usually expect. What is most surprising to me is the effect we can have on the physical realm when we invite the participation of the One who provides a different energy—one from outside our material realm. To illustrate, here's an example from the world of energy medicine.

The cells of the body communicate with minute amounts of electrical energy, signaling each other and passing along information. My father understood this when he developed microcurrent to whisper to the body in its own language, correcting incoherent signals by reestablishing proper frequencies. One of the men who helped pioneer microcurrent is Doug Casey, who took Daddy's machines to the Olympics a number of times and worked on pro-athletes and normal patients as well. Doug told me when an area is injured, it's as if the electricity is shut off to that area. The body's energy actually flows around it instead of going through it. I picture it as New York City during that historic power outage—nothing but a big blackness where lights should have been. When you saturate the area with microcurrent, it reestablishes the electrical terrain and the body's energy flows through the affected area, turning the lights back on.

In a way, the Body of Christ has been injured like that—areas where no power flows. My hope is this book will help reestablish the free flow of Holy Spirit power as these little stories remind us what Jesus said we're supposed to be doing and turn on the lights for His glory.

From quantum physics we learn there is a point at which energy and matter are interchangeable. Sound is energy—frequencies traveling through time and space. Considering these things, wouldn't it be likely that words spoken in cooperation with the Word who said, "Let there be..." would also have power to affect molecules and atomic structures? As John Lennox says, miracles don't violate natural laws, they simply introduce a different energy into the situation. Can we make a difference in the physical realm with words? Let me tell you a story from my friend Nancy. It changed the way I pray. As with the love bomb prayer, I didn't know we could do this. I'm not trying to give a scientific explanation for answered prayer; I only want to show you what happens when fervent prayer, inspired by the Holy Spirit, was offered in humility to the Creator of all things.

When an impatient driver decided to pass a vehicle on a narrow 2-lane road in the dark in the rain, he collided head-on into Parkie's car coming the other way. Amazingly, Parkie survived. Nancy kept a prayer vigil for her brother, monitoring all that was going on with him. The most recent crisis was lack of kidney function. Doctors discovered that Parkie's gallbladder had died and was poisoning his body. His kidneys couldn't keep up. But even weeks after they removed his gallbladder, Parkie's kidneys still weren't able to cleanse his blood. They had to give him daily dialysis, a debilitating procedure that left Parkie limp and exhausted. Alarmed, Nancy asked a doctor to tell her what the kidneys are supposed to do. The doctor showed her a diagram of the organ, explaining in detail the parts and their function. When Parkie returned from dialysis, Nancy sat by his bed praying, picturing each part of his kidneys, asking the Lord to restore their function according to His original design. I don't know how long she did that, but the part you need to know is that was the last time Parkie needed dialysis.

Who knew we could do that? I sure didn't! But, after that, I added sharpshooter prayers to my arsenal of weapons of warfare that are mighty through God. No more wimpy prayers: "Dear Lord, please give the surgeons wisdom in their hands. Please help our brother recover from this problem." Chuck Missler says prayer is the most powerful thing we can do. He said we can send long-range missiles into the battle from the safety of our homes. Distance healing. Too far-fetched? The Centurion understood it. He told Jesus, "Speak the word and my servant shall be healed." When you're praying, you're already operating in supernatural realms. It doesn't matter how far away you are.

Specific is better than general, not because God doesn't know how a kidney is supposed to function, but because there is something wonderful in the partnership of human and Holy Spirit. Missler says when you're calling for a salvo, you don't say, "Shoot the enemy." You specify the target. Maybe it's because the precision of the answer, so astonishing to see, is part of the joy of answered prayers. It is so much more impressive to me when I hear the detail of the answer. It shows me how near and caring our God is, and He has given power and authority to us, His children, made in His image, charged by Jesus to do what He did when He was here. Nancy prayed picturing each part of the kidney and asking God to restore its full function. There's power in our words. When we pray, molecules move and miracles can happen.

Supernatural from the Start

The Bible is founded on the supernatural. It begins with God speaking everything into being. If that's not supernatural, what is? Then He makes human beings in His image and enjoys talking with them. "Natural" would be human talking with human. Deity fellowshipping with His creation, that's supernatural—above and beyond the character of this material world. Beginning to End, the Bible is full of the supernatural. Without miracles, there is no Bible, and no redemptive death and resurrection. Here's a simple way to think of it: If we can bring it about, if we can do it in our own abilities, character and strength, it's not's supernatural. We cannot save ourselves. We cannot follow the ways of God, loving our enemies, forgiving those who hurt us, blessing those who curse us, doing good to those who hate us, praying for those who spitefully use and persecute us, trusting Him instead of taking matters into our own hands, hearing His Voice, receiving revelations from His Word, trusting Him in impossible difficulties, bearing up under crushing pressure, seeing things from heaven's point of view, walking after the Spirit instead of following the appetites and tyrannies of the flesh, doing what God says is best instead of what comes naturally, bringing about the things Jesus did on Earth and more.

There are some who say the passage from 1 Corinthians that says when that which is perfect has come, all the supernatural manifestations will be over. They're talking about prophecy and tongues and other manifestations of the Spirit. They say those things were necessary to get the Church established, but now they're no longer needed. All those healings, raisings from the dead, casting out of demons, messages from God spoken through human beings—that proved to the pagans and heathens that God is real and Jesus was who He said He was. But now all of that is settled. Now we can do church without that supernatural stuff going on. They claim the perfect that has come is the Bible, therefore everything amazing and beyond normal human life is also no longer necessary. I guess they ignore the last book in the Bible. But they also reject anything out of the ordinary in church, in Christian life, anything that disturbs the way things are and should always be. Do they really mean to ignore what Jesus said—that we are to do what He did and bring Father glory?

Miracles have always been a way God demonstrates that He is God. Why? Because He's not willing that any should perish, and miracles show this present world with all its chaos and sorrows is not all there is. He is here, a very present Help in trouble. He came to set at liberty those held captive in the prisons of their minds, and transform shipwrecked human beings into radiant men and women of God. There are documentaries, reports from all over the world, video footage of genuine, medically-verifiable miracle healings—thousands of them. Hundreds raised from the dead. We're not talking from CPR or Code Blue protocols; we're witnessing people raised up who have been dead long enough to begin to stink. Too far-fetched? What about Lazarus? Jesus said to do what He did and more. Why? We're His representatives on Earth. He came to destroy death.

"Forasmuch then as the children are partakers of flesh and blood, He also Himself likewise took part of the same; that through death He might destroy him that had the power of death, that is, the devil; and deliver them who through fear of death were all their lifetime subject to bondage." (Heb 2:14) That's an amazing freedom. Think of it. Fear of death keeps us in bondage, slaves to anxieties about irrevocable loss—of life, but also of dreams, possibilities, relationships, opportunities... Jesus came to defeat death, hell, and the grave. He came to save us from slavery to the fear of death. He came, not only to give us His life, but to share ours with us. It's quite a gift!

Sozo

When the Bible says Jesus came to seek and save, the word "save" in Greek is *sozo,* and means, among other things, "to make whole." Now look at what Hebrews 2 says about this salvation which cost heaven so much to make available to us. "Therefore we ought to give the more earnest heed to the things which we have heard, lest at any time we should let them slip. For if the word spoken by angels was steadfast, and every transgression and disobedience received a just recompense of reward; How shall we escape, if we neglect so great salvation; which at the first began to be spoken by the Lord, and was confirmed unto us by them that heard him; God also bearing them witness, both with signs and wonders, and with diverse miracles, and gifts of the Holy Ghost, according to his own will?" (Heb 2:1-4 KJV) Here's the part that God highlighted for me: "God also bearing them witness, both with signs and wonders, and with diverse miracles, and gifts of the Holy Ghost, according to his own will." It's part of that great salvation that we are so urgently warned to take seriously and not let slip. It seems obvious to me that God intends His miracles to be happening today. Early in His ministry, Jesus summoned to Him His twelve disciples and gave them power *and* authority over unclean spirits, to drive them out, and to cure all kinds of disease and all kinds of weakness *and* infirmity. Cure the sick, raise the dead, cleanse the lepers, drive out demons." (Matthew 10:6, 8 AMPC)

Many Christians don't believe in this reality—either what's possible for us to do through the Holy Spirit, or the part the dark side can play in the mess of today. What do they do with this passage? "And these signs shall follow them that believe; in my name shall they cast out devils; they shall speak with new tongues; They shall take up serpents; and if they drink any deadly thing, it shall not hurt them; they shall lay hands on the sick, and they shall recover. So then after the Lord had spoken unto them, he was received up into heaven, and sat on the right hand of God. And they went forth, and preached everywhere, the Lord working with them, and confirming the word with signs following. Amen." (Mark 16:14-20 KJV)

Mark 16 is not meant to be an exhaustive list; it just gives a range to the kinds of things available when you're on Kingdom business. Along those lines, I had a friend named Diana who was mentoring me when I was a new Christian before I got involved with the legalistic church. One day I was scheduled to be her last haircut following a packed schedule of back-to-back customers. Diana had been so busy she hadn't even had time to get a drink. As I settled myself in her chair, she reached under the sink, pulled out a white plastic gallon jug, and grabbed a big swig of the clear liquid. It was not water. Quickly we began to pray, citing this specific Scripture. Then we waited, ready to race Diana to the ER. But nothing happened. My doctor husband Dennis read the label. He said what she had ingested should have immediately burned her mouth and throat so severely her throat would have quickly swollen shut, but she didn't have any inflammation at all, and later she reported no problems with her digestive tract. It was pretty impressive for me, a brand-new Christian. I throw this in for free just in case you ever encounter an emergency like that. If you don't know there are things Jesus told us we can do in His name, you won't think to ask.

ANOTHER REALITY

There really is a supernatural realm beyond what we usually perceive. I think part of our problem, maybe a big part, is all of our experience living only in the "real" world. Maybe you didn't grow up in a family that prayed to God and saw Him answer those prayers. I didn't. My parents made their choices according to their best, educated judgments. I grew up doing what seemed right in my own eyes, and boy did I make a mess of it! How I wish I had known there was a God who loved me and would guide me when I floundered in my marriage! I had no idea there were two worlds—spirit life eternal in God: *zoe*, and flesh—*sarx*—like *carne*. Meat. Scripture says to be carnally-minded is death. It separates us from God life—*zoe*. The supernatural normal Christian life is there for whoever will seek it, but it does take effort and focus. Like searching for emeralds in the depths of the earth. There are wondrous treasures in spirit-life, but it's so familiar to walk as human beings and so hard to consider doing life aligning with an entirely different reality.

Scripture says to walk not after the flesh but after the Spirit. I used to think that meant not to indulge my flesh—you know, the drunk in the gutter. But what God showed me is flesh is confined to what we can reason on our own. It's that closed universe limited to the material world.

Here is the best example I know. Abram was promised an heir from his own body. After waiting about a decade, perhaps the couple reviewed God's words and noticed He hadn't said Sarah had to be the mom and decided He must have something else in mind. At that time, a barren woman could offer her husband a substitute who would bear a child to preserve his bloodline but be attributed to herself. It was legal, moral, ethical, socially acceptable, commonplace, and customary. Only one problem. It wasn't what God intended. The child of promise was meant to be a miracle, something that could not be explained by natural means. God wanted to begin His chosen people in such a memorable way. When we look at our circumstances and feel barren and impotent, other solutions will be available that are legal, moral, ethical, socially acceptable, commonplace, and customary. We have free will. We can take matters into our own hands and do what seems best according to what we know. And it will work, sort of. You may eventually get Isaac, but you may engender Ishmael in the process.

I think, "strait is the gate and narrow is the way and few there be who find it" (Matt 7:14) isn't only about salvation. I think it's about a Kingdom-mindedness that is sensitive to the presence of God, His voice, His fingerprints, His nudges, warnings, course-corrections, and inspirations. It's here that He gives us the treasures of darkness and hidden riches of secret places. You wouldn't tell your secrets to strangers, casual acquaintances, or even to friends, except those you consider close, tried and true, trustworthy to share your heart. It's the same with God. One amazing aspect of the supernatural normal Christian life is the privilege of friendship with God. It is with His friends that He shares His mysteries ("mystery" defined as "manifesting His private counsel"). But you know what's even more astonishing? He wants to. He's not hiding or being cagey. He doesn't play games or hard-to-get. That degree of friendship is available to anyone who wants it enough to make the effort to develop that relationship of intimacy, just as it is with anyone you want to be close to. He invites. He promises. Open the door when He knocks. He will come in and have dinner with you. (Rev 3:20)

"And ye shall seek me, and find me, when ye shall search for me with all your heart. And I will be found by you, saith the Lord." (Jeremiah 29:13, 14)

In 1988 I was fresh out of 10 years in a legalistic church, bewildered and depressed to the point of being suicidal. I had no idea who God was, and I was afraid of Him. Someone recommended A.W. Tozer's *The Pursuit of God.* I could hardly understand it. Tozer's thoughts were from a different realm. I read it twice. Then I asked the Lord, "Is the kind of relationship Tozer had with You something unique to him because You made him special, or can everyone know You like that?"

"Everyone," He said.

Since 1988, I have been looking for that communion that transforms my normal, mundane human world into the transcendent life of God. Tozer says every person has the relationship with God he wants, no more, no less. I want all I can get, and I put much of what I've learned into this book because I very much want you to also have all that He has available and waiting for you.

Prophecy

Some Christians get queasy at any supernatural manifestations in modern-day America. "We don't do that here," is a common reaction to the gifts the Holy Spirit wants to give the Body of Christ. My friend Debra used to go to a church like that. She wasn't aware of it until the pastor started insisting each member sign a covenant with the church. She read it, and told him she couldn't sign it because one of the statements was a rejection of the Holy Spirit. She said, "I can't agree to denying one-third of the Trinity." The pastor said that was okay, just keep it to herself. She said she couldn't do that either.

The Apostle Paul warned that in the last days there will be those who have the form of godliness but deny the power. (2 Tim. 3:5) And Jesus talked about the tares growing with the wheat, with all of the sorting out happening at the end. I wonder if that's what we're seeing here. I'm not making any statements about salvation; only God knows a person's heart. However, at the very least, a vital part of the intended life of the Body of Christ is cut off when the Breath of God is being suffocated into silence. Why would any Believer want to say to the Holy Spirit, "You're not welcome here"?

In the 1980s, a wonderful woman named Joyce was a regular at the church I was attending. She and her husband Mickey were from Zimbabwe (originally Rhodesia) and had seen the horrors of those brutal wars. Mickey belonged to an organization that kept him updated on the martyrs around the world. It's through him that I learned most of what I know about our suffering brethren in other countries.

Joyce was one of the most godly women I have ever known, a person Jesus could rely on to strengthen brothers and sisters with visions, prophecy, and words of knowledge. Scripture warns us to test the spirits, not just accept whatever we hear, and I'd heard enough bogus "messages from God" that I was careful to compare what was being spoken with the Bible and what God was speaking to my own heart. With Joyce, every time she brought messages from God, they rang true.

What does it take to be able to bring messages from God? Humility, for one. Alignment with His values, for another. And willingness. But mostly it takes relationship. Jesus told His disciples He was no longer calling them servants because servants don't know what their Master is doing. He said He was calling them friends. Abraham was called the friend of God and God told him what He was planning to do to Sodom and Gomorrah. Noah found grace in the eyes of the Lord and God told him to build the ark, and then when to get into it. The prophet Amos said God doesn't do anything without telling His prophets first. Now in the time of the New Covenant, Jesus is letting us know He will tell us first because we're His friends. And also because there are things we are called to do right now. Lately He has been emphasizing to me the need to be lights in the world. He wants to make a distinction between His people and the world, because those who don't know Him need to be aware there is a transcendent realm, an omnipotent God who loves them and invites them to take part in His magnificent Plan for this momentous time on Earth. Power with signs following will be needed to exemplify that Kingdom life, the miraculous, the supernatural, the outpouring of the glory of God.

When God's going to work, He speaks to His people. Nonetheless, I have to admit I was hesitant to bring up prophecy in this book, or quote any, because it's an area of automatic abhorrence for some. Prayer power? Yes! Let's go for it! Fingerprints of God? Bring it on. But prophecy from a human being in the twenty-first century? No thank you.

I like to feed my friends healthy and nutritious meals that are also delicious, and I never want to set before them anything they can't stand (Dan, for example, hates zucchini).

But when it comes to the Word of God, we are cautioned to present all of it—the whole counsel—not just the parts we're sure our friends will like, or what we want to push. Reminds me of going to a salad bar and filling a plate for you with favorite greens and toppings, but avoiding the beets and garbanzo beans because I'm not sure you'll want them. Then I remembered the title of this book which includes the words "mighty," "supernatural," and "normal." Dan tells me the title of a book is a promise. God, Himself, told me I was avoiding one of those very supernatural manifestations that is intended to be normal because it's so necessary—especially now.

All of the prophecies I'm including in this book came through Joyce. They are very special to me. For more than forty years they've helped me keep God's perspective on the time in which He placed me. They have guided and encouraged me and kept me aware of the need for communion and close communication with Him—especially now. The one I quote below helps me remember the value of quiet time in the secret place of the Most High, a very biblical principle presented here as a question and an invitation.

"Is there a place of quiet silence, a secret place that you have found? There needs to be a secret place in every human heart, a secret place that will cry out to Me, a secret place where you and I can speak. It is a necessary place, that is why it is prepared. It is a place of quiet rest, a place of peace, a place of comfort, a place of joy, a place of instruction. This instruction is necessary. It shall be given individually. This instruction can be used in life to reveal Me. I need the people who will reveal Me in their lives and so love one another that the world can see. I need people drawn by the power in your lives. Where does the power come from? It comes from Me and it comes from secret times with Me. Have you found that secret place?"

3

Glory

He Is the Light of the World

Since this book is on the supernatural nature of the Christian life, it's best to start at the top, with the most "other" of the otherworldy realms we're going to explore together. Who *is* this God who invites us into private conversation? James 1 says He is the Father of Lights in whom is no variableness or shadow of turning. He is consistent; He never changes. In Matthew 5:16, Jesus says "You are the light of the world." There's a connection here. Our Father is Light. We're supposed to be light too—visible so others may see our good works and give glory to our Heavenly Father. What does that mean? What is glory? And how can we give it to our God? That's what this chapter is about. Let's look at God's glory first.

The first place we see God's glory is in His creation. Psalm 19 says the heavens declare the glory of God. Our response to those glories is worship: "You're God; I'm not." Can't help it. You see a gorgeous sky full of purple, scarlet, and blue; curtains of colored lights undulating high in the northern sky; the sparkling display on a starry night, and it makes you say, "Wow!" They show His magnificence, creativity, flawless aesthetics. It's His bigness, imagination, and endless surprises. It's the Mind that designed 20,000 different kinds of butterflies, deep sea creatures that boggle the mind with their shapes and survival, rocks that look common and unremarkable until black light reveals startling fluorescence. Each creation indicates something of the creativity of God who hides glowing colors in the ordinary, enables soft and fragile animals to live under conditions of immense pressure, and provides ecological niches for so many kinds of butterflies to flourish without getting in each other's way. Everywhere He has hidden messages that say even the most ordinary-looking, the most vulnerable, the most ephemeral have surprising strengths and beauties. Each is unique and carefully designed. He is not less deliberate in crafting each of His beloved children. All of God's creations have properties yet to be discovered. It takes the right circumstances, the necessary timing. In days to come, some of us are going to be surprised to find He has furnished us with florescence, flourishing, and the ability to bear up under immense pressure. I don't know about you, but it makes my heart fall down and worship. He is mighty, able to provide for all of His precious creations, small and inconsequential as they may seem to a world in love with dominance, control, and power.

Doxa

So far I've talked about nature and God's creative genius, but the Bible gives us deeper insight into His glory. *Doxa* is the Greek word for "glory." Immediately I think in terms of breath-taking brilliance, a radiance of overwhelming beauty, but I want to be more specific. Other Scriptures don't seem to have anything to do with radiance and beauty. When Joshua confronted Achan after the defeat at Ai, He said, "My son, I beg you, give glory to the Lord God of Israel, and make confession to Him, and tell me now what you have done; do not hide it from me." (Joshua 7;19) That puzzled me. How does confession give glory to God? This, and other Scriptures seem to indicate that giving God glory is related to recognizing who He is, acknowledging His holiness, relating to Him appropriately, giving Him His due. It's perceiving God's true image and character.

In Exodus 22 and 24, Moses implores God to show him His glory. God responds, "I will make all My goodness pass before you, and I will proclaim My name." For the Hebrews, a name was the essence of the character. When God said He would show His glory, it was His goodness and His character Moses would be seeing.

This is what Yahweh said: "The Lord, the Lord God, merciful and gracious, longsuffering, and abounding in goodness and truth, keeping mercy for thousands, forgiving iniquity and transgressions and sin, by no means clearing the guilty, visiting the iniquity of the fathers upon the children and the children's children to the third and the fourth generation." (Exodus 34:6-8 NKJV)

It's interesting to me that God does not mention his holiness, His transcendence, His power, wisdom, pre-eminence, omniscience, or creativity. The only aspects of His goodness and essence He declares before Moses are relational. They're how He relates to people.

I noticed He declares "the good stuff" before bringing up "not clearing the guilty." How is punishing the guilty part of God's glory? It shows His true goodness. We make a mistake in equating grace, mercy, and long-suffering with leniency toward sin. As C.S. Lewis wrote, "He's not tame, but He's good." There's wisdom in fearing the Lord. God is not indulgent or lenient, letting things go because He knows we're weak. Sin hurts us. He wants us to be safe, whole, fulfilled, and none of that happens when we "miss the mark"—the archery term that is the definition of "sin."

Justice and righteousness are the foundations of His throne. The universe is constructed on firm principles that fit together like a building where everything has been measured, squared, plum. You start allowing things to be crooked or warped, and the organization, family, person, government, society begins to come apart. These days, that kind of absolute standard of right and wrong sounds judgmental and harsh, not allowing people the freedom to do what they want. Really? Ever seen a child that has never been taught to share or not hit other kids? To allow a child to run amuck would not be good for anyone, especially the child who grows up to be a spoiled brat destined for an unhappy life strewn with broken relationships. Sin has consequences, even though God is willing to forgive. Normalizing sin, replacing God's standard with your own is iniquity. It twists the spiritual DNA for three or four generations. Still, in His infinite mercy, Yahweh limits the carnage. By the time a family gets to great grandchildren, the effects of the transgressions of ancestors is diluted to the point it no longer has the power it once had to distort their original design.

In this day of leniency, "tolerance," and adjustable ethics, we may not see the goodness in God's judgments. Yet, what good Father allows his children to be violated, or, for that matter, to violate others? In God, nobody "gets away" with anything. Wrongs must be righted. But there is mercy and forgiveness and a very high price paid by the Judge Himself to give us grace and restoration to relationship with Him who keeps mercy to thousands. So when we see God's punishment of sin in His revelation of His glory, it shows us His nature, His character, His goodness. In the movies when the bad guys get theirs, don't you want to cheer? That's how it will be at the end of time. All evil will be destroyed. It's part of the glory of God.

I need to add this about *doxa*. Bible scholar Spiros Zodhiates says, "All have sinned and come short of the glory of God" means we have all lacked God's image and character. So true! We can all agree to that assessment. We may argue that we're good people and defend ourselves against the "S" word, but who among us can say we are full expressions of the image and character of God? Nobody. You probably figured out "All have sinned and come short of the glory of God" (Rom 3:23) is not the Good News. That simply exposes our deep deficiency. We're not welcomed into heaven on the basis of how we compare with other people; it's how we measure up to God. Are we holy enough to stand in His presence without being fried in the intensity of His holiness? Of course not. But, in Jesus, we are completely enveloped in His righteousness. But it gets even better. Scripture says we become more and more like Him, including His glory. We get transformed. Really? Is that even possible? Yes! Read on!

Jesus came to show us the Father. When we keep our eyes on Him, we are looking at Father God, now face to face. Once we are born again (transformed), washed in the blood of the Lamb, covered with His righteousness, we are able to look upon His beloved face without going up in a wisp of dark smoke. We can gaze upon His glory (as much as we are able to perceive while still in our mortal bodies). Wow! It changes us.

Paul says it this way, "But we all with unveiled faces beholding as in a glass the glory of the Lord, are changed into the same image from glory to glory, even as by the Spirit of the Lord." (2 Cor 3:18) Scripture says we become like Him—the *same image* as God, changed *from glory to glory*—a work of the Holy Spirit that happens when we keep our eyes on Him!

A word about the unveiled face. The reference is to Exodus 24:29-45. Moses had just spent his second 40 days and 40 nights on Mount Sinai with God, and when he returned with the second set of stone tablets (they were small enough to carry in one hand—sorry, Charlton Heston), his face shone with the glory of God. It so alarmed the people that they were afraid to go near him, so Moses put a veil over his face for their sakes. But whenever he met with God, Scripture says he removed the veil.

When Paul talks about beholding the glory of the Lord with unveiled faces, he's referring to face to face communication. The mirror part is the wistful acknowledgement that we are, for now, not able to see all of His glory. Why not? We're still in our rather limited physical Earth-suits. I think of it like this. My dad was an avid radio ham. In the 1930s, he talked regularly on shortwave with the king of Siam (that was before it became Thailand). The king so enjoyed talking with my dad that he invited him to visit him in his royal palace. They talked often enough that they recognized each other's voices, though the signal was uneven and the voices distorted by limitations in electronics and variations in atmospheric conditions. How different it would have been for my dad to step into the royal palace and speak with the king face to face! And how much more astonishing will it be when we see our King in His royal palace face to face!

Paul says, "For now we see through a glass, darkly; but then face to face: now I know in part; but then shall I know even as also I am known." (1 Corinthians 13:12 KJV).

I believe what the children of Israel saw on Moses' face was not the reflected glory of God. The moon reflects the light of the sun but is not substantially changed. In Moses' case, I believe the brightness was a resonance with God in the whole of Moses' being. He had to be physically altered in some way to be able to stand in God's presence 40 days and 40 nights (twice), eating and drinking nothing, receiving a multitude of detailed instructions and remembering and then conveying them to the people accurately in their entirety. But the biggest reason for the radiance on Moses' face was from seeing the glory of God. If being in sunlight can give you a tan (or a burn), wouldn't the brilliance of God's glory affect a human being in a tangible way? Scripture says when we gaze at Him intently, it transforms us.

In Romans 12:2, Paul provides additional insight into how this transformation takes place. "…do not be conformed to this world (pressured into its mold), but be transformed by the renewing of your mind, that you may prove what is that good and acceptable and perfect will of God." When we think like Him, it transforms us. Something supernatural happens when we align with God's ways and harmonize and resonate with His essence and character.

God told me there's a Mount Sinai for each of us—a sacred place where He wants to meet with us face to face. It's there that we behold His glory, and when we come back down to the flatland, there's a shine on our face everyone can see. It's the glory of God, the Light of the world, now so filling our being that it brings His character and transforming goodness into us and everything we do.

The goodness of God

The Greek word for "good" is *kalos.* It means much more than morally pure. It always carries with it the sense of loveliness, of something admirable. In the marketplace, *kalos* is used to describe grapes that are full of sweet juice, fragrant, and a deep, rich color; horses that are strong, well-proportioned, intelligent, gentle, and good-tempered. It describes a man who is honest, known for integrity, a man of his word. It's used for what is noble, praiseworthy, charming, winsome, lovely and has intrinsic beauty. When Jesus says "I AM the Good Shepherd," the word is *kalos.* He's the *Kalos* Shepherd. His deeds are morally good, but also gracious and beautiful.

Now let's look at that Scripture in Matthew about our charge from Jesus to be lights of the world. Here is how it reads in the Amplified Bible: "Let your light so shine before men that they may see your moral excellence and your praiseworthy, noble, and good (*kalos*) deeds and recognize and honor and praise and glorify your Father who is in heaven."(Matthew 5:16 AMPC)

I think any time we reveal God's image and character in our actions, words, relationships, business practices, projects, choices, and expressions, we give Him glory. We are meant to think and move and have our being resonant with His heart. Wherever we are, His Life shines through us.

Okay, that's an interesting theory, but what does this look like in real life?

I think of the bedpan nurse who was so kind and gracious to my mom that she transformed what could have been totally humiliating into what felt to my mom as safe and loving as a visit from a dear and treasured friend. Then there's the time I was having some trees cut down on my property. I could hear the foreman giving instructions to his crew. A lot of people have done work around my place, and the last tree guys were sullen, surly, and did a lot of swearing. So this group surprised me. James was the guy in charge. He was so cheerful and respectful to his crew, and he called everyone "Brother." When he came to tell me they would be back to finish up the next day, I told him I appreciated the way he spoke to his crew. He was pleased and said he tried really hard to treat others the way he wanted to be treated. Turns out he's a Christian dedicating every moment of his life to the glory of God. It's a deliberate choice, and it certainly shows.

Most recently, there's José, a handyman gifted with many skills and the ability to solve perplexing problems. When I commented on that, he said he prays before each job because there are often things he's never seen before. He asks God to show him what has to be done, and he always gets the help he needs. José is fast, efficient, an artisan in the quality of his finish work. Whenever he's around, I can feel the joy of the Lord.

My neighbor Cathy is a gentle person, a dog-lover who is able to make animals feel safe. She is the only person who can clip Hedy's nails without turning her into a Tasmanian Devil. Cathy never forces Hedy. Over the years they have become good friends. When it's time for the nail trim, Hedy cooperates. She has even been known to offer Cathy her paw. Cathy's husband Dan is a long-time general contractor who has rescued me more than once with emergency-level problems in my home. He has also done a lot of work on the cabin next door. Since my office is a few yards from the current projects, I have often heard him directing his crews through difficult and tricky situations. Two words come to mind: "competence" and "kindness." When I hear such gracious respect for fellow humans, it shows me (and others) there are better ways to get the job done than yelling, cursing, and berating. Dan has been responsible for hundreds of crews, some quite numerous, on some very big jobs. He is always the same. He operates this way: "Lead by example."

These people impress me with the *kalos* way they do their work. Their words to one another are like song; their movements together are like dance. They are not trying to impress or influence anyone. They are just doing their jobs, but the way they do them changes the atmosphere for Good. Whatever we're doing, we can do it in *kalos* ways. It isn't something that's seen much these days, I'm afraid, so it's even more important that we let our little lights shine.

Up here on the mountain, sound travels far. I can hear clearly the words spoken by neighbors two streets below. You never know who's watching or listening. I've heard it said people become Christians because they've met one, and people don't become Christians because they've met one. Both of those happpened to me. I'm so thankful that Myrtle and Marge loved me into the Kingdom by showing me the true nature and character of God. I saw Him in their eyes. I heard Him in their voices. Their kindness melted my defenses. Who wants to fight against absolute, unconditional love? They weren't famous, dazzlingly talented, powerful, or rich. But the flame of God, bright inside them, drew me from darkness into His marvelous Light.

Here are three more stories about people who live their lives for the glory of God. Others saw their good works and it made them wonder why they did what they did. Notice that the Light of God shined in the darkness of each circumstance, using the opportunities at hand to show a different way to live, like turning on a light. Being the light of the world always changes the way things look. It enables people to see in the ordinary mundanities of life the supernatural transcendent *kalos* Life of God.

Chocolate Cream Pie

I have known Stephanie since she was eleven years old when her mom, Carol, enrolled her in our Christian school back in the 1980s. I watched her grow up, hired her to work as a graphic artist at Earthen Vessel Productions, and followed her life as she became a wife and mother. In all those years, the one thing I've seen is how consistently thoughtful and gracious Stephanie has been to everyone. Even when she was a little girl, she had that type of personality that caused people to like her immediately. That's why I was mystified when she told me her new neighbor couldn't stand her and made sure she knew it.

Most people would have ignored that neighbor, but not Stephanie. She prayed and prayed. She went to her neighbor and said, "If I have offended you in some way, please forgive me." That only made the neighbor more annoyed.

Time went on. Things didn't get better. Stephanie was still mystified. She asked God if she had offended the woman. Had she done something wrong? The Lord said, "Make her a chocolate cream pie. It's her favorite." Stephanie had never made one before. Did she rush to the grocery store and find a frozen pie to defrost for the unhappy neighbor? No. She found a recipe and made one from scratch with very good ingredients. As she made it, she prayed for God to bless it because she knew it was special from Him. Though it was her first one, it came out well. Then she took it to the neighbor's house. The woman wasn't home, but her daughter answered the door. When Stephanie handed her the pie, the daughter exclaimed, "It's her favorite!" Did the neighbor suddenly realize what a wonderful person Stephanie is? No. But she was just a touch less hostile.

I told you this story because it exemplifies the *kalos* life, one where the good deed is not only morally pure, it's lovely, winsome, and delicious. The Apostle Paul wrote, "See that none render evil for evil unto any man; but ever follow that which is good, both among yourselves, and to all men." (1 Thessalonians 5:15 KJV) Jesus told His disciples, "Do good to those who hate you." Why? Because when we obey what Jesus said, He can do surprising things not possible when we operate solely on human reasoning. When we follow the Spirit instead of our flesh, it releases a different energy into the situation. I have the feeling that neighbor is as mystified by Stephanie's behavior as Stephanie is about hers, and you never know where that will lead.

The other thing that impresses me about this story is God knew the neighbor's favorite dessert and told Stephanie to make one for her. It touches me that God woos cranky people in such *kalos* and gentle ways.

"Let us not lose heart and grow weary in acting nobly and doing right, for in due time we shall reap if we faint not (if we do not loosen and relax our courage, if we don't become unraveled)." (Gal 6:9)

Rice and the Christian Chinese

God wants there to be a distinction between His people and everybody else. How are we different when we follow Jesus? One of the best examples is this story Chuck Smith shared from his time in China in the 1990s.

"The Communist officials were telling us there is one province in China that is just about all Christian, and they decided they would give to the government the full quota of rice, but they would make it the finest rice they could as a witness for Jesus Christ. This government official was telling me where they bring their truckloads of rice to this government depot there's always a long line of trucks because the government has to go through and inspect each truck that comes before they weigh them because the people would put rocks and gravel all through the rice so it has more weight. But when they come from this province, they just signal them, 'Go ahead and dump it.' And the others say, 'Wait a minute! How come they don't have to wait in line? We've been here for two days.' And they say, 'Well, they're Christians and their rice we can trust. It's always good.' The government is aware that being a Christian makes a difference."

George and the Orphans

In the 1800s, George Mueller founded an orphanage that clothed, housed, fed, and educated thousands of orphans. Over the decades he provided for them with means supplied by the Lord Himself. From the beginning, Mueller decided he would never tell anyone the needs, and the Lord always supplied without fail, though it was sometimes at the very last minute.

Why did Mueller do it this way? It was the days of the deification of intellect. People were no longer interested in living for God. In fact, they didn't even believe in Him. They discarded the Bible as fairy tales and moral lessons that no longer applied to civilized, enlightened, scientifically-minded, educated people. Compassion left the streets of England. Orphans died in the dust. Charles Dickens wrote *Oliver Twist,* but it did not awaken pity or concern. Then George Mueller, a playboy who stole shamelessly from his father and friends, encountered the living God in the person of the risen Christ who love bombed him. A peace came over the heart that had never felt satisfied. He stopped striving for self-satisfaction. Instead, he gave himself and everything he had to Jesus. Why did George Mueller go to such extremes to feed orphans without having one fundraiser or ever appealing to others to help in this ministry of compassion? He wanted people to know God is real, and He still does miracles.

When Mueller was able to have a large complex of buildings built without asking for or owing a penny, he showed everyone the miracle-working God who loves the lowest of the low. Charles Dickens had his doubts that Mueller's homes were treating these street kids so well, so he dropped in unannounced. Mueller gave a staff member his keys and told him to let Mr. Dickens into any room he wanted. There Dickens observed well-fed, well-dressed children playing happily and being educated in trades and skills "above their class." Mueller's homes demonstrated God's heart, His image and character, and they gave God glory.

When our deeds are lovely, when they carry the fragrance of Christ, people are drawn. We were designed for such a time as this. God has chosen us for good deeds—*kalos*, and mighty. Jesus showed us the Father in a full expression of His mercy and grace. It's a supernatural—above natural—transcendent life we're called to live before others so they will know there is a God in heaven who is gracious, kind, compassionate, merciful, patient, forgiving, generous, wise, good, powerful, glorious—and He loves them.

4

The God of Words

In the Bible, from Beginning to End, God speaks and things happen. Galaxies are flung into space, a plethora of phyla and species with their individual body plans and commands for unique epigenetics ordering the formation of various types of cells at just the right moments for the person or beetle or grass to develop and function as designed. But even more wondrous to me is the fact that God speaks to people. In the Garden, they heard Him. Even throughout the times of judges and kings and captivities, He was speaking, though fewer and fewer were open to His voice. Eventually they relied on prophets because they didn't want to deal with Him directly, probably starting at Mount Sinai where they told Moses Yahweh was too frightening and they would be perfectly satisfied just having him tell them what Yahweh said.

People like Daniel and other prophets received so many words from the mouth of God that they filled books with specifics of what He wanted to say. Then, after Jesus came, after Pentecost when the Holy Spirit arrived to indwell and empower believers, individuals hearing the voice of God personally was once more expected and normal. And now? Most people don't even believe God is real, so why would they expect to hear from Him? I'm including in that "most" Christians who go regularly to church, as reported in that survey I told you about.

Our souls are meant to yearn for Him. There's that God-shaped vacuum that only He can fill. We are created to know Him and enjoy Him forever. We are designed for rich communication overflowing with treasures of wisdom that color our lives with vibrant beauty. Sunsets are glorious, a feast for the eyes, but talking with the One who paints a new one every evening? That enlarges our innermost beings, enabling us to receive more and more without feeling overwhelmed.

I'm not saying it's a voice you hear, though God does choose to do that sometimes. It depends on the circumstances. The most stunning example of the audible voice is this next story, which my friend Nathan told me.

Dannie, Nathan's dad, was trudging through the jungle, exhausted and bleary. He stopped to lean against a tree when the Voice said loudly, "Get down!" Dannie was so tired he didn't want to. "Get down!" the Voice said more insistently. Again he ignored it. A third time the Voice ordered, "GET DOWN!" so forcefully that Dannie obeyed. A millisecond after that a volley of bullets hit the tree right where his head had been.

Dannie said, "If it hadn't been for God, Nathan would not be here." He looked at his son with fond eyes. "He's the best thing I've ever done. He saved my life." I asked Nathan what that meant. He told me when his dad came back from Vietnam, he was angry and violent. In order to survive, he shut off his heart. In Vietnam, he decided he would never cry again. But when he held his little baby son, he cried. And later, when the relationship with Nate's mother ended and she took the boy away from him, Dannie cried for two weeks straight. That flood of grief released the lock on Dannie's heart and enabled him to love again.

Every baby is a very intentional creation designed by God for a specific time on Earth. He saved Dannie's life and Nathan came into being, a blessing to an awful lot of us whose lives have been made better because of him.

In Dannie's case, a still, small voice wouldn't have done the job. He needed to hear words that were loud and external. But

I, and most of my friends, get words inside our hearts. We just know what He said. If you're wary of hearing voices, there's another way to hear Him regularly. It's called "The Bible." God has loaded it with messages to you. Here's an example: One time I was reading along in Isaiah and suddenly stumbled over words I don't remember having ever read before. God said, "I will give you the treasures of darkness and hidden riches of secret places that you may know it is I, Yahweh, the God of Israel, who calls you by your name." (Isaiah 45:3)

I was shocked. The words leaped off the page straight into my heart. I knew God was speaking those words directly to me. I knew He was going to give me the secret riches hidden in dark places, treasures that can only be found during times of greatest distress and despair. The reason for this revelation of the good things hidden there? That I may know—from experience—that it is the Great I AM, the God who keeps His promises to His people, who calls me by my name. He knows my name, but He also knows my real name. "Israel" is the name He gave Jacob, changing "Supplanter" to "Prince with God." That was Jacob's true name and destiny. And God knows mine.

In its historical context, that passage from Isaiah was directed to Cyrus, who must have been shocked to read his name in a papyrus scroll written hundreds of years before he rode into Babylon. But the Word of God is alive and supernatural. The Holy Spirit can activate ink and paper, breathing into them a *rhema* word from God to a human thousands of years after it was originally written. He also activates words we speak, empowering them to bring into situations the miraculous.

There's an incident in Homer's *The Odyssey* where Odysseus is standing on a high place shouting down to the people below. Behind him Athena, goddess of wisdom and war, is shouting through him. The word for her action comes from *spirare*, Late Latin for "spirit," from which we get our word "inspire." It means "to breathe into." It also has the sense of "breathing religious or divine feeling into." Of course, Athena shouting through Odysseus is ancient fiction, but it always struck me as a powerful visual of what Holy Spirit does when we pray. He breathes into our words. It's not just us feeble human beings saying words. Those words change things. It's not something we can do ourselves. It's supernatural—the intervention of Almighty God because we, His beloved children, are asking for wrongs to be righted, wisdom and clarity to come, alignment be reestablished where things are off-kilter, light to reveal truth and reality, and Kingdom life to be released on Earth. When it is, people see God is real. He truly is who He says He is, and it brings Him glory.

Here's another truth about the power of prayer. When we agree together the power increases. We see this in the Tower of Babel. When people are of one mind, they can get a lot more done—even if it's for ungodly purposes. It is also in the Scripture that says one will put a thousand to flight and two will put ten thousand. The context of Deuteronomy 32:30 has to do with Israel's rebellion, but it also shows me a multiplication of effectiveness when there are additional people involved. When Carol, Debra, and I pray, we get 3-D coverage because each of us has different gifts and perspectives. There's a lot more power. We can feel it. It's when we're together that words from God start flowing, triggered by need and our focus on connecting with Him. That's when He says things there's no way we could otherwise know, things which are confirmed later in astonishing ways to our amazement and delight. Hearing from God is an adventure, and kind of a wild ride.

How do I know He wants to talk? The Bible confirms it. And I've heard Him. I know it's God because He says things I couldn't know, and nothing ever contradicts the Bible.

They're usually short statements, encouragement or course-correction, and I always feel strengthened and uplifted even if I'm being corrected. My time with God is like being in a garden. It's never a woodshed.

Here's an example: Sunlight was coming through the window, lovely and inviting in the summer afternoon. I stepped over to look out, and immediately noticed a small black spot on the glass. I kept looking at it. Then, after a moment, the Lord asked, "What do you see?"

"There's this little black spot," I said. "I think it's a fly speck."

"What else?"

Hmmmm... All I saw was the little black speck. Then I felt a nudging..."Look beyond...

"Oh," I said, feeling I had been snapped out of a trance. "There's a tree. And some grass. And, oh, there's blue sky, a really nice blue, and big white clouds and birds flying and..."

"Yes," He said. "There's so much more than a speck on the glass, but that's what you chose to look at."

I hung my head. "I'm sorry, Lord," I said. "I know I always focus on what's wrong. I guess I'm just a negative person..."

He said gently, "Why do you insist on seeing yourself in the worst possible way? I'd rather you saw yourself the way I do."

"How's that?" I asked.

He said, "In progress."

Here's another: "Did you think there wouldn't be a fight?"And occasionally, when I'm particularly impressed with something He's done, He'll say, "You ain't seen nothin' yet!"

But what if I want something really, really badly and think God might say no? There have been times I handled that problem quite simply. I didn't ask. I don't recommend it. My friend Dan says, "God always chooses the best for us." To us humans, however, it doesn't always look that way. Below are four quotes that help me accept God's answers in the context of the Big Picture, not just what I want. I suppose you could say God gives us, not what He knows we want, but what He knows we want most.

Singer/Songwriter Bryan Duncan says God has three answers to prayer:

"Yes," "Not yet," and, "I have something better."

Bible teacher Chuck Missler says, "The worst thing we can do is choose our will instead of His."

My friend Bob Cull told me, "'No' is as good an answer as 'Yes' if we know His heart."

And someone whose name I don't remember said, "God's will is what we would always choose if we knew all the facts."

Why does this matter? Most human beings live adequately functioning lives without God saying things to them. They believe it isn't necessary to have additional input from Him. In the past, I would have agreed. That was before. That was when we could count on things being as they were. That was before God told me, "Now the only thing 'new' about normal is it will always be something new." We won't be able to guess. It isn't that we won't have help. God wants to guide us. But He doesn't grab your steering wheel and force you onto a road He knows is better than the one you're choosing. This story from my friend Rhonda illustrates the point.

Rhonda and her husband Charlie had just been invited to a special getaway with two of their dearest friends. The friends had rented two condos at Oceanside, each with two rooms, so they told Rhonda and Charlie they could invite another couple if they wanted. Rhonda knew exactly who to ask, and that couple was delighted at the chance to go to the ocean with them. All of them were very close friends.

What Rhonda didn't know was the woman she invited was fighting off some bug. She thought it would be over soon, so she didn't mention it, but as the road trip went on, Rhonda's friend began to feel worse. Not long after, she was very sick. Then her husband got sick. Then Rhonda and Charlie got sick. It was miserable for all of them, and other things went wrong as well. When they got back, the woman was so ill she had to go to the hospital. She had pneumonia. It took weeks for all of them to get well.

One day when Rhonda was worshiping at church, she thought, *I guess I should have asked You first before I invited them.* Clearly she heard the Lord say, "A time is coming when you won't make a move without asking Me first."

That incident was three years ago. When Rhonda told me about it, I had some thoughts of how that might happen, what life might be like in the coming days. Nothing could have prepared me for what happened in 2020. All through 2019, the Lord kept saying to me, "Enjoy normal because, starting next year, it will never be normal again." And now, half-way through the second year of pandemic confusion, Rhonda's story is more meaningful than ever, and what the Lord told her is becoming more applicable every day. The wonderful thing about that is He wants us to ask Him. James 1 says we can ask for wisdom and He'll give it without ever scolding us. Yes, the days are shaky and scary, but we have a big God, and He always knows the best thing to do.

One more story about God's answers—and our ability to accept them with confidence.

I happened to be standing in the parking lot of Claremont High School when my classmate, a new driver, backed her car directly into my station wagon. She jumped out of the driver's seat and gasped in horror as she ran her hand over the dent in my car. "I'm so sorry!" she said, tears starting to run down her cheeks. "I'm so-so sorry!"

I wasn't nearly as upset as she. Reassuringly I patted her arm. "Don't worry," I said, "It'll be okay. My daddy can fix anything."

Years later when I asked my father to tell me his favorite memory of my childhood, that's the story he recalled. He was extraordinarily gifted at fixing things and I think it pleased him to know his little daughter had such confidence in his ability to make things right, no matter what.

5

Communion With The Most High

Communication with Almighty God is supernatural. As human beings living in a temporal world, we don't know what to expect. How many people listen for the thunder and continue to miss the still, small voice? Recently my son John told me something that I think explains why some people don't hear from Him. He said he was grumbling about all the people who pass him and flagrantly ignore posted speed limits. God told him, "It's not about obeying that one particular law. It's about the mindset. Why does a person speed? Are they saying, 'You can't tell me what to do; I'll do what I want'? If you disregard earthly authority and the rules put in for your safety, how easy is it for you to disregard other rules? How can you hear My still, small voice when you have your fingers in your ears, shouting, 'You're not my boss! You can't tell me what to do!'?"

But He still wants to talk, not only *to* us, but *with* us. Even so, it's hard for people to hear Him these days, even if they want to. One of my young friends told me he's given up on hearing God. He said the anxiety of waiting for Him was too much. It was better not to expect anything anymore. This young man is not being rebellious. He earnestly desires contact with God, but it's been fifteen years and he hasn't heard a word. When he talks, I can't help thinking what he says about Father God sounds a lot like what he says about his earthly dad. Many of us have that problem. We're wounded in the daddy-place and it affects our ability to interact with Father God. I think this is one of the saddest things about Christianity today. No wonder there's so little power in the Church, so much weakness in the Body, so little radiance in the Bride. It's hard to connect with someone you don't want to listen to, or to get excited about someone you think doesn't want to talk to you.

I've struggled with prayer for most of my Christian life. I didn't even realize it was a problem. Actually, there are two things that hindered my communication with Father God. The first came from my Confucian upbringing. There was a strict expectation of how I was to interact with my dad. It was one-sided. He'd speak. I'd obey. Not long ago, it occurred to me there was a part of me that still yearned to be on my daddy's lap, cuddled and comforted, able to tell him everything I was thinking and feeling, so I decided to try it. I sat on the floor of my prayer place and pictured myself as a little girl, not an adult approaching a monarch, but as a beloved child. I didn't try to edit my words for maximum respect and acceptability. I just spewed. It was certainly a different kind of prayer—more honest and heartfelt, less guarded and protective. I told Him my sorrows. What a remarkable change! I experienced the unique love of God who no longer felt like my dad.

When I told my sweet neighbor Cathy about this, she said, "He knows what we're thinking anyway, so why do we have to tell Him?" I said I think He is interested in hearing what we will choose to say. There's something about speaking our thoughts and feelings out loud that helps us know better what we're really dealing with. As long as it's swirling around in our heads, it hasn't a form, a substance, a solidity. Words have power to make clear and visible things that have been hidden even from ourselves. But when we speak them, we can hear them, disentangled from the threads of thought and association that curl around them in the mental swirl. One thought at a time, laid before the throne of God. It reduces the confusion and invites Almighty God into the mess.

This other issue is insidious and severely limiting. It's about capacity. To explain this, let me tell you a story.

I remember the time my friend Dan took me to meet his mother. It was lunchtime and she fixed us sandwiches, the kind Dan had eaten all his childhood. The sandwich consisted of two slices of white bread a small smear of mayonnaise in the center of one slice, and a single piece of baloney. That was it. I looked at Dan to see if it was a joke. It wasn't. My mother was the "pile-it-high" kind of gal, so when Dan came over, I made him a sandwich Kay Wing-style. It was an inch of thin-sliced pastrami with lettuce, tomatoes, and a generous spread of mayonnaise that extended all the way to the four edges of the fragrant rye bread. Proudly, I set it on the table before him. He thanked me, tried to take a bite, and set it back on the plate. "I can't," he said apologetically. "It overwhelms me."

When God began showing me things, I enjoyed it at first, but I'd quickly feel satiated. I'd think He was done, but there would be more. It would make me anxious. I'd feel, *I shouldn't be receiving all of this.* It was an embarrassment of riches and I didn't deserve it. Who was I to receive such bounty? I did not have the capacity to accept what God wanted to give me. My spirit was small. My appetite was small. My expectation was small. I was satisfied with far less than God wanted to give me. In my father's house, I never had a choice of what or how much I would receive. I was expected to be grateful and never ask for more. So I didn't. I think this is another reason people don't hear from God. There is damage in their daddy-place and they've managed as best they could, compensating for the lack of connection by reducing their expectation—and need. It was not rebellion that kept my spiritual ears closed; I was satisfied with a single slice of baloney between two pieces of white bread. That was then. Now when I go into my prayer place I expect a banquet—and He always gives one to me.

Over the years, God has spoken to me through various circumstances and also in words and pictures. In this book, I'll be suggesting ways to tune your spiritual ears and give you sharper, clearer spiritual vision. Like anything, it takes practice. The stories in this chapter may give you insight into ways He can communicate with you. Through them, I'm hoping you will also have a greater understanding of His heart.

Tuning Up

I have a very good electronic tuner for my guitar, but sometimes I just don't want to deal with it so I tune my guitar by ear to the high E, adjusting all the strings till they sound okay together.

One day I was leading an old Gospel song at church and Jeanine, a veteran of Gospel music, decided to play along. I love her playing, so full of energy and joy. The only problem was the piano was tuned to standard pitch and my guitar was tuned to itself. Jeanine couldn't hear the cacophony over the loud soundboard of the baby grand, but I was standing near the monitor and my guitar was amplified. It and the piano were equal in volume and it was, as you can imagine, simply awful. I finally stopped playing and let Jeanine continue. Thankfully, the congregation was very forgiving, but since then I always tune to standard pitch, just in case somebody wants to play along.

I am reminded that, before playing a symphony, the orchestra members tune their instruments to one standard pitch (A 440). Then, when they play, they're automatically in harmony with one another. The Lord told me He's the Standard, and when we tune our hearts to His, we're not only going to make beautiful music with Him, we will automatically be in harmony with one another—at least with those who have also tuned their hearts to His.

I hate conflict. All of my life I have tried to make peace, even if it meant compromising or minimizing myself. I want no dissonance; I want everybody to get along. But there are those who tune up using themselves as the standard. What God showed me is I am not meant to harmonize with everyone. Many are tuning up to themselves, the world, or each other. There's no way I can be resonant with them and God too. Jesus is the Way, the Truth, the Life. Why would I want to tune my heart to any but the one whose heart is the absolute Perfect Pitch?

What is the song God is singing over us? Scripture says it's joy. It's also love. How do I know that? Because God is love. His essence is love. Everything He does is from a heart of love. When we are tuned to His heart, that is what our lives will be also.

At the Last Supper, Jesus told His disciples, "A new commandment I give you: Love one another. As I have loved you, so you must love one another. By this everyone will know that you are my disciples, if you love one another." (John 13:34-35) Years later, one of those disciples would write, "Beloved, let us love one another: for love is of God; and every one that loveth is born of God, and knoweth God. He that loveth not knoweth not God; for God is love." (1 John 4: 7-8)

In Greek, the verb tense that means "continues to" is translated in the King James Version with the "-eth" suffix. It's not a one-time heroic act of love, but continual loving, always in harmony with God's own song of joy and love.

Both of these commands about loving one another require supernatural help. People can be downright cranky, short-tempered, hostile, hateful, critical, unreasonable, blaming, nasty… We, the *ecclesia*, the church, the chosen called-out ones are not the ones assembling in buildings on Sundays and Wednesdays and holidays. We're all over the world. And we're supposed to love one another. Do we? Think of Northern Ireland where John Lennox's father's store was bombed because he hired equal numbers of Catholic and Protestant believers.

I know of friendships between Christians that have ended in bitterness because of political differences. Churches have split over very small matters, and, frankly, we who call ourselves by the name of the one who forgave everyone, look and sound and behave just like those who don't believe in God. Is it because we've stopped tuning our hearts to His? Or maybe we never did. 1 John says the one who does not love does not know God because God is love. Maybe we don't really know God. Or maybe we don't know He is love. God once told me, "Honey, the reason you keep sinning like this is you simply don't know how much I love *you.*" That kind of unconditional acceptance transforms us—if we believe it and let Him show us how to love the way He does. Only with Holy Spirit power can we love our enemies, bless those who curse us, pray for those who persecute, torture, falsely accuse, berate, belittle, despise, demean, insult, reject, betray, abandon, kick us to the curb, or throw us under the bus. When we do things His way, we will be in harmony with God and each other.

Pastor Don Piper was thoroughly dead after an 18-wheeler ran over his little Ford Escort. He spent the next ninety minutes in heaven. Most of what he felt and saw was beyond his ability to describe, but one thing stood out to him, the music. It was everywhere, full of words extolling the holiness of God and praising Him. He said it was incredibly beautiful, but surprising because each song (and there were thousands) was different from the others, but they were perfectly harmonious and wonderful together. That's the way it will be in heaven, and that's the way it can be on Earth when our hearts are tuned to our Savior, and what comes out of us are words of edification, exhortation, and comfort, of speaking the truth in love.

Light of the World

We were making good time. The 2-lane highway was smooth and traffic was sparse and often non-existent. We sped along on our way to the annual Women Writing the West conference. This year it was in Walla Walla, Washington. We were driving up through eastern Oregon to see the countryside. As we passed through a small town, I noticed a gas station and asked Dan if he thought we should stop. He looked at the gauge. "It's just under half a tank," he said. "I don't like that type of gas. We can get gas in the next town." When we were down to under a quarter of a tank, Dan told me to keep my eyes open for a gas station. I did. There were none. In fact, there wasn't much of anything out there. No towns. No houses. No gas stations or cell service.

The sky grew dark. We drove on. The road was empty, as was the land. Outside, the temperature was dropping. It was late October. The gas tank read Empty. In the car, it was very quiet. Softly I began to pray. Eyes on the gas gauge, Dan had already been silently praying. Every time we rounded a curve or came up over a rise, we strained our eyes in hopes of seeing some lights or signs of civilization. But we didn't. No lights. No cars. Nothing but black. We had been on Empty quite awhile now. Dan was making noises of dismay. I was reminding God of the widow and cruse of oil. He could multiply loaves and fishes; He could make the little Honda CR-V run on fumes. It's amazing how driving on a deserted road in the dark in the cold with no cell service and no signs of life can so quickly improve one's prayer life. Then, faintly in the distance we thought we saw lights—not many, but something that looked like hope. They were a long way off. As we got closer, we could see car lights moving across another highway. Oooh! Signs of life! Miles later we came to a dark T intersection. Dan turned right because he could see a few lights and dark buildings that way. As we got closer, he spotted a faint light in one of the buildings. He figured it was coming from a sign or night light and pulled into the dirt parking lot. "Maybe I can get cell service now," he said.

When he got out of the car he noticed some old-style gas pumps there, like the kind we had in the '50s. We were at a store with pumps without credit card terminals. Here was gas but there was no way to get it.

Out from the shadows, a man approached. "They're closed," he said, "but they're still in there." Dan peered in the window and saw a lady sitting at a desk with a lamp on. This was the light he had seen from the road. He knocked desperately on the window. Through the glass, he said, "We need gas!" The woman came to the door and Dan told her our plight. She called to her husband to turn on the pumps. Light poured out of the windows then, and she came and filled our tank. Gratefully I grabbed one of my Scripture song albums, hopped out of the car, and handed it to her with effusive thanks. "You're an answer to prayer!" I told her. Turns out they were Christians and we had a big hug as family members do.

I thought of this story—God's provision of enough fuel for us to get to a station after being past Empty for over 50 miles, then the relief and joy of seeing lights and having the tank filled by the owners who just happened to still be in their store, though it was closed. I thought of how we had longed for lights around every curve and over every hill, searching in the vast blank blackness for some sign of help. And I thought of the words of Jesus who said, "You are the light of the world. A city on a hill cannot be hidden."

We are not meant to be hidden. People are searching for hope in the darkness. Jesus said we are the light of the world—we carry His Light. Just as we looked for lights to show us where help was, people need to see the Light of God in us, and God, Himself, has placed us on a hill—in plain sight—that we might beckon to the frightened and weary traveler that there is help, hope, and a hug waiting to help them get where they need to go.

Person to Person

Through the ages, and all throughout the New Testament, people have brought people to God. From Andrew to the Samaritan woman at the well, from Philip interpreting Isaiah for the official in the chariot, to the "foolishness of preaching" that brought thousands to Jesus in a day, God reached people through people, hence the call for us to be the light of the world. It's getting so dark, and lights can signal hope and help. This is a good thing because many humans are afraid of God, especially if they've been beaten with the Bible. The angry God of the Old Testament is the one I was taught, and I've spent thirty-five years trying to find who God really is and what He's truly like.

Here are some things I've learned. God is not mean, tyrannical, petty, vengeful, vicious, bombastic, boring, demanding, bullying, irritated, disappointed, or needy. He's not a megalomaniac craving praise, insisting that everyone bow down to Him or end up in the fiery furnace. God doesn't need us to tell Him how great He is. He is not ego-centric. He is who He is and He has nothing to prove. He is God, and He is definitely worth knowing.

God knows how to reach a person's heart. George MacDonald (one of the authors who most inspired C.S. Lewis) understood this. In *The Musician's Quest,* he wrote a line I love because of how beautifully it shows the heart of Father God. Here is my paraphrase—-God is like an ocean surrounding a man, always looking for a crack in the wall through which He can rush and reveal Himself to him. And He will use whatever He can, whether the fragrance of a rose or a few strains on a violin.

C.S. Lewis was an avowed atheist, arrogant in his academic prowess, secure in his fortress of reason and intellect. There was no room for the supernatural in his life, and certainly not the mythology of Jesus, a God-man come to Earth. But J.R.R. Tolkien was his friend. Through Tolkien, Lewis became a Christian, one whose books have changed millions of lives through his clear logic and exquisite, God-honoring prose. I can't help noticing that God brought these two great minds together with such mutual respect and enjoyment of the same literary genres that Tolkien could reason with Lewis in language the atheist could understand. It was Divine perfect placement. What riches would have been lost had Lewis not embraced Jesus and had the desire and inspiration to make Him accessible through Aslan, King of the Beasts, and dozens of books of apologetics and fiction! *Mere Christianity* is still changing lives, and all of Lewis's many, many books, are still in print.

Tolkien's books, too, have affected millions with their message of eternal hope where it seems there is none. He coined a word, "eucatastrophe" That's where overwhelming circumstances are suddenly turned to good, against all odds, because what you see at the Black Gates is not all there is. Out of the view of the flaming eye are two insignificant persons who are struggling to destroy the Ring of Power, something the power-mad evil Sauron would never guess anyone would do.

Eucatastrophe. It's what Jesus did on the cross. Aslan—he's not a tame lion, but he's good. Two friends, one drawing the other to the Truth that is the Light of the world. Two superb minds writing books of fiction that are able to draw readers into that truth because the hearts of the writers belonged to God.

Each of us is positioned in life with Yahweh's meticulous Divine Placement. When I was a young Christian, I didn't think I had anything special to offer people who were unaware of the God who came to give them a brand new life—meaningful, purposeful, eternal—even as they live on this physical Earth. After reading *The Cross and the Switchblade* I told God I couldn't do that. I was a wimp. I told Him, "I feel pretty silly trying to wage war with a rose." He said each person has a specific design. One person is like a hammer. One is like a toothpick. One is not better than the other. When you need a toothpick to get a bothersome shred of lettuce from between your teeth, a hammer simply won't do. A rose is non-threatening and I can get places other people can't. Since then, I have found ways to share His love with writers, poets, artists, musicians, and, my favorites, the community of blind and other disabled people partnering with service dogs. It's a niche I fit well. I know how to speak their language. I share their struggles. And in their times of darkness, I can turn on the lights and help them get off Empty.

Listening

It was Dog Day. The instructor escorted me to the library. "Sit here," he said, patting the seat so I could locate the chair. "I'll be right back." I sat, tense with excitement, awaiting the moment when I would meet the guide dog that had been chosen for me. Would we like each other? We had to be partners. If we didn't get along, we could not be a team. Everything depended on the bond. "Here she is," the instructor said. "This is Hedy." A small black Lab was at his side. He walked over and handed me her leash. "From now on, unless there's a need for it, no one else touches this leash, not even me."

The leather was stiff and new in my hand as I walked Hedy on heel back to my room. The rest of the day would be spent getting to know one another. I was to stroke her, talk to her, and work on establishing a connection. My roommate had already received her dog—Bogart. She was cooing over him as he lay with his head on her lap, looking supremely happy to be hers. I glanced at them enviously. Hedy was not nearly as thrilled to be with me. I turned my attention to her. From now on, it was all about exclusivity. We had been instructed not to interact with any dog but our own—not to pet or talk, or make eye contact. It was crucial for our safety.

By the way, I think the dogs in our group were named for movie stars because there was Hedy (Lamarr), Bogart (as in Humphrey), and a silly little blonde Lab named "Harlowe," who was as ditsy as could be. Oh, and a shapely, leggy German Shepherd named Sheena, as in Sheena of the Jungle. We knew the name of every dog in our class, but, of course, we knew better than to make any contact, and especially we must not talk to them. I found this mystifying. I could understand the need for not petting, because that would interfere with their bond, but what harm could come from greeting my roommate's dog?

I won't go into what it took to bond with Hedy. I'll just say it was a chore, and I had my doubts whether she really was God's choice for me. She was always so interested in what everyone else was doing even though I kept talking to her, stroking her, doing everything I could think of to convince her we belonged together. Talking was a big part of the process. They told us our dog had to respond to our voice alone. That's why no one, not even the trainers and instructors, talked to our dogs.

In case you don't know, no one can force a guide dog to work. It's a calling, a love of purpose designed into that particular animal by God. If they don't want to work, they simply sit down. Or pee in harness. Or, if they don't think you're getting the message, they will run you into garbage cans and telephone poles. So if you see working guide dogs, you know they want to. The other thing is you can't make a guide dog love you, and if she doesn't, she won't be vigilant to listen to you, cooperate with you, or keep you safe.

Every day we put our guide through specific movements. We gave them commands and made sure they obeyed. We corrected them when they were distracted and rewarded them when they did a good job. Every day for hours and hours we worked with our dogs. It wasn't for their sakes; they already knew what to do. I think most of the training was for us. We had to manage our dogs in all sorts of situations. Of course, being a well-disciplined daughter of a Confucian scholar, I was diligent in every exercise, doing my best to execute it perfectly, which is not as easy as you'd think with a bright, assertive, strong-minded little sentient being on the other end of the leash.

One day we went to the airport to learn how to go through the x-ray machine. Each of us would get to practice, and then we would line up in a queue to exit the building. For this, we would be making a moving turn. That means we would say the name of the dog (to make sure she was paying attention), then we would say the direction and make a movement with our hand to reinforce the direction. In a stationary turn, it would be like this. Hedy would be in a sit. I would say, "Hedy, right," and make a sweeping gesture that direction. She would get up and go to the right. But in a moving turn, you're walking and repeating the instructions, "Hedy, right, Hedy, right, Hedy, right" with the gesture. The dog will look for the first opportunity to turn right.

Finally all of us had successfully been through the machine. The line of guide dog teams waiting to leave was long. Hedy and I were near the back. On our right were rows of chairs with passengers waiting for their flights. We would be moving past the chairs, turning right as soon as the way was clear, and heading out the automatic doors. As soon as each team was about three feet from the end of the chairs, the person started giving the command. "Harlowe, right!" "Bogart, right!" "Sheena, right!" all at the same time. Such a confusion of voices, a cacophony of sound! But one by one they cleared the chairs and turned to the right. Hedy and I moved forward. I began the commands. She was guiding me straight ahead. "Hedy, right, Hedy, right." As we passed the last row of chairs, Hedy swung to the right and out the automatic doors which closed with a triumphant, victorious swoosh behind us. I felt fabulous and so proud of Hedy.

That was the most convincing demonstration to me of why my dog had to respond to my voice alone. A lot of voices were giving commands, firm, authoritative, insistent, but Hedy didn't listen to them. The only voice she obeyed was mine.

I bet you can see the application. There are a lot of voices and people going on their way, but being able to walk a supernatural life requires a strong relationship, a choice to accept the Call, and the desire to listen to one Beloved Voice alone. Then you can truly be a team, bonded in love. Then let the adventures begin!

6

Seeing In New Ways

"Without a vision the people perish." (Proverbs 29:18) "Perish" also means "cast off restraint" and "are uncontrolled." The subtitle of this book is "Vision for the supernatural normal Christian life." It's not "a vision," it's "vision for." It has taken me decades to have the vision I have now—not the loss of it that qualifies me for a guide dog, but the clear view from heaven's perspective of what life in God can look like. I'd read accounts in the Bible, but it's not the same as seeing God Life (*zoe*) demonstrated in people I know and others who have lived in recent times. If we never see *zoe* lived out in front of us, it probably won't occur to us that it's possible in this day and age and that we're meant to have it. What you see depends on what you're looking for. Before I go on, there's a principle I want to share with you. It's about learning how to see what's really there.

A bunch of high school students from surrounding cities were invited to study every Saturday with curators at the Museum of Natural History in Los Angeles. One of the students from my high school chose to study with a marine biologist. For their last session, the scientist took them to the coast. There he instructed them to search the tide pools and collect creatures they found. They had three hours.

Off they went, glass jars in hand, bounding from one pool to another, exclaiming over starfish and anemones. At the end of their time, back they came, animals crowded into their jars of salt water. One by one, they presented their finds. All of them had the same things—muscles, limpets, starfish, anemones, snails. Then the curator produced his jar. It was full of the most amazing creatures—small, delicate, unusual, rare. His students were stunned. How did he find them? He told them he had not moved from the place he had been when they left him. Patiently he waited, looking for those hours into the still water. Slowly, tiny sea creatures began to emerge. The entire collection of amazing animals came from that one pool. All he did was wait and watch. The students had gone pool to pool scooping up whatever they saw, and because they were hasty, they found only things that were large, common, and slow.

When you're looking for the supernatural in your daily life, you won't ever see the treasures if you're watching for the big and the obvious. God reveals His treasures when we're willing to wait quietly, watching with bright, sharp eyes for what is hidden there.

Along those lines, I want to tell you a couple of stories that changed my view of what this supernatural normal Christian life looks like.

Bea Cull

My first ten years of Christianity were spent in a very legalistic church. It was all about keeping the rules, maintaining my righteousness, and proving it was worth it to Jesus to pay such a high price to buy me back. When I left that church, bewildered and depressed, God sent me some mentors. One was Bob Cull and another was his grandma, Bea.

Bob told me, "Jesus sits on my grandma's bed in the morning waiting for her to wake up so they can talk." She was definitely the most unusual person I'd ever met. Her answers to my questions were never something I could guess. They just came out of her decades of deep friendship with Jesus.

Bea and her husband planted churches, and sometimes the churches were in remote places. (She told me she didn't get any credit for doing that because she loved to camp). One location required a ferry and a couple of days of travel to get there. They didn't have much money. One day they ran out of kerosene. That very day, some friends showed up at their door with a big can of kerosene. Bea calculated that God would have had to prompt these friends two weeks ahead of time in order to get them there on the exact day they ran out. Another time they were low on groceries. Bea said she was particularly missing the taste of ketchup. That day, someone showed up at her door with food, and sticking out of the bag right on top was a bottle of ketchup.

I sighed and said I had always wished I could have those kinds of experiences with God, but they seemed reserved for the faithful in places of great need. Bea smiled and said, "but you *have* had those things in your life. Have you ever had a phone call from a friend just when you needed it? It's the same thing. You don't need ketchup, but sometimes you desperately need good counsel from a godly friend." Bea opened my eyes to God's care. Sometimes we miss those little supernatural gifts because we don't recognize what they really mean. It's the More so many long to see, and not seeing it in Christian life, seek it earnestly elsewhere. Many end up in the occult because there spiritual power is openly acknowledged and cultivated. We miss so much when we insist Christianity today is safe, sophisticated, and civilized. We tend not to expect anything supernatural from God.

There are spectacular accounts of God's interventions in the Bible and in stories we've all heard. I have included some of my favorites in this book. But I want to also help you see the interventions in small ways, in what I call "The Daily Divine." That level of discernment takes practice, and you have to be paying attention. But once you start to see God's fingerprints, you'll soon be seeing them everywhere. That's when life stops being mundane and becomes an exciting adventure.

Seeing in New Ways

Pop Art was brand new when I was in college. Andy Warhol made headlines (and a lot of money) by making large paintings of Campbell's soup cans. I remember seeing hanging on a gallery wall a black iron skillet with a fried egg (made of some plastic material) in the middle. On a pedestal there was a white porcelain modern sculpture. It turned out to be a toilet. At the same time, Action Drama was also making its statement in live theater. The audience would be seated, the play would begin, and the audience would follow the actors into the street. The play was staged along the route and the audience didn't know if the couple arguing in the parked car were part of the drama or not. So they noticed everything. I don't think this type of theater presentation lasted long, but it made an important point. Everything is drama. It's all around you. Life is drama. Open your eyes.

A lot of people thought this kind of thing was ridiculous, but it struck me as a new way to see the world. Everything could be art—a fried egg in a black skillet. Open your eyes. Art is everywhere.

When I became a professional free-lance photographer, I carried this concept with me. Anything could be worth capturing on film—a black garden hose lying on red tiles, my father's tools on a solder-stained workbench. It made my everyday life richer because I was always looking for the ordinary that I could help others see was something worth noticing. My own daily life was full of searching for beauty in the mundane, and because I was looking, I found it. It fed my soul because all day long I was looking for, and finding, lovely things around me.

I believe this applies nicely to our ability to see the fingerprints of God in small things in our lives. Here's an example from an email that came recently from my friend Darda. "The Lord took care of my rain spout that had fallen down and my son, John, is too busy right now to fix it. Because a piece of mail for my neighbor was delivered in my mail box, I called them to meet me and said I would give it to them. When she came, she saw my rain spout and said her husband would take a look at it. He did, and was able to put it back in place and screw it together. All because God put a piece of mail in the wrong box." You could call this coincidence, serendipity, or luck. Many do. Darda did not. She immediately attributed this blessing to God watching out for her. Is He? Or is it just the goodness of neighbors?

It makes me think of the time I was looking out my kitchen window. There was a strong wind that day, and the branches of the pine trees were waving, looking like long, shaggy arms. I was thinking how much it seemed as if they were moving their limbs on their own. Someone who knew nothing about atmospheric phenomena would not automatically attribute that gesturing to something external to them. We've seen people wave. It looks just like that. So, through empirical evidence, we can make that association of cause and effect.

How would I explain wind to someone who cannot see it and has never felt it or even heard it? The only way that person can be convinced is by standing outside and feeling it for themselves. I think it's the same with the supernatural. Many times the Daily Divine goes unrecognized, the good that happens to us being attributed to coincidence, or even the goodness of other people. I don't go with coincidence, which rabbis say is not a kosher word, but yes, certainly the goodness of people. But, behind it all, Scripture says every good and perfect gift comes down from the Father of Lights. We are created in His image, and when we do good for one another, we're acting like Him, and the world is a better place.

I think the way you see this kind of thing reveals the way you see your life's journey. Are you going it alone, or is God alongside you as Scripture says He promises to be? I think of the well-timed phone call or the neighbor's misplaced letter as fingerprints of God because they're small, and you have to want to see them. You have to open your spiritual eyes. It takes a certain willingness to see things in a new way—the egg in the frying pan, the couple in the car at the curb. We tend to go blandly on our way, oblivious to all that surrounds us, and we miss the fingerprints of God—and the delight of knowing He is leaving evidences of His presence and caring in the mundane of our daily lives. These next stories show the fingerprints of God in small things.

Carol's Story

My friend Carol had a special pair of earrings that her daughter Stephanie had given her. They weren't expensive, just sentimental and much enjoyed. Then, somehow, one was missing. Carol searched her house and yard and even the walkways around her neighborhood where she walked Angel and Fritz.

"About two weeks later," Carol said, "I happened to be sitting on the couch talking on the phone to a lady from church and something caught my eye. One of those little stuffed animals that the dogs play with was sitting there on the floor near the sliding glass door, and between its two front paws I saw something shiny. I thought, *That can't be.* It was that earring! I saw it and I screamed, and I still had this lady on the phone. I said, 'My earring!' and told her the story." Goodness of God. I knew it was a miracle."

In this case, the earring Carol lost wasn't a family heirloom. Carol loved them, and God cared about her distress. He also has a great sense of humor. I have a picture of the earring there between the front legs of the stuffed animal. Makes me laugh inside to think of it. Carol lives a vibrant spiritual life in full view of God, neighbors, and whoever happens to be around. And I bet it gives God a chuckle when she reacts to His surprises with such enthusiasm. Only He would have thought of placing her missing earring in a setting like that. Cute. Sometimes He's just so cute!

Sandy's Story

"My mother did not go to church. I wanted to, but couldn't. I can never remember her talking about God or reading the Bible. Then my sister started going to church and soon after I had enough strength to start going too. That was the start of a new life. I finally was strong enough to put God before my mother and her bad spirit. I had a *very controlling* mother and was never allowed to date, have friends over or live a normal life. At times she would lock me in the yard even at age 30. I had such fear of her. I never thought I would ever get to meet a man and get married. I did believe in God all my life though and loved Him.

"One day I was praying and I said to God, 'Please send someone to me that I could be a good wife to.'

"My mother had a back problem and was always complaining. I remembered hearing about Dr. Pace and how good of a doctor he was, so I called and that day we went to see him. I liked him right away as a person as he was very kind to all that I saw. God had this happen as my mother had such control of me. God was working in Bill's life also. Bill had a loving, God-loving mother who took him to church as a child and taught him God's ways and was always reading the Bible. So Bill had a good start and loved God all his life and went to church even as a teenager. When we got together we both had love for God which no one could take away.

"Shortly after getting married, we started attending church together and down the road Bill became a minister and still is to this day. That was our most precious gift. The rest of the story had trials from my mother and other people, but we learned a lot and grew even closer to God. People can see how we love each other and it keeps growing even to this day. All through our lives God has been the center."

I met Dr. Bill Pace in the 1980s when he began working with my father pioneering microcurrent with my dad's new inventions. Dr. Pace was able to innovate applications for this ground-breaking modality, and soon he was helping teach seminars my father was offering to eager practitioners. I remember watching Dr. Pace demonstrate techniques, all the while explaining the principles behind the protocols. And he was funny. My dad said it was because of all his experience keeping congregations engaged as he preached. He was competent, professional, but not flashy, brash, or acting like a celebrity. He had the integrity that made people trust him, he had the gentleness that made women feel safe in his presence, and he was kind.

I'm telling you this because one of the miraculous parts of Sandy's story is God kept Bill Pace, an extremely eligible and desirable bachelor, reserved for her. He wasn't a kid when she met him. He'd been in practice long enough to have gained a stellar reputation. I'm sure there were women who would have loved to have his attention, but God kept him for the young woman who prayed, "Please send someone to me that I could be a good wife to."

I met Sandy years later when my mother was ill. My father was taking care of her at home and Dr. Pace would come to treat her. He brought Sandy with him to visit with Mom. Sometimes I'd be there helping my dad. That's how we got to know each other and became friends.

I don't know how many people ask God to pick their spouse for them, but I'll tell you, Bill and Sandy Pace are lights like a city on a hill. They have a gentleness together that isn't common in these times of pushy, self-promoting striving for preeminence. They come like servants and serve with love. Whenever they walked into my parents' house, the atmosphere changed in the room and whatever frustrations or exhaustions my mom, dad, or I might be feeling disappeared.

I didn't know Sandy's story. I figured she was brought up in a supportive family, going to church since she was a little girl. She had such sweet goodness about her. So when she sent me the story of how she met Bill, I was shocked. I think there are many ways for a life to give glory to God, and not all supernatural interventions are front page news. Some are quiet and gentle, but their influences are powerful and they keep going on and on like little ripples across the pond.

The Boy Left Behind

This story is not small but I included it here because it's about seeing in new ways. Sometimes we face situations that make no sense to us. It's in those times that we can become discouraged, disappointed, offended, and begin to distrust and desert God. Chuck Smith told this story at one of the Calvary Chapel pastors' conferences I attended in the 1990s. I was so deeply moved that I went up to him afterwards and asked, "May I repeat that story in print?" Looking directly into my eyes and taking both of my hands in his, he said in his deep, kind voice, "You may do whatever you like with anything I say. You have my total permission." This is what he said:

"I was invited by the Chinese government to talk to them about Jesus. To get there, the Lord opened the door in a very unusual and miraculous way. We have a Korean fellowship at our church. One of the members is a woman whose family was living in North Korea under Communist rule. They had made plans for escape and, when she was just two years old, they got word that they had to leave immediately. No time to do anything, not even pack. If you're going to get out, you have to just go. It so happened that their oldest son wasn't home at that particular time, so they had to make a decision: Do we leave with the rest of the family and leave the son here or do we just lose our opportunity to escape? They decided they would escape in hopes of getting their son out later. So the family escaped minus the one son. Unfortunately, the parents were never able to contact him. They spent their lives praying that God would somehow help them, but both mother and father died without ever having heard from that one boy again.

"This Korean lady and her sister had been meeting at our church every Wednesday and praying that God would help them to somehow contact their brother who was somewhere over there, they didn't know where. As they were praying one Wednesday afternoon, the Lord gave this lady a telephone number. She called it. It was a Manchurian prefix. She dialed it and her brother answered. She didn't know if it was him so she started asking questions. He couldn't believe it was his sister on the phone. It was a thing incredulous for both of them. But as they talked they realized, yes, it was her brother. He was a general in the Communist army. He was over the whole Manchurian area. And he said, 'You *must* come and see me.' He got visas for her and her sister and they went over and visited him in China. It was actually through him that we got the official government invitation to come. And through him we had the State Dinner in the State House. We went into this place where the big wigs go. I ate all kinds of stuff that I don't know what I ate and I really don't want to know either, but I liked it.

"I had a chance to meet her brother and talk to him. I said, 'You know, years ago when you were a boy and your family escaped and you were left, no doubt in your mind you became bitter against God. How could God take away your family? Maybe you even became angry with God. Turned against Him because you were left behind all alone. No doubt through the years you've wondered and wondered why God would allow that. You know, God was wanting to reach this nation for Jesus Christ, and I believe that He has chosen you as an instrument to open the doors for the Gospel to be brought. And all that, though you didn't understand it and it was so hard for you to work it out, yet it was all a part of God's plan to put things together.' Tears came into his eyes. The bitterness that he'd felt against God began to melt. He began to see that

God's hand was in the whole thing for the purpose of opening the door to this vast number of people. He accepted the Lord while we were there. It was just a glorious experience.

"The government is inviting us to come back. In fact they want us to have a pastors' conference for all of the three Self Movement pastors and they said 'We will also invite the house church pastors.'

"The Lord does work in interesting ways. In our own lives there are times we go through experiences that we don't understand. It would seem that God has forsaken us, that God isn't hearing us. We sometimes question God's love because we just don't understand the things we're going through—the pain or the hurt or the suffering that we might be experiencing, but we must be careful not to judge God until we know the whole story. So often in the midst of the story we're prone to jump to conclusions that are wrong. God's hand is on our lives. God's hands are in these things. And though we don't understand the disappointment or the pain or the sorrow or the problems that we've been going through, God's got a purpose. All things are working together for good. That you've gotta know.

"There's got to be certain foundational truths that we have established in our hearts that are unshakable. Whenever you come up against what you don't understand, you've got to have those foundations that you can fall back on—things that I *do* understand.

"What do I understand? I understand that God is good. I understand that God loves me, and that whatever has happened in my life, God has allowed it to happen for good. I may not understand what good can come out of this, but that doesn't matter. If God has allowed it to happen, it's happened for good.

I understand that God is far wiser than I am. The problem is that God is always working from the eternal perspective and I'm always living in the temporal. God is interested in my eternal good and I'm interested in my temporal good. Sometimes things that are not temporally good for me are eternally good for me. And God in His love is working from the eternal. That's why we don't always understand.

"The 73rd Psalm is a classic example. He begins with an affirmation, 'Truly God is good. But as for me, my foot almost slipped. I was almost wiped out. I was observing the prosperity of the wicked. They seem to have everything they want. No problems. They're blasphemous. They're horrible people, and yet they seem to have more than their hearts could wish. And here am I trying to live the right kind of life, do the right thing. I have nothing but trouble. Problems vexing me all the time.' He began to draw false conclusions. He began to think, *Well, it really doesn't pay to try to live the right kind of life.* He said it was too painful for him until…'until I went into the sanctuary of God and then I saw their end.'

You see, going into the sanctuary of God, he got the right perspective. Make sure when people come into the sanctuary of God they get the eternal perspective. They're living out there in that temporal world getting bloody, bruised, and sometimes they just crawl into church, beaten by the world and their contact with the world. But when they come into the church, they should come into the consciousness and the awareness of the eternal. What a difference it makes when you begin to look at things from the eternal perspective!

"Rather than envying the wicked, he now feels sorry for them. 'Surely Thou hast set them in slippery places. They're caught up with terrors. In a moment they're going to be destroyed. But, Lord, You're continually with me. You hold me by the right hand and You're going to receive me into glory.' He says he'd begun to think like an animal. He'd begun to lose the spiritual dimension, but the sanctuary of God was the answer, seeing things from the eternal perspective. And this General began to see things from the eternal perspective and God did a real number on him. And God will do a number on us when we can come into the eternal perspective and see the eternal Plan of God."

7

Prayer

We stood at the gravesite with its freshly opened earth, having just buried the 16 year-old daughter of a Chinese couple I knew. I wanted to support them in their time of devastation even though I didn't know their daughter. There's a Chinese custom of sending things to the loved one in the afterworld by burning paper representations of the things you want them to have, such as special paper money, glasses, clothes, cars. The parents weren't burning anything at this Lake County cemetery, but the father came up to me after the service and said he had been burning things for his daughter at home. "I don't know if it really does anything," he confessed with an embarrassed look, "but it makes me feel better."

A lot of people treat prayer like that. I don't know if it actually does anything, but it makes me feel better.

As you know from my love bomb stories, we've seen it definitely does something. Prayer has power, not because we do, but because we're inviting Almighty God to intervene in our lives. But if He already knows what we need before we ask, why should we have to say anything? Because we have free will, and He will not violate it. He does not intrude. And another thing, it's always about relationship. We get to partner with the Creator of everything by making our requests and then seeing the results. Jesus said to ask the Father that He might be glorified and our joy may be full. That's quite wonderful, 'way better than sending paper cars and clothes in smoke.

Someone said each prayer is like a single snowflake. These snowflakes pile up in the mountains until they become massive deposits of snowpack. When summer comes, the heat causes them to melt and run down to water the dry places. I prayed for thirty years for my father to come to the Lord, and at the end, he did.

As I'm writing this book, I'm seeing how often prayer comes up as a crucial part of the story. Prayer, as conversations with God, is probably the most supernatural aspect of the Christian life. Think of it. We little frail, often stupid, short-sighted, ordinary human beings can commune with the Creator of the universe, the One who invented quantum physics and the composition of stars. Do you enjoy talking with creative people? physicists? farmers? animal lovers? musicians? philosophers? writers? People who have the joy of life? He is all of that and more. He's the most fascinating Being you will ever meet, and He loves you and understands you better than anyone else ever can. When you talk to this marvelous Being, sometimes He reveals things you couldn't possibly know—things that help you in your griefs and struggles. And He will use pictures, words, stories that will be meaningful to you alone—at your level, in your language. It's one of the most wonderful ways He lets you know you are completely known, understood, and perfectly loved.

By the way, at the time of their daughter's car crash, her mom and dad were estranged. Their daughter had been praying for their reconciliation. At her grave site, her mom and dad came together in their grief, and more than twenty years later, they are still together.

Connections

"Andrew," was born with a rare blood disease, like leukemia. His grandma was beside herself with worry and asked for prayer. Doctors had told the family the tiny, fragile newborn was not likely to survive. But God loves babies, and I had been on the prayer team for enough years to know He did surprising and impossible things for them. After a few months, Andrew's grandma said he was stable and, amazingly, his blood was normal. He was still underweight, but he was beginning to grow.

Over the years, I continued to pray for Andrew as the Lord brought him to mind. One day his grandma approached me as I sat waiting for the Sunday service to begin. "I want you to meet someone," she said. Out from behind her peeked a shy, slender little blonde boy. "This is Andrew," she said. Andrew looked at me, then rushed over, threw his arms around my neck, and kissed me on the cheek. Then he took a step away, smiled sweetly, his eyes shining, and returned to his grandma's side. She was astonished. "He never does anything like that," she said.

I knew why. It's happened before. When we pray for someone, a connection is made in the spiritual realm. It's invisible as a single silk thread, insistent as spider web. The more you pray for that one, the more strands are added til it can become as thick and strong as a steel cable. When you finally meet face to face, your spirits recognize each other. There's something familiar that can be felt. It's a lovely, gracious comfort in each other's presence. Too far-fetched? Let me tell you another story.

For a few years I'd been working with Matthew and Amie Chapman, puppy raisers preparing dogs for service organizations. Puppies who have problems with fear, aggression, distractibility, or other behavioral issues get dropped from the program quickly in order to keep from using important resources on dogs who choose not to work with a disabled person. About 50% of puppies who start off being socialized for service never make it to graduation. Therefore, there is always a shortage of service dogs available. As a member of a guide dog team, I know what a blessing it is to have a canine partner, so I started working with the Chapmans to see if I could help with behavioral issues in their puppies. That's how I started praying with them for the healing of Penny's problems. She is a black Great Dane mix—a formidable animal who had issues with fear and unpredictable aggression. She wasn't shy, but she was wary around strangers and particular about whom she would trust. The Chapmans believed she would be a good service animal if she could be relieved of her fear and aggression, so we met several times by phone and prayed for her together.

One day the Chapmans came for a visit. They brought all their dogs—Ozzy, Ricki, Pixie, and Penny. When everyone was settled in my house, Penny decided she needed to be in my lap. She managed her huge head and her right foreleg because that's all that would fit. Amie and Matthew made some sounds of amazement. They said it was very unusual for her to be in my lap.

I'm including this story about Penny because dogs don't do placebo. When you pray for someone, their spirit knows. Even if you've never met in person, there is a recognition that is deep and strong. Even when a person is in a coma or has advanced Alzheimer's, their spirit knows. So go ahead and pray. They will hear you and it will matter.

Daniel

Three times a day, at the time of prayers back home, Daniel prayed. Ever wonder why? When King Solomon dedicated the temple in Jerusalem, Daniel was listening. When the enemy carried him away to Babylon, he was remembering. Throughout his captivity, Daniel faithfully prayed towards Jerusalem, towards the temple that was no longer standing, not one stone upon another.

Here's what Solomon prayed: "When they sin against You (for there is no one who does not sin), and You become angry with them and deliver them to the enemy, and they take them captive to a land far or near; yet when they come to themselves in the land where they were carried captive, and repent, and make supplication to You in the land of their captivity, saying, 'We have sinned, we have done wrong, and have committed wickedness'; and when they return to You with all their heart and with all their soul in the land of their captivity, where they have been carried captive, and pray toward their land which You gave to their fathers, the city which You have chosen, and toward the temple which I have built for Your name: then hear from heaven Your dwelling place their prayer and their supplications, and maintain their cause, and forgive Your people who have sinned against You." (2 Chron 6:36-39 NKJV)

Daniel had been praying from the land of their captivity for seventy years, one silken thread at a time, he was connecting with God. By the time he had to face the lions, Daniel's connection with Yahweh was strong as a thick steel cable. It's a good thing to remember as we live in a society that wants to change our names, give us alien identities, force us to bow down to their gods and forsake our own. Prayer can keep us connected to Jesus in powerful ways that can shut the mouths of lions. Scripture says God chooses our leaders, and all through the Bible we see Him using wicked leaders to wake His people up, proving to them their need for Him, the one true God. It also brings opportunities for God to make a distinction between His people and the wicked culture around them—lights shining in the darkness—the deeper the darkness, the brighter the light.

The Worth of One Person's Prayers

I just got this amazing insight from God. I asked about Peter's release from jail (the angel had to kick him to wake him up). I asked if he would have been rescued if the people hadn't prayed. I got No. Really? I asked if there had been one person praying would he have been rescued. I got Yes. Hmmmm... Better double check that. Is it in the Bible? Yes. Scriptural confirmation is Abraham talking to God about the destruction of Sodom and Gomorrah. "If there are 10 righteous?" Well, there really weren't any, not even Lot, who showed by his actions he still had his heart in the world, but Lot was rescued as a result of that conversation. "And it came to pass, when God destroyed the cities of the plain, that God remembered Abraham, and sent Lot out of the midst of the overthrow, when He overthrew the cities in which Lot had dwelt." (Genesis 19:29 NKJV) Scripture says, "God remembered Abraham." They'd talked about it. One person can make that kind of difference in the rescue of another from impossible circumstances, including despair, depression, fear, anger, and anxiety.

Participation Prophecy

So here's Daniel reading the scroll of Jeremiah. He sees these words, "This is what the Lord says: 'When seventy years are completed for Babylon, I will come to you and fulfill my good promise to bring you back to this place. For I know the plans I have for you,' declares the Lord, 'plans to prosper you and not to harm you, plans to give you hope and a future. Then you will call on me and come and pray to me, and I will listen to you. You will seek me and find me when you seek me with all your heart. I will be found by you,' declares the Lord, 'and will bring you back from captivity. I will gather you from all the nations and places where I have banished you,' declares the Lord, 'and will bring you back to the place from which I carried you into exile.'" (Jeremiah 29:10-14 NKJV)

Daniel was carried off in the first group of captives, a teenager who has now served in the courts of four kings. He is elderly—possibly in his late 80s, and realizes it's been about seventy years since he was taken from Jerusalem. He reads, "You will call to Me and come and pray to Me and I will listen to you and bring you back to the place from which I carried you into exile." So Daniel begins to seek the Lord with all his heart. He puts on sackcloth. He fasts. He earnestly prays and seeks the face of God, and Gabriel comes and delivers the most astonishing prophecies about End Times to be found in the entire Bible (Daniel 9).

I've read that account before. I knew Daniel prayed and Gabriel came with details of what God intended to do, not just in bringing back His people, but all the way to their intended End. What I missed was the connection between the return to the land and Daniel's prayers. Before this, I assumed when God said it, it was sure to happen a certain way no matter what. Just sit back and see how He brings it about. But what if it's not that prescribed? What if God extends to people of that era an invitation to contribute? My friend Dan calls it "participation prophecy." He said, "The final outcome is always the same with God, but how you get there can be totally different. The prophecy in Jeremiah is a participation prophecy. 'If you do this, I will do this.' So if you don't do it, He's not going to do it because He doesn't lie. He's not going to say, 'Well, I'll do it anyway. You were supposed to do it, but you didn't. But I'm the forgiving parent. I understand. You can go out, even though you're on restriction, I'll let you out for the night.' No. It has to happen some other way. The outcome's the same, and we could get lazy in knowing that, but what we go through is going to be completely different if we participate or not. Your life, what you go through, and what the world around you is like will be different. These are prophecies that affect millions of people. They affect the country, the world. If you participate, you can make things better. You can make things happen. If you don't, you could be delaying it, you're putting it off, or it won't happen at all through you, and now it has to happen a different way. They're not prophecies you can look at and go, 'Oh, it'll be interesting to see how that happens.' That's what I do. I look at these prophecies and say, 'Oh, that's interesting. How's that going to work?' God always does things that come about in ways I could never imagine. I couldn't imagine COVID-19 or lockdowns. Now we're going into the stage of the vaccine—the vaxxed and the unvaxxed. Things come about that you can't imagine, such as how the Jews were going to go back to Jerusalem after World War II and become a nation."

I wonder how many others were seeking God's face at the end of the seventy years. In Jeremiah 29:1, it says, "This is the text of the letter that the prophet Jeremiah sent from Jerusalem to the surviving elders among the exiles and to the priests, the prophets and all the other people Nebuchadnezzar had carried into exile from Jerusalem to Babylon."The ones who would have known about this letter were already old enough to be elders, priests, and prophets. Most likely they were dead, but what about "all the others that were carried off"? Who knows? The only thing Scripture tells us is Daniel had a copy, studied it, and took the prophecy seriously enough to do what God said. If you do this, I will do that. Daniel did the first part, God did the rest.

Why does this matter? I've been reading prophecies that have yet to be fulfilled. It never occurred to me that I could actually contribute to bringing them about. Daniel might have been the only one in Babylon seeking God's face at the end of the seventy years, and yet because of that one man praying earnestly, a surprising freedom was granted to them. I'm only one small person who feels more and more like a captive in a foreign land. I have the sense that this is God's choice for us for now, and it may be that we won't get to go to our real country till it's over, but I can pray and seek the face of God and my life, the lives around me, and my part of the world will be better because of it. Here's one example. These are God's instructions to His people, newly captured and carried off to Babylon. They may very well apply to us as well. "… seek the peace and prosperity of the city to which I have carried you into exile. Pray to the Lord for it, because if it prospers, you too will prosper." (Jeremiah 29:7) We may not be able to affect the outpourings of wrath on obdurate earth-dwellers, but we can love bomb our communities, making it possible for them to become areas where natural light is seen in dwelling places no matter how thick the darkness is outside.

Of course, Daniel wasn't just any person off the street deciding to ask God for something huge. As I reported above, Daniel had been connecting with God every day for seventy years. He had a very strong relationship with the Most High. It's possible that Daniel was the only one in Babylon seeking God's face about the release at the end of the seventy years, and yet because of that one man praying earnestly, a whole bunch of people got to go back to their promised land.

But wait. There's More. Daniel asked about Jeremiah's prophecy and Gabriel was dispatched to answer him, but he surprised Daniel by also giving him insight into the future for his people —information that could decode events for those who would be living at the time of the End. That information is so critical that Jesus quoted it to His disciples in the private briefing on the Mount of Olives.

The night of His betrayal, Jesus told His disciples He would tell them what was going to happen because they were His friends. Daniel was also God's friend. Gabriel said,"At the beginning of thy supplications the commandment came forth, and I am come to shew thee; for thou art greatly beloved: therefore understand the matter, and consider the vision." (Daniel 9:23KJV) When you're God's trusted friend, He tells you things, sometimes really big ones. Another one of God's faithful friends was John. Look at what Jesus revealed to him! In these days, it's helpful to hear from Jesus what we need to know. But you have to be His trusted friend.

What if you haven't gotten there yet? What if you're barely starting to be interested in a deeper relationship? Prayer is the best way to build a bond with God. The Bible gives Him many names, and each one represents an aspect of His character and offers a point of connection. Jesus called heavenly Father "Abba." It's Hebrew for "Papa." Ravi calls God "Daddy." It's a wonderful thing to be able to feel close enough to the creator of everything to call Him by a name that embodies a full wealth of close and loving relationship. In no other religion may devotees call their god "Father." It's too intimate, too familiar. But here's what the Apostle Paul writes in this wonderful prayer:

"For this reason [seeing the greatness of this plan by which you are built together in Christ], I bow my knees before the Father of our Lord Jesus Christ, For whom every family in heaven and on earth is named [that Father from whom all fatherhood takes its title and derives its name]. May He grant you out of the rich treasury of His glory to be strengthened and reinforced with mighty power in the inner man by the [Holy] Spirit [Himself indwelling your innermost being]. May Christ through your faith [actually] dwell (settle down, abide, make His permanent home) in your hearts! May you be rooted deep in love and founded securely on love, That you may have the power and be strong to apprehend and grasp with all the saints [God's devoted people, the experience of that love] what is the breadth and length and height and depth [of it];" (Ephesians 3:14-18 AMPC)

But wait! What if you really don't want to talk to Father? What if "father" is not a comforting name, one reassuring a child there is a protective, providing, guiding relationship, a guaranteed special place in the family under the shelter of his care? What if your father was absent, abusive, demanding, critical, unstable, unpredictable, inconsistent unreliable, obsessive, controlling, violent, volatile, uncaring, impossible to please? I know too many people, Christians and not, who cannot relate to Father God. Some of these wounded Christians wouldn't pray at all if it weren't for Jesus. They can huddle behind the "good Son" and thus escape the wrath of angry, judgmental, disappointed Father.

Jesus said He came to make connection with Father possible for the first time after the Fall. That sounds good, unless you really don't want to be connected to Him. What if your father was distant, untrustworthy, a tyrannical bully? What if you never felt safe with him? What if, when you were left alone with him, he said terrible things to you, or, possibly worse, you found you had nothing to say to one another?

My first decades of prayer were a matter of dutifully showing up for orders, faithfully carrying out my responsibilities, respectfully thanking Father for His provision and forgiveness, and putting myself through the spiritual MRI to scan for that which required corrective measures. I had no idea I could be His friend. I finally had to call Him Papa because "Father" was too much like my Confucian/legalistic relationship—formal, respectful, always conscious of being in the proper demeanor to approach the Most High.

I missed out on years of wonderful fellowship with Papa God because of my early training in a legalistic church, but other churches also make the God of the Old Covenant formidable and scary and the God of the New Covenant gracious and forgiving. Wait. Aren't they the same? Jesus said, "I and the Father are One." That's not to say they are one person, but one in essence, power, and intention. "When you've seen Me," Jesus said, "you've seen the Father." One God. One unity of being. One heart of love.

I admit I've had to work at this. All of the artistic representations reinforce the intimidating image of Father. In the Sistine Chapel, Adam lies naked and inert watching the approach of a powerful white-bearded stern Ancient of Days. Then you have all the wrath, starting with the curses in Genesis 3 as soon as He is disobeyed. Many of us have hidden from the one so quick to punish any disobedience. I'm not going to go into a lot of theology here. I just want to say there are reasons for everything God does. My friend Dan says, "He always does what's best." God is love. That's repeated throughout the Bible. He's not schizophrenic. His motivation is always love. His character is love. His essence is love. Therefore, there is love and the best for everyone behind everything He does.

Most of us have been told God sees everything and you'd better behave. "He sees you when you're sleeping. He knows when you're awake. He knows if you've been bad or good so… watch out!" When Dan told me about some really crummy things a big company was doing, I said, "Nobody gets away with anything." I didn't mean whatever you've done will be found out and punished, which is something Dan was taught when he was a little kid. I meant this is not all there is. They may feel powerful and important, but someday they will die. Someday they will stand before the Lord and give an account of what they did with the life He gave them. And we will also stand before the Lord. We'll be robed in the righteousness of Christ, forgiven and welcomed Home, but we didn't "get away" with anything. The debt to God had to be paid, and Jesus did it. And we were wise enough to accept the gift.

Father never intended humans to go to hell. It was prepared for the devil and his angels. He created each one of us before time began and provided unlimited possibilities for us to explore and have fruitful life . Do you realize what would have happened if Jesus hadn't taken our sin debt on Himself and paid it all? There's no reincarnation, no endless chances to get everything right. It's appointed once for us to die, and then the judgment. Without Jesus, there would be no forgiveness, only judgment. No escape. No atonement. No reconciliation with God. No possibility of heaven. "But," you say, "maybe things would have been different and we wouldn't have been born." Too late. As Dan says, "We were already in the queue."

But Yahweh, I AM, Father, Son, and Holy Spirit, in oneness of agreement, purpose, essence, and love, saved us. It wasn't only the Passover Lamb, but all members of the Godhead together. All of them were involved. You can see them active in the *Tanakh* (the Old Testament), preparing the way for Messiah's incarnation. I encourage you to explore this astounding holy ground and discover the wonders of the God of Genesis to Malachai, who is gracious, long-suffering, forgiving, generous, and full of love. In Him is light and there is no darkness at all, not even a shadow of turning. He is all good, and it's *kalos* good as well as morally pure. Being around that God is delightful. You can be your entire authentic self and He will embrace you in grace, then when you pray, you have such confidence in His power, wisdom and goodness. Here indeed is Someone you can trust—completely. Abba.

Okay, but there's a lot of wrath, judgment, people dropping dead, thunder and fire and plagues and stuff in the Old Testament, not to mention the ground opening up and swallowing a crowd of dissenters and waters covering the entire globe.

Yeah. I know. I've been thinking about that for years. I've written some of my understandings in this book, but for now I want to offer you a chance to experience Papa a different way. Rather than giving you a treatise on why I no longer think of Papa as stern and mean, I'm offering some stories—some mine and some from others—that represent the heart of Papa God in different situations and in different ways. God is multifaceted—He can't be known from a single encounter—so here is a composite view, more like what a butterfly can see with its 180 degree field of vision through round compound eyes. I'm hoping they give you a gestalt where the whole is more than the sum of the parts. May they help you perceive God in greater fullness and invite you into a deeper relationship with the Father of Eternities, the One who is mighty to save, and whose every thought and deed towards you comes from His heart of love.

8

Papa's Heart

The Bolshoi Master

We were excited and scared. Students from dance schools all over Southern California were given the opportunity of going to a big studio in Los Angeles to study for one day with a master of the famous Bolshoi Ballet. We stood before the wall of mirrors, all of us looking small and anxious in our black leotards and soft ballet slippers. I was one of the smallest, a scrawny six-year-old with inflexible feet who was only taking ballet because I fell so often my mother thought dance lessons might help me be less clumsy.

The master strode around in his heavy black street shoes, barking out ballet terms in a thick Russian accent. I could see him in the mirrored wall walking among the dancers, smacking with his stick their legs, feet, buttocks, arms—whatever wasn't positioned perfectly. I was very nervous. When he got to me, he seemed a huge, stocky bear all in black. He whacked me smartly with his stick. My calf stung. My eyes stung from tears I tried very hard to hold back. I didn't want him to know I was crying, but tears slid down my face and I couldn't wipe them away because I was trying to keep my hands in the right positions. I could hear his gruff voice firing orders amidst the swishing of slippers lightly brushing the worn wooden floor. His footsteps were getting farther away. But then he was back. Somehow he had seen my face. I was mortified. He took my hand and led me to a chair. Surely he was going to make me sit there the rest of the day. I was humiliated. But the chair was not for me. He took a seat and lifted me onto his lap. He held me in his arms and spoke to me very softly, as gently and kindly as if he were my grandfather. I didn't understand a word of Russian and don't remember anything else about that day—only his gentleness and the immense comfort and security of his arms. Without understanding a word, I realized that a person can seem harsh and demanding, but he doesn't hate you. Behind the kind of training necessary for you to be your best is a heart of love tender as a loving father cherishing his much beloved child.

Carie

For most of his life, Dan has had dogs, but in more recent years his lifestyle and living conditions weren't the best for having pets. Then he moved. The new place had a nice little house by the lake with some acreage and lots of room for a dog to roam and play. Off he went to the Pound. When he returned, he had a sweet little black and white puppy, so small she fit into his two cupped hands. "She's so quiet," he told me, "I think she's going to be a very calm dog. I'm going to call her 'Carie.'"

Carie was quiet because she was sick. Terribly sick. She began to cough. Soon it was obvious she needed help, but Dan was raised where you didn't spend a lot of money on your pets. Animals were animals. You saved your money to take care of your kids. He thought maybe Carie would get well on her own. He fixed her a box on the front porch, made her as comfortable as possible, and went to the store. When he returned, she wasn't in her box. He called for her, but of course, he'd had her only a day and she didn't know her name or his voice.

Dan was worried. He knew sometimes sick animals would find a place to hide and die. He scanned the uneven slopes, tawny with weeds and dried grasses. Carie was small, but she was black and white. He figured if she was there he would see her. He didn't. There were so many places to look. He decided to walk up the hill behind the house, the loose rocks and dirt uneven under his feet. He was starting to think maybe he wasn't meant to find her when he stepped directly on an old glass bottle that rolled under his foot and sent him headlong onto hands and knees, his face just inches from the ground. Right there, hardly visible through a covering of dry grass, was something black and white. It was Carie. She had found a hole and curled into it. She was barely alive. At that moment God spoke to Dan. "You chose her. She is your responsibility. Take care of her."

It was Parvo. Carie was on an IV drip for a week at the vet's office. Dan drove there every day to spend an hour or two with the tiny puppy, massaging her, talking to her, encouraging her to live. Surprisingly, she did. He found out later that all the other puppies in her litter had died.

There are lots of directions I could go now. I could tell you about Carie's life with Dan, and how she wasn't quiet or calm. When he was throwing sticks for her, she would get so excited and loud she'd sound as if she were being tortured. Everyone loved Carie except my elderly black lab Velvet, whom Carie, a McNab Shepard, insisted on herding. Still, with her jaunty personality and happy energy, Carie became a neighborhood favorite and eventually brought joy to a bitter and isolated man who lived nearby. But that doesn't answer the "So what?" question. You told me this story. So what?

When I asked Dan what he thought the "So what?" of this story is, he said, "God cares about little sick puppies. He wanted me to find her." When I heard that, tears came to my eyes. Yes. That's the heart of Papa God. He knows every sparrow that falls. Death was not part of His Plan. Still isn't. In His eyes, each life is precious, even a Parvo-sick Pound Puppy hiding in a hole in the ground.

One more thing comes to mind as I write. Dan went looking for her. When he found her, he didn't leave her there. He took her out of the hole and spent a week of care and a lot of money to save her life. We were all Pound Puppies. Jesus chose us, adopted us, and welcomed us into His Family. He spent a lot of effort and it cost Him plenty to save our lives. He did not leave us in a hole to die. Now He invites us to help Him pull others out of the Pit and welcome them to vibrant life as a much-beloved child of God.

My Time

My son John and his wife Shelly have been going through probably the worst trial of their adult lives. John told me the only thing he could bear to listen to, the only thing that gave him strength and peace, as he drove the hour and fifteen minutes to work and back was worship music and the Bible. Nothing else brought him any relief. This is from a boy whose first word was "booka." He has been an avid reader since early childhood, and discovered the joys of audio books on those long commutes in his car. However, in this time of extreme stress and pain, even the availability of the book he had been eagerly awaiting had no appeal. He needed worship. He needed the Bible. He needed time with God.

Five months passed. The sharp anguish diminished enough that John began to feel less desperate, more normal. One morning as he started to turn on that audio book he'd been wanting to hear, the Lord spoke clearly to his heart. "This is MY time," He told him. "You gave it to Me and I want it. You can listen to the book on the way back."

Epilogue

It's now months after John told me about his conversation with God. He said he still treasures that time with God on the long drive to work. The palpable sense of God's presence beside him continues with him all through the day and into the night. It's something wonderful that's now an integral part of his life, something that came about because of, not in spite of, his present difficulties. No wonder James said to count it all joy when you fall into diverse trials. Who would have guessed that the intense suffering would bring about indestructible joy? The Lord, your God, who is right there in the midst of your pain, is mighty. He is able to save you from hopeless despair. In His presence is fullness of joy. And the joy of the Lord is your strength.

John at Taco Bell

This incident happened when my son John was working at Taco Bell. It was the summer before he started his education at Bethany College and would be leaving home for the very first time. Here's what he told me.

"I was working the drive through at Taco Bell. There's a pad you lean against that opens the glass doors of the window. If you step away, it closes it. Some clown decided he'd be funny. After I gave him his order, he shot water at me with a water gun. I had already stepped back and the doors had closed, but I saw the water on the glass. I don't like water fights and I don't like to get wet. So I got a little angry and I felt a tap on my shoulder and an impression like God was saying to me, 'That is how it will be for you. Before you even know it, I will be there and I will protect you. That's who I will be for you.' And He's spent the last thirty years proving that He meant it."

Knowing that God is a very present help in trouble, our strengthener, our comforter, our peace, the one who cares deeply about the details of our lives no matter how small—that's the kind of supernatural relationship that transforms "normal" life into an adventure, one delightful with awareness that the God of the Universe is watching out for you, no matter how far away from home you must go.

At The Sea Wall

I was standing at the sea wall at Anchor Bay next to my husband's diving partner, Ron, a large, loud, Italian man who loved pasta and good beer. In his wetsuit, he looked like a big, black sea lion. He was gazing at his little daughter as she wandered at the edge of the water looking for interesting things to bring home. The love in his eyes was so deep that I said to myself, *I wish my dad would look at me like that.*

"But I do," I heard in my heart.

"I know," I answered, somewhat guardedly in case it was my imagination and not the voice of God. I recited a bit of Psalm 139—"Your thoughts towards me are as many as the grains of sands…"

"No," came the voice.

"No?" Suddenly I was disappointed. I wanted it to be Papa God looking at me with that much love.

"Look it up," the voice said.

I rushed back to my camper, turned in my Bible to Psalms and read, "How precious also are Your thoughts to me, O God! How great is the sum of them! If I count them, they would be more in number than the sand."

"Oh," I said, tears brimming in my eyes, "*more.*"

TEXTING "RACHEL"

A difficult and heart-breaking divorce left "Mark" a wreck and his family in a shambles. He tried to keep connected with his daughter, "Rachel," but she was being poisoned, and Mark was blamed for it all. Time increased the distance between them until there was only silence.

Recently Mark sent me this email: "I received a text from my daughter's mom. She said that Rachel was unhappy with me. I used to text her every day and I had stopped. At first I was annoyed. Yes, I had stopped my daily text to her. I stopped because she had stopped. At first I would receive prompt and loving responses to my texts. Then the replies came later in the day. Replies started to come the next day or the day after. Days would pass by between replies. It was soon clear to me that she wasn't interested in communicating with me. So I stopped. When Rachel's mom said she wanted the texts to resume and made it sound like my fault that our communication had halted, my first instinct was to ignore the message.

Why should I reach out when I had been so ignored? So I asked God. How do I respond to my daughter? He said to me, "I reach out to you every day all day long. There is frequently no response. But when you call out to Me, I am there for you. Be there for your daughter."

Update: A few months after sharing this story, Mark told me he had texted Rachel and had recently heard back from her. They texted back and forth all weekend, and he is getting to answer her questions about how to survive the hard parts of being an adult. As Mark told me this news, tears came to my eyes, and I heard them in his voice as well. For years I had been praying that they would be reconciled and be lovingly in one another's lives. Jesus died to redeem all that was lost even when it looks impossible. And I can tell you from experience: little girls need their daddy.

If You're Willing

My teenaged son, John, was miserably sick. He had a fever and a headache so severe he couldn't bear any light. He lay in the darkness, shades pulled shut, feeling totally wretched. Dennis and I had done all we knew to do. Helplessly we waited for the sickness to run its course.

Checking on him one evening, I was surprised to hear his cheerful voice. "Hi, Mom. I'm well," he said. Really? The last time I saw John, he was practically unconscious. "I prayed," he said. He told Jesus, "The leper said, 'if You're willing You can heal me,' and You said You were willing. If You're willing, Jesus, You can heal me." John said, "I heard, 'I'm willing' and felt something like a sticker being peeled off my forehead. And now I'm well."

Indeed he was. Suddenly. Totally.

It wasn't a huge emergency or a serious illness, but I think it's significant that Jesus doesn't have to be begged or implored, and the need doesn't have to be huge. He answered the quiet request of a suffering teenaged boy in a way that was so startlingly sweet that I remember it to this day.

The Ugly Phone Call

Back when I could still see pretty well, I had a portrait studio. One morning I noticed the flashing red light on the answering machine and pushed the button. I heard the voice of a young woman saying vile, disgusting things. Quickly I hit Erase, but I kept hearing the words even as I tried to work. At first I rebuked them. They came back relentlessly. Finally I decided every time I heard those words I would pray for her. And I did.

On the third day a most amazing thing happened. As I began to pray for the young woman, an overwhelming feeling of love for her came over me. Right then the Lord spoke. He said, "Of all the businesses in Lake County, I had her call you because I knew you would pray for her."

My friend Sheri says, "Most people have been hit by exploding bullets and what we hear coming out of their mouths are cries for help and screams of pain." Jesus said, "Father, forgive them, for they know not what they do." He charged us saying, "Love one another as I have loved you." He loved me when I was hostile and profane. Then He showed me how to love that young woman as He loved me. It's a great Plan, this passing along of the grace we've received. It's what He did, and so can we.

Wounded Animal

Today John told me he felt like a mortally wounded animal thrashing around on the ground. He said it didn't really do any good, but he did it anyway. The pressing need is for him to find another place to live, his landlords having given him notice that he has to be out by the 15th. It is now getting down to the wire, and all the doors he's tried have slammed shut. In a way, it's been surreal because doors that usually fly open haven't. For example, companies that finance real estate are usually like ravening wolves tracking and stalking you once they notice you near their lair. John called two, and both promised to call him back. Neither did. Houses would come up on his real estate search app and disappear before he had a chance to check them out. And friends who have recently found places and said they'd see if other rentals nearby were available have not. It really does appear that God is giving no options, hence the thrashing. John told me today God was saying, "Are you getting anything out of that? Are we done now?"

This evening, John sent me this email:

"I was thinking about the image I got of the mortally wounded animal in its death throes. It was a deer or an elk. I could see the big dark eye that was nearest to me as it lay on its side. It blinked in incomprehension as the life ebbed out of it. I could see the eye as the glimmer of life gradually faded out like a dwindling spark from a once roaring fire. God said to me, 'That is your Flesh. That is your scientific, logical, rational, reasonable, foolish human mind. That is your unbelief. It's dying. It has to. Then you can truly believe.'

"'Um…wow. Well, it hasn't served me very well so far. I'd say I'll miss it but I bet I won't. So, yeah, Lord, I guess I'm done.'"

The Boy on the Boat

"I'm so glad you're finally going to meet my pastor," Linda said, beaming. She had arranged for me to do a concert for the Easter morning service at the little church on the coast that she and her husband had attended for years before they moved to Lake County. I was excited too. She had told me about this pastor and the wondrous things he had done. One story in particular stuck in my memory, though I don't remember the pastor's name or the name of the woman, so I'll call him "Joe" and the woman "Helen." I'll call the boy "Toby."

Joe was a young pastor, gifted and charismatic in personality. He had been invited to preach at several churches scattered among the islands in the Philippines. Just as he was about to make reservations for flights, the Holy Spirit told him to go by boat instead. "But it will take much longer!" he protested, reluctantly giving in.

Pastor Joe was bored. He was a go-getter and this leisurely boat trip to the next island felt like such a waste of time. He wandered aimlessly around the deck. There was a map on the wall showing the route the boat was taking, a red line threading its way to each port. Pastor Joe studied it, tracing the red line with his finger. Then he flopped down on one of the deck chairs and laid back, hoping to at least catch a nap.

"Excuse me," a woman's voice said. Joe sat up. "Are you a pastor?" Joe said he was, and wondered how she knew. "My name is Helen," she said. They chatted a little. He noticed she had her brown hair in a tight bun—-kind of an old-fashioned hairstyle in those days. Then she left.

Joe settled back into the lounge chair and closed his eyes, but soon he heard Helen's voice again. "Pastor," she said, "This is Toby." When Joe opened his eyes he saw a woman and a little boy standing with Helen. "His mother would like you to pray for him." There was a napkin over the boy's face.

"What's wrong with him," he asked, lifting the napkin. Hastily he dropped it. The boy had no eyes.

"A battery blew up in his face," Helen said. "Please, Pastor. She wants you to pray for him." Backing away, Pastor Joe began stammering, making noises about prayer and what God does and doesn't do... "Please," Helen said again. "Please pray."

So he did, reluctantly, with a lot of disclaimers. He was making yet another excuse when he noticed the boy had gone to the wall and was tracing with his finger the red line of the path the boat was taking. With one move, Pastor Joe was at his side, whipped off the napkin, and there, looking back at him, were two bright blue eyes.

I had heard of reconstructive miracles, but nobody I knew personally had ever seen or been involved in one, so I was interested to meet this amazing pastor whose ministry started with such a spectacular miracle.

Easter Sunday came and I did my concert at the church. After the congregation left, I told Pastor Joe Linda had told me the story. "Is it true?" I asked. He assured me it was. "Would you tell me?" I said, "I'd love to hear it from you personally." Eagerly we pulled up chairs and sat in a circle with Linda and her husband and a few close friends. In a well-practiced voice, Pastor Joe began his narrative.

At the end, he said, "When it was time to leave the boat, I stood by the gangplank and waited to talk to Helen, but I never saw her get off, and when I described her to the crew, none of them recalled seeing her. I believe she was an angel."

Right then the Lord spoke to me. "Yes, she was an angel, and you notice she had to ask him three times to pray. It wasn't his great faith that healed the boy. The boy was healed because I wanted to heal him so badly."

I've heard it said that Jesus does not respond to need; He responds to faith. That's true. Plenty of accounts in the Bible where Jesus points that out. But then there's the funeral procession where the widow's only son is being carried through town. Jesus stops them and raises the dead. Same with Lazarus, already four days in his tomb. Whose faith was in operation there? Not Martha's or Mary's. I remember being taught the magic formulas that would cause God to act on our behalf—faith and no doubt spoken from a heart purified from selfish motives and a lifestyle of hidden sins… If we get the formula right, then He is obliged to perform as required.

What this story of Toby's healing says to me is God does want us to ask so our joy may be full, but it's always His sovereign grace that is behind each interaction between human and Almighty God. There's a danger here any time miracles happen. When we think it's our great faith that moves the hands of God, we might feel powerful and cause others to think we are too. What a disaster for everyone! We can end up more blind than a boy with no eyes.

I know a pastor who had a miracle healing early in his life. He was in the first year of seminary, struggling to study with eyes so weak he had to peer through thick lenses to read. One day he saw the story of the blind men who asked Jesus to heal them. He said, "According to your faith be it unto you." The words leaped off the page and the young man took off his glasses and threw them in the trash. For two weeks he bumped into walls and stumbled over steps while his classmates laughed at him, but suddenly he could see. They stopped laughing.

The problem was, he took that as proof of his great faith, and it was just enough off-course that it ended up taking the pastor far from the heart of God. He didn't start off that way, which is why I didn't suspect anything was wrong with his teaching until it almost killed me. I had heard his story and believed him when he said he was a man of great faith.

Just in case you've been contaminated with that kind of teaching—that you have to build your faith and become a faith giant to do great things for God, I want to quote a little something I just found in Matthew. It's the moment that Jesus answers the two blind men. He touches their eyes and says, "According to your faith and trust and reliance [on the power invested in Me] be it done to you." (Matt 9:29 AMPC) See? It's not your faith in your faith. It's your faith in *Him*. Isn't that a lot better? He heals because that's what He does. We don't have to work it up. Remember that in case Jesus urges you to pray for someone. With your obedience you provide the human connection. He provides the rest.

I've also heard it said that God always wants to heal. I asked Him about that. Yes, He wants to heal. Everyone who asked Jesus was healed, and the way He achieved that healing was not always the same. Sometimes it takes praying more than once, even by Jesus. If the blind man He prayed for is seeing men walking as trees, there's more to be done. I believe the Holy Spirit made sure Jesus's healing of blind eyes was done more than one way. The point is not to give us a formula, but a freedom to let Him do what He knows is most needed for that healing to be complete. Along those lines, I want to tell you three stories.

After Hedy and I graduated from guide dog school, I published a book of twelve stories I collected from my classmates. Each interview told the nature of the blindness, its effect on the person, and what having a guide dog did for their attitude towards their life ahead. I got invitations from radio and TV, and for one of them, I invited a classmate who lived in the area. Her blindness had been caused from severe Type 2 Diabetes, but she had recently received a transplant and, with her brand-new pancreas, she was feeling fabulous.

We did the TV interview and then I took her to breakfast. She ordered a huge pile of pancakes upon which she poured both containers of maple-flavored syrup. Having had a very diabetic husband, I found this alarming, but it got worse. She signaled the server and requested two more containers of syrup. They were promptly delivered, and she emptied them on her already swimming pancakes. Then she ate every bit of that breakfast and mopped up all the syrup so none of it was left.

I didn't hear from my classmate for a long time. Finally, after repeated emails, she answered, saying her new pancreas had failed. Since it was her second transplant, they told her she was not eligible for another, so she said I probably wouldn't hear from her again since she felt lousy and hadn't much time left to live. I thought about that. My classmate had received her healing, a miracle of sorts because it takes so long to receive an organ for a transplant, but she had not changed her lifestyle. She continued to indulge her unhealthy appetites, and the consequences were fatal.

This story has a happier outcome. I had been at a meeting where I was asked to pray for a woman who was having trouble with her eyes. She was scheduled for cataract surgery, but she would rather have God heal her. I thought it was odd that they would ask a blind lady to pray for the eyes of another, but I truly believe in God's ability to heal, so I agreed. When I prayed for her, my hands got so hot I was shocked. Since I expected to hear she was healed, I was surprised when she said she was going to have the surgery. She said God had provided a miracle in that regard—her insurance was going to pay for it. I told her I'd like to treat her with microcurrent after her surgery to help speed up the healing.

I treated the woman several times, making sure that all the tissue around her eyes was transmitting coherent signals and restored to its proper frequency. Each session took about an hour. During that hour, there was opportunity to talk, and it came out that she was struggling with resentment against her husband. For the next weeks we talked and prayed and worked through the issues. By the time her tissues were healed, so was her marriage. It was then that God told me she had needed something more important than an instant healing of her eyes, and for that depth of healing, she needed time—repeated times of time—with a Christian sister who would listen and guide her in the truth that makes us free, including the supernatural ability to forgive resentments built up over many years. And that, He said, is as much a miracle as receiving new eyeballs. Healing isn't about having perfectly functioning body parts. It's about restoration, redemption, reconciliation. It's being whole in the most eternal way possible.

Through lifestyle choices, my classmate from guide dog school lost her chance for more years of better health. But what if you have something hereditary, something that's not your fault? In view of a lifetime of having to deal with a difficult disease, wouldn't the God of love and compassion touch you and heal you so you can be like all the other children? Why would He let you suffer?

My friend Dustin was diagnosed as having Type 1 diabetes when he was eleven. That meant his pancreas would not make insulin. He would have to depend on external sources of that vital substance the rest of his life. It was a lot for a youngster to deal with.

Did he become depressed, bitter, resentful? I don't know. His family moved to another state and we lost touch. What I do know is what he did about it to get where he is now. Dustin studied nutrition, adjusted his food choices, became a fitness professional, and earned a Masters in dance. Not only has he become an impressive example of overcoming what could be considered severe physical limitations, he inspires others as a personal trainer. Earned Authority is something you can't buy or learn by advanced education. You can only get it by the way you deal with hard things. Few can tell Dustin, "No, I can't. It's just too hard."

Could God have healed Dustin? Would that have been better? There's no way to know. All I can say is there's depth to this young man, a maturity rare in people his age, and a combination of wisdom and compassion and the ability to encounter devastating things with *hupomeno*, the Greek word for patience. It means bearing up under pressure. Like weight lifting. Dustin has done a lot of heavy lifting through the years, and he has strength that comes through in the authority and authenticity of his words, his movement, his creative endeavors. Would he have it had he grown up "normal" like all the other boys? I don't think so. His choices—in food, in attitude, in lifestyle—will inform his art and inspire others all his long, healthy life. And what he creates in movement, words, and story will communicate the wisdom and endurance gained from years of choosing to walk the path of life with courage and grace.

Walking Grounded

When my mother was nearing her last weeks, she worried about me. "Who will take care of you in your blindness? Dennis can't. He's too sick himself."

I said, "Don't worry, Mom. I'll get one of those cool dogs."

In 2004, my mom died, and my husband's health continued to plummet until, in 2006, he had two strokes. I tried to care for him at home, but stairs were nearly impossible for him, and I couldn't see well enough to clean up after him. Finally he went to live with my son John, and when I tried to go back to work, I discovered I could no longer read. Fifteen years of unremitting stress had ravaged the retinas that were already damaged from the progression of Retinitis Pigmentosa.

I was devastated. I had been slowly losing sight since I was in my twenties, but this drastic drop was a shock. Changes in my life were quickly forced upon me. My son Thomas and his very concerned wife urged me, implored me, not to drive anymore. I didn't want to give up the last vestige of freedom. But within a week, God made it clear I was no longer safe to drive, so I stopped. Then came an avalanche of losses. I couldn't read my mail. I was dependent on others to do almost everything. My privacy, my independence, my capabilities as an artist, even my identity as a human being, were gone like a vapor in the wind. It made me want to lie down in the snow and go to sleep.

But I had promised my mother. She always said, "A promise made is a debt unpaid." I had promised her I would get a guide dog, so I started investigating how to do that. It turned out you have to be totally able to get around with a cane. That required some significant training. I was assigned an O&M, an Orientation and Mobility Specialist. His name was Scott Kies.

I had been a professional photographer. I had written a dozen books. Now when I tried to see text, all I saw was vague, pale gray smudges against a blinding background that hurt my eyes. I was vulnerable as a newborn mouse, blind and helpless and unable to care for myself. I felt worthless, useless, a burden to anyone who had to drive me, find things for me, or lead me around. I mention this because Scott came into my life when I most wanted to give up. He wouldn't let me.

Scott was thorough, his explanations clear and easy to remember. He was encouraging, but refused to settle for "close enough." Since the person's life depended on the skills he was teaching, he couldn't settle for less than what would keep the person most safe. Even so, Scott was gentle and incredibly kind, watching out for me always.

You might say Scott was that attentive because it was his job, and I would tell you I had cane training six years before and the O&M wasn't nearly as thorough or as caring, and when Scott asked me what I already knew of the skill, he was shocked at how little I'd been taught. In fact, I'd found the cane kind of a nuisance instead of a viable aid, so I'd stopped using it.

Immediately Scott set out to teach me how to travel confidently and independently. It took awhile. But, because it took so long, a strange thing began to happen. Because I had many opportunities to do it very badly, because there were times I was completely confused and wanted to quit, and because he nudged me gently back into trying again, I began to think I must have some value. Why else would he invest this much time and energy in me?

Some people think time is money. We use words such as "spend" or "invest." But when you're feeling devalued, time means love. Time means caring, there's something here worth saving, nurturing, enabling and equipping to return to the land of the living. Scott did more than teach me how to travel safely; he showed me my life mattered to him. And so it also began to matter to me.

Scott taught me how to evaluate the surface I was walking on. Was it dirt, pavement, loose gravel, macadam, blacktop, cement, bark, river rock, grass, cobblestone, not to forget truncated domes, metal grates, and storm drains. What's that soft, loose stuff? Pine needles obscuring the path? It's amazing what you can learn from a stick if you know what you're feeling.

I still had some residual sight so I could see where I was, but Scott said I couldn't rely on that. He explained, "You have to be a confident traveler to be able to get a guide dog, as the dog looks to you for guidance. If you aren't confident in yourself and your decisions the dog won't trust you."

So we practiced on my street with my eyes closed. "Hear that change in sound?" Scott said. "That's how you know you've passed the open lot three houses from yours. Feel that change in the road? You're on the dirt shoulder. Smell that bay tree? You're almost home."

I had to be present at all times, pay attention to every detail of sensory information. Whenever I'd walked on my street before, I was always thinking of other things, mostly what I had to do that day. I had never paid attention to any of these things, and suddenly I was noticing the light breeze that came from the lake, the sun warming the side of my face, telling me which way I was facing, the rich aroma of the bay tree like an herbal bouquet in the lovely outdoors. Suddenly I realized I felt completely alive. I was living in the present moment, fully there, fully engaged, fully aware. Instead of being only in my head, and my head being elsewhere, I was right there, every bit of me, my whole being alert and connected with present time. It was thrilling.

Scott wanted to make sure I was safe at every moment, and he made a point of educating me in reading the surfaces with my cane. That way I would be aware of every hazard, every possible place of loose footing or edges of sidewalks or paving stones sticking up. He wanted to be sure nothing tripped me or caused me to stumble. He was teaching me to walk circumspectly, not as a fool, carelessly nonchalant and unaware, but wise, conscious of what was all around me, sights, sounds, smells, and especially under my feet. He wanted me to be alert for holes, edges, sudden drops, the beginnings and endings of stairs. It's kind of a God-thing—learning to discern and pay attention and keep your balance on all kinds of tricky terrain, being in the moment every step of the way. He wants us to know where we are at all times. He is always there, walking beside us, watching out for us, patient, kind, and gracious, investing time and energy in us every moment because we matter, we are deeply loved, and He is there guiding us, making sure we make it safely all the way Home.

One day, Scott showed up with a monocular. It did for one eye what binoculars do for two. He taught me how to rotate the barrel in order to bring the desired object into focus. Scott said, "My joy comes from the 'light bulb' moment when something hits just right for the person I am with. Like for the monocular when someone can not even look through it, then seeing the light coming through the barrel, to be able to scan to find and describe an object for the prize."

To help me practice sighting on small objects, Scott took me to the State Park near my home. We stood on the bridge, greenish water flowing slowly below us.

Scott said, "There's a light-colored branch sticking out of the water at about 9:00 o'clock on your left. It's kind of like a letter 'L.' Do you see it? Good. Now continue following it to the right." I did what he said, sighting through the barrel of the monocular, focusing, then moving it to the right, careful to keep the branch in view. Suddenly I gave a delighted squeal. There on the end of the branch were four snoozing black turtles.

I think God has tools and techniques that enable us to see what we could not see before. I think He looks for the light bulb moment when we figure out how to see the light that comes through the new tool, enabling us to focus and see clearly what He has magnified for us. But the best part of this story for me is the absolute delight I had when I followed Scott's directions and found the turtles. I think Scott may have enjoyed that moment too, both because I was successful using the monocular, and because he was pleased I was so delighted with the surprise he had prepared for me.

God has things He can see that we can't unless He directs us in how to find them. And I have such a strong feeling that He enjoys our enjoyment of what He has prepared for us. I think it delights His heart.

Vetch

In the countryside of Lake County, California, vetch grows in tangles of creeping vines, propagating with runners that invade everything. It's a pest. But one day I took a closer look at the flowers that clustered on its stems, small purple trumpets with golden throats inside. "It was nice of You to put pretty flowers on the weeds," I told God. "You could have made everything gray."

"I'm so glad you noticed," came the reply. "I made them for hope." Then He said, "Have you ever noticed that the first things out of bare branches after winter are not leaves, but blossoms? I made them for hope."

This next part came in a flurry of images that take longer to describe than to see. I saw puppies and kittens and fuzzy yellow duckies and cute little baby chicks. He said again, "I made them for hope."

Then I saw an old man in dirty, ragged clothes, his face lined and grizzled with unshaved stubble. Under the torn brim of his old slouch hat was a sad face that had lived through many troubles.

Nearby on the wooden porch where he was standing, a small kitten rolled on its back, batting at a piece of lint that floated in the sunlight. A tiny hint of a smile crossed the old man's face.

God showed me He had carefully designed blossoms, adorable baby animals, and flowers on weeds to reach past the sufferings, no matter how great, and touch us deeply with hope.

Many years later, my mother was dying slowly of a pernicious neurological degenerative disease. I was exhausted physically, mentally, but mostly emotionally, from multiple trips to Southern California to help my dad take care of her at their home. I was worn out with grief.

On one of my few weeks back in Lake County, I came across some kittens that needed adoption, and I let the girl at the vet's office talk me into taking two. "They can entertain each other," she said. I named the gray tabby Joshua. His little Siamese-looking sister I named Hope. They made me laugh, and I really needed to. Somehow they broke into the sadness that locked my heart in sorrow just as Father God in His wisdom had designed them to do. Only He could have thought of "cute" to defeat despair. Cute, blossoms, Spring. He made them for hope.

9

Suffering

November is a hard month for me. Time can hold memories, triggered by the weather, the color and scent of the sky. Autumn is a transition time when trees pull their sap into their centers, exposing the colors in the leaves that have always been there, disguised by the green of chlorophyll during days of sunlight and plenty. It's symbolic to us, and actual as well.

My husband Dennis said autumn is the season when those who are frail will pass to the Other Side. He did. On October 27, his father's birthday, Dennis got his heart's desire and entered heaven at last, no longer troubled by the losses from strokes or the mental torment of advanced dementia, wondering why Jesus didn't take him Home. Exactly two weeks later, my father also had his heart's desire. He went to sleep and woke up in heaven. I was, and am, so happy for both of them, and it comforts me to picture them reunited with those they loved and missed on Earth. But the sky is gray and chill is in the air, and I remember them, and I feel the loss still. My friend Dan says he hates death so much because it's so unnatural. God never intended it to be like this. It's the middle of November as I write this part of the book. I still feel the ache. I still miss my mom, though she died in 2004. I was tearful this morning as I felt the gray even in my own heart. And gently, the Holy Spirit reminded me of something He showed me many years ago.

When my son John was a teenager and still living at home, we had a cat that we both loved. Alexander was silky white with black splotches down his back. We were his favorite humans, and he always found one of our laps to curl into and purr. Then one day I noticed he was very hot and weighed almost nothing. The vet diagnosed feline leukemia and that was the end of our life with Alexander. We cried together, John and I. No one else understood.

I thought I'd be okay after that, but I wasn't. When I noticed on a bulletin board a photo of a smiling woman holding a cat, a flash of rage shot through me. Why did she get to have a cat when my cat was dead? I felt so violent I was shocked and frightened. Why was I that angry? He was only a cat. But the anger continued, fierce and severe and scorching. I asked the Lord, "What is this about?"

Suddenly I was standing inside an artisan's shop. Sunlight poured through the glass wall where bowls and vases and other wonderful ceramics were displayed on shelves and could be seen from either the shop or the street. In the corner a few yards from me sat a young man, sleeves rolled up. I could see his muscular brown arms as he steadied the wet clay turning on the wheel in front of him.

Then the door opened and in came a very thin man dressed all in black, his sharp features and black eyes hard and mean. He stepped to the display shelf, took down a vase, turned and faced the potter. Without taking his eyes off him, he held the vase straight out to the side shoulder high, and opened his fingers. The vase crashed to the floor and shattered. The potter said nothing. Neither did he look away from the man or stop what he was doing.

The man turned back to the displays, selected another piece, returned to face the potter, held it straight out and, without taking his eyes off the potter's, let go. Loudly the pot smashed on the hard floor. I saw the muscle in the potter's jaw tighten, but he said nothing and he did not stop what he was doing. Then I heard these words. "Whenever you feel anger over death, you're feeling a tiny bit of what I feel every time something dies. It was never meant to be like this, but for now it must be so. That is why I came, and that is why I died."

Why did God allow evil to enter His perfect creation? Why did He give angels free will? Didn't He know Lucifer would rebel? Didn't He realize Eve would fall for the seduction? Occupying the Eternal Now, God could see all of history with its wars and hideous cruelties and expressions of wickedness that boggle the mind. Didn't He care? Why didn't He stop it from the start?

We could argue about what a good God would, should, could have done about evil and the suffering it brings, but we'd be missing the point. He gave us free will and respects us too much to violate it. Does that make Him weak? Hardly. It proves irrefutably He is not a tyrannical bully forcing humans to obey Him or suffer His wrath. At the same time, He is righteous. Wickedness must be judged, and the wages of sin is death. Nobody gets away with anything. The price had to be paid, and instead of abandoning us to our rebellions and their consequences, Jesus paid for all transgressions and every evil devised by the heart of humankind. He didn't remain aloof from suffering. He entered into it and took it upon Himself, even knowing many would never receive this gift.

Think of it. Jesus paid for every sin Nero committed, and they were as numerous as the sands. Scripture says He paid the full price for each human. If Nero had received that gift, he would have been welcomed into heaven. Hard as this is to believe, God loved him that much. God is love, an incomprehensible enormity of love we can't understand, a love so vast it's not willing that a single human being would be lost. When God gave us free will, He took a terrible risk. So do we when we have children. There's always a chance we could engender a child who would grow up to hate us. But we take that risk, hoping for love freely given, a connection unique to each child, unlike any other relationship with any other being.

I think God's love is something we can't comprehend, something on the cosmic scale where free will makes evil possible, but, even so, He is able to turn it to astonishing Good and demonstrate His wisdom, power, goodness, and glory through it all. Too big for my puny brain. All I know is He was willing to pay for each violation so we would have a choice. Then, as the poem says, He as the Hound of Heaven tirelessly pursues us on wounded feet. He didn't pay the bill and leave us to figure it out. He actively woos each one, and many especially wicked sinners have turned around and found a life significant with meaning and fruitfulness—George Mueller, Matthew the tax collector, and me.

But that's not all. John Lennox says if we saw what God did subsequently for those who have suffered because of the greed and selfishness of other people, all our questions would disappear and we would fall down and worship Him.

Sometimes You Never Get Something You Want

I've heard it said suffering is getting what you don't want and wanting what you don't get. God is love. It's His nature. But sometimes it doesn't feel like it. This little story helps me see the loving Father-heart of God in the context of what looks like harsh and painful punishment while withholding very desirable good from one who wants it very much.

When my son John was about six months old, he went from contentedly sitting wherever I left him to crawling as fast as he could to the farthest regions in the house. That was fine, until he discovered an intriguing shiny black thing. It was an electrical cord. And it was plugged in. I caught him just as he lifted it to his sweet little wet mouth. "No!" I said firmly, but gently. "Don't touch that." I moved him several feet away. Quick as he could crawl, he was back, reaching for the cord. "No!" I said more firmly, in a darker tone. I picked him up and carried him across the room. Immediately John turned and crawled surprisingly fast back to the enticing black cord. "No! Don't touch it!" I said louder. One more time I picked him up, this time carrying him into another room. I figured that was that and went back to folding laundry.

I looked up just in time to see John with the cord in both hands, raising it to his already open mouth. "No!" I yelled, snatching it out of his hands. Without looking up, he reached for it again. Alarmed, I slapped his arm. "No!"

It stung. It had to. John looked up at me, his large brown eyes wide with surprise. I had never hurt him before. I had never even yelled at him. I watched those bewildered eyes brim with tears that filled and then spilled while the corners of his usually happy mouth began to turn down and he started to cry. It broke my heart and I wanted to cry too, but I said again sternly, "No. Don't touch that." He slumped into sobs. I couldn't have felt worse. I pulled my little boy to me, hugging him, rocking him, wordless as I stifled my own sobs and silent tears ran down my face.

There are times you have to hurt someone you love and there's no way you can explain it or help them understand why. And there are times God has to do the same. C.S. Lewis says pain is the megaphone of God. Sometimes we're so intent on what we want that we don't realize it can kill us.

Purification

When God talks about purifying, He uses words such as "fire" and "refine as silver." You probably already know that precious metals are refined in crucibles that are heated to higher and higher temperatures. Throughout the process, dross is released and skimmed off. But recently God gave me a different picture.

Sandalwood is a fragrant, highly-prized wood that is made into decorative objects and furniture. My grandmother gave me a sandalwood fan that had a lovely scent. In the Bible, sandalwood is also translated "aloes." That's not the aloes of the spike-leafed plant whose liquid is good for burns; it's a tree whose sap can be distilled by heat and pressure into an oil with powerful healing properties. It has one of the highest percentages of sesquiterpenes, sub-atomic particles that can pass the blood brain barrier and instantly oxygenate both the blood and the brain. The Lord pointed out to me that sandalwood can be used for decorations, utilitarian objects such as tables and chairs, or it can be transformed by heat and pressure into something that is many times the worth of nicely carved furniture or objects of art. In ancient times, kings counted their wealth more in quantities of essential oils than in silver and gold. Okay, but what does this mean? And why do I need to know this right now as I work on this chapter on suffering?

The Christian life is practical. We can rest our weight on it. Life with God is attractive and able to exude the fragrance of Christ. But under pressure, in the furnace of affliction, godly character is purified within us. That treasure, like essential oils, is released, pure and precious. It cannot be produced any other way. And the King counts it among His most cherished treasures. Behind all things are God's intentions to bring about good for us—even working for us a far more exceeding and eternal weight of glory. But John Lennox has brought up something I never considered—that the God of infinite love and goodness would, in some way, "make it up" to those who have suffered because of the greed and selfishness and disregard for human life that comes from a worldview without God. I thought of the Holocaust and the Killing Fields and the martyrs across the centuries. We only see people from the outside. God sees individuals, each one so precious He gave His life for them. And we only know what happens till the curtain comes down. We don't see beyond the veil. Chuck Smith says, "We're always thinking of our temporal good, but God is always thinking of our eternal good." In the next chapter, I'm going to share stories with you from the inside of suffering so you may know what God can do with His transforming love.

10

Inside Suffering

A rabbi who interviewed survivors of the Holocaust concluded it's meaningless suffering that defeats us. In the midst of the worst, if you can still believe in the goodness of God you can come out with your soul intact, and many times, even this side of the veil, you get to see some of that goodness taking place right before your eyes. The next stories show you what God did to change what could have seemed like meaningless suffering into obvious and astonishing good—both temporal and eternal.

Mom

I remember standing at the foot of my mother's bed the morning after her death. I had spent the last seven years making trips to Southern California to help my father take care of her at home as she steadily sank deeper into neurological degeneration that took her ability to walk, then swallow, talk, or move.

My dad arranged for Dr. Bill Pace to come treat Mom with medical devices my dad had invented. Dr. Pace was one of the first to try microcurrent, and remained one of my dad's respected and trusted colleagues. Since my dad had retired from doctoring and Dr. Pace was still practicing, he always gave him his latest medical inventions to try out. But there was more to this than respect between them as health professionals. My dad told me Dr. Pace was a Christian, a pastor who refused to work on the Sabbath. It impressed him enough that he remarked about it to me more than once over the years.

Once a week, Dr. Pace came, accompanied by his wife Sandy. While Dr. Pace treated Mom, Sandy would visit with her. Mom needed friendship. Her life had been so busy she didn't have time for any, and when they retired, my dad chased any friends away, saying he would be her friend, the only one she would ever need. But he was very hard of hearing, and Mom's voice was faint. At last he recognized he could not give her this vital part of her life—conversation. But somehow Sandy, bending close, understood the garbled words and responded in ways that let my mother know she was really listening and understanding what she was trying to say. My dad told me he thought what Sandy did in those gentle visits did more for Mom than Dr. Pace's expert treatments. It's true. A life needs more than comfort in the body. It needs to be lovingly connected with others, and Sandy did that with her unique, sweet grace.

My father had told me his family mocked Christians, saying they needed a crutch because they were so weak, but he had immense respect for Dr. Pace and Sandy. They were such a loving couple, so ready to help in any way they could. I knew they had an unusual effect on him. It was more than respect or even the friendship they developed over a period of thirty years; it was a kind of awe. I have no doubt it affected my dad's choice at the end to give his own heart to Jesus.

Eventually my mother lost control of almost all her muscles. My father and I had to turn her every two hours, feed her through a G-tube connected to her stomach, and struggle to understand the sounds she was making that were trying to be words. Sometimes I had to suction her all night long through hours of what must have felt to her like drowning. My sister dropped by one day, took a look at our once elegant and brilliantly gifted multi-tasking mother, now slumped in a Hoya Lift, and pronounced flatly, "She has no quality of life." The implication was there was no reason for her to continue to live. She would be better off dead.

I knew better. There were parts of my mom that were being healed that never could have been reached if she had been healthy. There were relationships that were being mended that could not have been repaired under any other circumstances.

My mother had been the unloved child among her five siblings, and I had been her unfavorite in the family of two daughters. She was expert at finding fault, flaws, and inadequacies, spotting weaknesses and imperfections in everything from the performance of a prima ballerina to the fit in a custom suit. She, herself, was dressed and groomed magnificently, the glamorous, exceptional Kay Wing who single-handedly kept everything in good order at their three offices and at home. And she'd wash all the walls and ceilings of all the rooms of the large custom house every week. She expected a lot of perfection, and demanded the same from us and herself. Trouble was, she could actually do it. And I couldn't. So I was always facing the truth of my inadequacies, ineptitudes, and insufficiencies. I came to believe I just wasn't very good—at or for anything. I think she knew it and wanted to stop, but didn't know how. Once she told me, "Chinese mothers are never gentle, never kind." She bemoaned her inability to love, never having received it from her mother.

In the second year of her confinement, my mother asked Jesus into her heart. "But I don't know if He accepted me," she told me the next morning, "Maybe I should fax Him."

Mom was not your typical sinner-type person. Hers was a life of impeccable integrity. She wouldn't tolerate exaggeration in a story, even to help make the point. Facts had to be verifiable and unembellished. Everything she did was squeaky clean. She demanded that from everyone around her, plus excellence in whatever they did. Because of that, and because of her own mother, she had what she called "a flailing tongue." Aside from that, she was an assiduous keeper of the law, so I wondered if she would notice any difference after the simple prayer I'd led her in. I'd heard testimonies of drug addicts suddenly delivered, and there was my own testimony of Jesus rescuing me from the demons I didn't realize I was serving. Except for being over-critical, there was nothing obvious in my mother's life that needed to be changed.

A few days after the prayer I asked if she'd noticed any difference. "Yes," she said. "Immediately." Since childhood she had seen demon faces—hideous, menacing faces coming at her whenever she closed her eyes. After the prayer they began to fade away. She never told me she had seen them all her life until after Jesus sent them away. A peace came over her mind.

But the losses were grievous. She would tell me it frightened her that now she couldn't move her legs, then her arms, then fingers. I would say, "I understand. I keep losing more of my sight, and it frightens me when I can't do something that was easy before." In this way my blindness became a source of comfort to her as we shared the fellowship of losses, and for that I was grateful. And there were times she agonized, saying she couldn't even brush her teeth or wipe her nose. As I wiped her nose, I told her on the cross, Jesus couldn't move His arms either, not to wipe the spittle or blood off His face. It seemed to reach an untouched place inside her. She knew He understood.

One particularly difficult day when she had needed almost nonstop care, I grieved before the Lord. "If only she hadn't insisted on trying to move that heavy thing she wouldn't have fractured her back and brought on this terrible illness!"

The Lord answered quietly, "And she might not be saved."

Now my mom, for whom nothing I did was ever good enough, became grateful for every little thing I did. She called me her Angelette and, when she could no longer speak, looked at me with such love that I almost couldn't bear it. She had never felt worthy of love unless she performed superhumanly and looked incredibly gorgeous. But the lovely clothes and jewels were no longer practical. Now she couldn't do anything for anyone. Instead, Daddy and I had to do everything for her. And then she found she was loved just for being who she was. She realized Jesus loved her like that, and so did her husband and daughter. And then she had that same kind of love to give to me. She became the mom of my dreams.

There are many kinds of wholeness, not just vibrancy of body and mind. Impulsively one day, I, who had always been afraid of her, climbed up onto her bed and lay beside her, holding her lovingly as the child she never got to be, and she held me lovingly in return, as the child I never got to be. I asked if she was afraid to die. She answered "No," and we talked about heaven and how we would be there together some day. She said, "Now we just have to get Daddy to come with us." Facing this terrible illness together, chasms in our relationship were being filled with the love of God. He was making us whole. Through it, Jesus healed us both.

Transformations were also happening with my dad. He had been King of the Castle with Mom waiting on him. He never washed a dish or cooked a meal. But when she could no longer rise from her bed, he promised her she would never go to a nursing home. He would take care of her in the home they had designed and built together—all the way to the end. "I took vows," he told her, "In sickness and in health. For better or for worse. And I intend to keep them." And he did. He learned how to do laundry and cook and do dishes. He completely left microcurrent so he could pour all his love and attention on his wife, who saw at last that she was, of all he loved, truly his number one. It healed them too.

Death strips us down to the things that matter most, and sometimes gives us opportunities to make amends and a chance to cherish every moment of God's gift of remaining time. It's hard to believe, but I know it's true—the last six months of my mother's life were the happiest of her entire eighty-three years. She had nothing that the world would value. Her looks were gone. She couldn't do anything. She needed care in every function. She wasn't productive. She wasn't useful. But the Lord used all that suffering and loss to convince her that our love, and the love she received from God, was real.

Now I stood at the foot of my mother's bed, her race at last having come to an end. The Lord spoke. "The blessings will far exceed the suffering and sorrow," He said.

"There was a lot of suffering and sorrow," I said. But it has been as He said. I know things I could not know—about Him, about my parents, about myself, about life and death and the value of suffering to the end with a person you love—things I could not know under any other circumstances. And I know how to comfort those who mourn.

One day my dad asked me, "What do you think happens after you die?" I was so shocked that I stammered first. He had always been so hostile at any mention of sin (Taoists don't believe in sin) that I avoided the subject, the plan of salvation, the afterlife in His presence. Now here was my dad asking me outright.

I told him carefully about heaven and that Mom was there. I reminded him about visions she had seen of her dad and mom being reunited after Grandma's death, and seeing her sister dancing in sunlight after her terrible death from ITP. "It isn't that I don't believe in those things," Daddy said, thinking about my words. "I don't doubt them, I've just never seen any of them myself."

For four glorious, golden years, my dad and I spent weeks at a time together, helping each other grieve and heal. We went on trips together. There was a cruise to Eastern Europe, a marathon drive to Cape Cod, and three road trips to Women Writing the West conferences where my dad was an instant hit among all those gifted and gracious writers. And I was important to him. And he was thankful. He noticed me. He appreciated my help. He became the dad of my dreams. He said, "Mom and I love you," though she was gone. He had never used the "L" word before, and even though it wasn't an unprotected, "I love you," at least he gave me that much. I know none of this would have happened except for the suffering we shared as we cared for Mom in the hardest of times. There was no meaningless suffering in my mother's disease. It remains as one of the strongest proofs to me of the truth of Romans 8:28. God truly worked all things together for my good, and in the lives of countless others who went through that time with us.

One day my father called me on the phone. I knew he hadn't much time left. He had shown me the aneurysm in his belly, the bulge under his skin that was enlarging almost every day. My father said he wasn't afraid to die. And he told me what I'd been waiting a lifetime to hear, "You're a good daughter," he said, "and I love you."

Tina

Lots of people have faced cancer. My dad had it. I don't know many families that haven't struggled together for the sake of a loved one going through procedures to fight off this invader. But few have had the severity and suddenness of onslaught that my friend Tina has been facing. I asked her to tell her story and she said she would because she wants her experiences to help other people.

As adults, we get prayer requests—"Pray for Tina with Stage 4 cancer. Pray for Kay, who can no longer eat, move, or talk." We grieve that these brilliant, energetic women could be so tragically struck down. When we pray for them, what can we say? So often all we get is a brief description of the problem, and often no updates unless it's bad. We don't know the wonderful ways God is bringing healing, reconciliation, and even salvation as He lovingly draws us closer in all circumstances to Himself. I think these stories will help strengthen your confidence in God's ability to work all things together for good. Instead of being left in shock from hearing the bad news, we get to see close-ups of radiant, smiling faces, and sufferings transformed into spiritual wholeness of breathtaking beauty.

Tina's Story

"How many times had I heard people complain about their aches and pains growing older, listened compassionately and thought to myself: *If he or she would only exercise a bit more and eat a bit less sugar...*

"Teaching Pilates for almost 20 years I was in the best shape of my life at age 62 and felt invincible when out of the blue I was diagnosed with stage 4 Ovarian Cancer. My life turned upside down. Most often Ovarian Cancer is not diagnosed until it reaches stage 3 or 4 (there is no stage 5...). The symptoms are very subtle and easily confused with indigestion. At this late stage it has spread and requires extensive surgery and chemotherapy, and even if the treatment is successful it is likely to come back in the majority of cases. Realizing that this diagnosis was way too big for me to handle I could do nothing else but give it over to God. And that was what I did in my car on the way back from the gynecologist office, and ever since.

"A few days later I was sitting with my husband in the surgeon's office when we got the news that our insurance was cancelled. In that moment I felt as if I was sitting under a golden tent or pyramid and everything was going to be ok. My poor husband meanwhile went through a couple of grueling hours on the phone until the insurance company figured out that someone had checked the wrong box. This is just one of the amazing experiences of divine intervention I had during the last topsy-turvy year full of challenges and triumphs. All throughout my life I had a somewhat loose connection to God. But now I am living in a much deeper, comforting and fulfilling relationship with God.

"The surgery was short – they closed right back up and sent me to chemotherapy because the cancer was all over and it would have been useless and too risky to operate. Several months of chemotherapy and another attempt of surgery brought a much different outcome: Although I was scheduled for an open-ended surgery I was wheeled into the recovery room just 4 hours later. My surgeon was able to remove all visible cancer in record time, taking out 8 organs and resecting several others. More rounds of chemotherapy over the next months and my cancer marker was down to 6 from 7200 (up to 35 is normal).

"When I was diagnosed my gynecologist asked me who my support system was, and I could only think of my husband. This last year showed me how much people care, even strangers I have never met. Cards, letters, notes, little gifts I put on our king-size bed after the last treatment covered it in several layers.

"Unfortunately the cancer came back in just 5 months, but every day and particularly in those times when I feel desperate and overwhelmed I take a few moments to look for the connection with God, align with and surrender to His will with a grateful heart. Each time I experience that same comforting ease from my "dis-ease." It had not failed me once. It sounds like a cliché, but I am living a happier and more fulfilled life now than before the diagnosis.

"Next to my bed sits a little clay angel guarding a piece of paper. These items had their home on the nightstand of my stepmother in my homeland of Germany while she was battling cancer. I took them with me after her funeral. Written on that old and wrinkly paper is the last verse of one of Bonhoeffer's most famous prayers: "Von guten Maechten wunderbar geborgen…"

(…*By loving forces wonderfully sheltered,*
we are awaiting fearlessly what comes.

God is with us at dusk and in the morning
and most assuredly on ev'ry day.)

"Since I was a little girl this prayer was part of our family's tradition. We sang it at bedtime, family weddings, birthdays, funerals, at Christmas or just because. Coming full circle."

Pastor Richard Wurmbrand

Richard Wurmbrand was in solitary confinement for a total of fourteen years. He said there were no windows in his small, bare cell. The only light was a single dim bulb in the ceiling. The only faces he saw were those of his torturers who came at unexpected times to use whatever means they could to make him recant his faith. His crime? He was an evangelical pastor in Communist Romania who believed that Jesus is God incarnate and died in our place to pay for our sins. He was also a Jew and a former atheist who refused to be silent about the reality of God who spared no expense in bringing us His offer of forgiveness and eternal life. I heard his talk. I spoke with him afterwards. When I came near where he sat, he smiled, stood up painfully, took both of my hands in his, and looked directly into my eyes. I saw there such gentle kindness and love that I was surprised and somewhat overwhelmed.

I read his book, *Tortured for Christ.* It was brutal. They even drugged him to trick him into signing a confession denying his belief in Jesus as God. All he could remember was, "Our Father," and that, he said, was enough.

But God met his beloved son in that small, bleak cell. Though they had broken every one of his bones at least twice and he was in constant pain, he rose up and danced with the Lord, whose presence was so strong that tears of joy flowed down his cheeks and nothing else mattered.

I'm mentioning this because it's not something that happened two thousand years ago. I met the pastor and Sabina, his dear wife, in the 1980s. Both of them had been through years of horror and torture, and yet they were kind, gentle, loving—and wonderfully funny. There was not a trace of bitterness, anger, resentment, or unforgiveness toward their captors, and there was not a trace of accusation of abandonment or betrayal against the Lord. Both of them continued to declare His goodness, His wisdom, His love. And they were radiant with His glory.

Bonhoeffer

My friend Tina told me Bonhoeffer was a Christian imprisoned for his faith. She said they didn't want any other god in Germany. When I said I had heard in college that Hitler was a Christian, which is why he hated Jews, she replied with surprise, "Oh no! He wanted to *be* God!" Tina said in the camp, Bonhoeffer did good to people, sharing his food and doing other Christian things. "That made them mad," she said, "so they put him in the cell by himself and cold without light." I thought it would be helpful to share this poem, which is so unprotected in its honesty. Bonhoeffer's poems give us a chance to hear his heart's cry, and see the kinds of things God can bring us through with a song even in the dark.

Who Am I?

Who am I? They often tell me
I step out from my cell,
Composed, contented and sure,
Like a lord from his manor.
Who am I? They often tell me.
I speak with my jailers,
Frankly, familiar and firm,
As though I was in command.
Who am I? They also tell me,

I bear the days of hardship,
Unconcerned, amused and proud,
  like one who usually wins.
Am I really what others tell me?
Or am I only what I myself know of me?
Troubled, homesick, ill, like a bird in a cage,
Gasping for breath, as though one strangled me,
Hungering for colors, for flowers, for songs of birds,
Thirsting for kind words, for human company,
Quivering with anger at despotism and petty insults,
Anxiously waiting for great events,
Helplessly worrying about friends far away,
  empty and tired of praying, of thinking, of working,
Exhausted and ready to bid farewell to it all.
Who am I? This or the other?
Am I then, this today and the other tomorrow?
Am I both at the same time? In public, a hypocrite
And by myself, a contemptible, whining weakling?
Or am I to myself, like a beaten army,
Flying in disorder from a victory already won?
Who am I? Lonely questions mock me,
Who I really am, you know me, I am thine, O God!

God Knows Me

When we have nothing left of ourselves but doubts even of who we believe we are, that's when we find it doesn't matter. God keeps loving us. He didn't bankrupt heaven to buy the pearl of great price, get it home, take a closer look, and decide it was not so great after all. Nope. Doesn't measure up. I think of my mom, nothing left of the formerly fabulous Kay Wing, confronted hourly by the face of unabashed, extravagant love. It changed her. God doesn't waste a thing. There is nothing futile in the Christian life. There's always More, and I don't mean in the sweet old by and by. It's now. Eternal Life is now. And this is Eternal Life, that you know God and the One He sent. Bonhoeffer wrote, "Who I really am, you know me, I am thine, O God!" In a prison cell, in a hospital bed, in a cancer ward, You know me, O God. You know who I really am. And I know You. Eternal Life is now. It's here in this isolation, this torture, this unhappy body, in this humiliating disease. And I know now I am never alone. I am perfectly loved, and forever and ever I am Thine, O God!

Job

When it comes to suffering, one of the first names to come to mind is Job's. In the last two years, as I've worked on books dealing specifically with the unprecedented suffering and uncertainties brought about by a mysterious virus and the multitudes of ways the world has decided to deal with it, I've thought a lot about Job. Below are my musings, random, but hopefully helpful to you.

I remember when 9-11 happened. People didn't write essays; they wrote poems and songs. When a loved one dies, often a relative or friend will write a poem. I think it's significant that the Book of Job has only three chapters that are written in prose: the first two and the last one. The rest are poetry. Sometimes we read the words of Job's "comforters" and think how arrogant and judgmental they were, but they were only expressing the beliefs of the day, and I believe they truly wanted to help him. I know when I can't help my friends with my counsel, I feel helpless because it hurts me to see them hurting, and sad that I can't get them out of it. So it makes sense to me that even the arguments of all the friends would be poetry, which gives me more understanding of their caring intentions towards their friend. It also occurs to me that the Word, Himself, the One who created all languages, thought to give us a genre, a literary vehicle, that is able to carry our hearts' cries, words in the only form that can contain immense and overwhelming anguish—a way to say what is too big to get out any other way. And it would be beautiful.

I find it significant that Job never blamed God for all his suffering, and God never answered his questions. Instead, perhaps as a response to Job's choice not to accuse Him of wrongdoing, He gave him what is undoubtedly one of the most spectacular panoramic views of His magnificence in detail and scope, with insight into His concern for His creation. Dr. Eleonore Stump noted that much of the language and examples God chose to reveal to Job had to do with nurture, birthing, and the care of everything from the universe to the tiny newborns hidden where no one can find them. What Job got for trusting God's goodness is an indelible revelation of God Himself, a gift beyond measure that changed everything for Job, even though, at that moment, nothing external in his life had been restored at all. If Job hadn't gone through his suffering, we would not have this detailed insight into God's creativity, intention, and nature.

I have always thought of the voice out of the whirlwind as a thunderous, irritated one. "Where were you when I…?" Overpowered, Job collapses in a heap of repentance and shame, crushed by God's huge, imposing divine presence. But re-reading and reconsidering, I no longer hear it that way. Of course, any voice out of a whirlwind is bound to be impressive, but, when I asked God about it, He said He wasn't yelling and He wasn't angry. His voice was firm, but not in the least demeaning. We make a mistake when we stop at the first words—"Where were you…" which is easy to imagine as sounding as furious as the swirling wind. But, just for fun, try saying the rest of Job 38 in that same, furious voice. "Where were you when I laid the cornerstone of the Earth when the morning stars sang together and all the sons of God shouted for joy?" Now I ask you, does that sound angry to you? Then there are those jaw-dropping recapitulations of the works within these original creations. When God made it, all of it was perfect. It was as if He said, "I made it vast, various, magnificent, detailed, intricate, synchronous, harmonious, glorious, and good." When he describes the way the scales of leviathan are so close together nothing can penetrate between them, I have the feeling He delighted in sharing with Job the thought He had taken in designing this formidable creature. There are also all those questions about the location of the dwelling of light, the commanding of mornings and the encroaching of the seas, with the implied message: "You wouldn't understand if I told you." There are expressions of design and how everything in the universe (grass to galaxies) fits together, with the repeating overtones that say, "If (since) I can keep all of this going, I can certainly take care of you." That is His heart still towards all He made.

Job sees his own smallness, but also recognizes this new understanding of Divine intent and heart so lavishly imparted to him, accepts the gift, and worships. Now I see You with the eyes of my heart. Something transformative happened to Job when he saw God as He really is. The same thing happens to us when we are able to see God in the midst of our suffering, and it's not something we can guess.

"But we all, with open face beholding as in a glass the glory of the Lord, are changed into the same image from glory to glory, even as by the Spirit of the Lord." (2 Corinthians 3:18) Notice it says "from glory to glory." It doesn't say "from icky to glory." In God, our lives are glorious, and He keeps revealing more as we turn not our backs on Him, but concentrate our gaze on Him, thus becoming more and more like Him, the God we worship.

Thinking about those four chapters in Job—38 to 41, it seems to me that God gave Job a revelation of Himself much greater than the amount of Job's suffering. It wasn't only a restoration and doubling of herds and flocks and children and status; it was an exponential gift of Himself. Without Job, we would not have any of these descriptions of sea monsters and treasuries of snow, much less that He set the ordinances of heaven, placed gifts of wisdom in the mind, or that He knew how to establish the doors of the shadow of death. Wow! And Job got to hear it straight from the mouth of the One who created it all! As a very, very, very small comparison, it would be like having Rembrandt tell you about his favorite paintings.

I wonder if Job realized God didn't have to tell him anything. He could have said, "Because I said so."

When I was in the legalistic church, I was in agreement with the logic of Job's three friends: "Bad happens when we sin, so repent of the sin and all will be well." The fact that the most horrible things for all time happened to the One least deserving of calamities, suffering, disgrace—well, somehow I missed that part. Perhaps it's our human reason that says if I'm obedient, only good things will happen to me. In a pre-Fall world, that would be absolutely true. But that's no longer applicable. After the Fall, evil entered the world and all sorts of bad things have happened since—by our own choices and the choices of others, including input from the dark side of the invisible realm.

One of my biggest concerns about things that can destroy our faith is disappointment from thinking a good God would not have allowed that ______ (fill in the blank) to happen. This is where we have to accept God as sovereign in what He allows, choosing to believe He is as good as He says He is, not expecting He is who we think He ought to be. It's difficult, His thoughts not being our thoughts, His ways not being our ways. This confrontation with suffering always offers a crossroads, a crisis which contains with it danger and opportunity—danger because we can pass judgment on God, saying,

"This is hard. Who can bear it?" But there is opportunity to say, "This is a hard thing, but where can we go? You have the Words of Life." Each time we trust through our freewill choice to believe He is good and intends good for us in every situation, we prove it can be done. And He can bring such astonishing good from it that all those who see it will give Him glory.

I realize the Book of Job is not primarily about God's revelation of Himself in proportion to Job's suffering, though that is magnificent and wonderful in itself. It's the wider frame that shows the invisible realm in interactions we could never guess. In this oldest book in the Bible, God wanted to make sure we knew this aspect of reality—something foundational for our understanding of the nature of human life. He revealed things we couldn't possibly perceive or figure out. There's another arena besides what we know on Earth. In that place, angels come and go, reporting to Almighty God. Satan has access to the throne room and is granted audience with the Lord of the Universe. He can be in only one place at a time. He is not omnipotent, omniscient, or omnipresent. His power is limited to what God authorizes. When limitations are placed on permissions, he cannot violate them.

The other thing God exposes in the Book of Job is human logic regarding bad things happening. Job's friends speak pages and pages of reasons for his suffering. They expressed what everyone thought back then, and, in many cases, they still do. God listens to all of it. Then, after the stunning revelation of Himself, He tells Job's friends they're wrong. Flat wrong. It isn't that simple. What you can figure out with your brilliant human mind isn't even close. So don't try. Trust God. He will give you the treasures of darkness and hidden riches of secret places that you may know Yahweh is actively at work in the situation, and He knows your needs and name.

Last thoughts on Job and the dialogue with God, I tried another voice on the words. I'm not doing violence to the text or disrespecting or diminishing God in any way; I'm trying to understand God in a tone different from what I've believed for 45 years. Please come along and see if it resonates with the truth of God's nature and character that you hold in your heart.

Picture Job as a very small child (God kind of says that when He refers to Job's age). We don't hear God shouting over the noise of the rushing, swirling wind, but distinct with whirlwind background sound. We hear God saying, "Where were you, little one, when I laid the foundations of the earth, stretched out the line upon it, and fastened its foundations? When I laid its cornerstone, the morning stars sang together and all the sons of God shouted for joy. Where were you, little one, when I made it all? I'll tell you. You were in My heart."

11

Agency

When we look at anything from a distance, individuality is lost. From 37,000 feet in the air, a forest looks like a dark green shag carpet. Freeways become patterns of thin, gray lines, and buildings, seen from above, are little geometric shapes without purpose or significance. And if all you see on the news and social media are mobs and crowds and masses, they seem an overwhelming force of anger and violence. One Russian filmmaker realized what an inaccurate view of reality this is. In his day, Russian filmmakers shot scenes of crowds with wide angle lenses. From that distance, humans don't even have faces; they're just a surging tide, a force. The filmmaker called this generalization "people as caviar" and shocked viewers with his close-ups of the face of an old peasant woman struggling to get up after being knocked down by rioters who were ignoring her plight. Now suffering had a human face and could no longer be ignored.

God sees individuals—down to the number of hairs on each head and the thoughts and intents of their hearts. We do well to remember we are not simply part of the crowd—helplessly swept up in the rushing waters of anger and violence that is so loud and present around us. We have free will. Each of us can choose to bring the will of God to Earth. We can make a difference.

History. When I was going to school, it was the subject I disliked almost as much as algebra. History was dates of battles, lists of presidents, treaties, reigns of kings, significant world events which bored me to death, and wars. Kingdoms rose and fell within a few pages, or even a few paragraphs.

Time swept across my years of education with broad strokes and, as the Russian filmmaker said, "people as caviar." My concept of history changed in 1998 when Theresa Hanley, Director of the Ontario Museum of History and Art, told me that history was now being considered in terms of agency. People are individuals who make choices. It is no longer a matter of governments whooshing through their lands knocking over everything in their way. It was no longer lists of dates and names. History was made of people choosing to do or not do, stay, or not stay. Their choices changed history. I saw that I, too, made history—maybe not as swooshingly as kings, but certainly life-changing enough in my own small world. Agency. That's the word. Free will. What do we do with it? We have much more effect on others than we know. And what we do and say and how we are, the tone in our voice, the look in our eye, can affect someone's eternity. Our children are watching, seeing how we respond to each difficult thing, learning from us how to navigate unprecedented uncertainty. It's exciting to know we can prepare them to be bright lights in this dark and scary time. In fact, because they are less threatening, children and young people can often be even more effective at shining in the darkness than grown-ups.

Crisis

First a word about judgment. In Greek the word is "*krisis*," as in "crossroads" or "crisis." All throughout the Bible, when you see judgment, you see God shaking up the people and circumstances so they can see more clearly that what they are trusting in will stand. Whether it's idols or Egypt or the riches of this world, God in His love and persistent pursuit of willful, rebellious, autonomous mankind dismantles self-sufficiency with famine, pestilence, the sword, earthquakes, drought, frogs, floods…well, you know. When God brings judgment, He's not venting His bad temper on the ones who displease Him. He's trying to bring them to their senses. There is only one place that is truly safe. There is only one God who is outside of our limitations. Only Yahweh, the I AM God, can make the desert flower and rescue our lives from futility. God is love. It's His essence, His nature, His way of being. Everything He does is an expression of that love, even the most severe forms of judgment.

The Straight Wall

God had told the prophet Amos to speak judgment over the children of Israel who were totally given to idolatry. Amos told the Lord he couldn't do that because the standard was too difficult for the people to meet. So the Lord gave him another judgment to deliver. Again, Amos refused, saying the people were "too small." Finally, God showed Amos a straight wall with a man holding a plumb line up to it. Without further objection, Amos delivered the Lord's words to His rebellious people.

Why a straight wall? If the wall had been crooked, wouldn't that have made more sense? Judgment would have been totally justified by showing how the people were not measuring up. Amos' objection had been based on his assertion that God's requirements were too difficult. What God showed His prophet was there were those among the people who were meeting His standard and living upright lives, thus proving it could be done. Evolution tells us we're just another phylum of animal. There is no higher purpose for our lives—just live, reproduce, get all you can, die.

Once God told me, "It's not a box. It only looks like a box." There's a distinct advantage in communicating with the Maker of heaven and earth who knows how to get us through whatever boxes us in, even if He has to fight for us Himself. When Joshua was summoned by God to lead His children into the Promised Land, God said to him, "Have I not commanded thee? Be strong and of good courage; be not afraid, neither be dismayed for the Lord thy God is with thee withersoever thou goest." (Joshua 1:9) God was reassuring Joshua He would be with him, though they would be facing the giants the ten spies had reported, saying they were as grasshoppers in their sight. I have to add that they weren't kidding. The original Hebrew word which English scholars translated as "giants" is actually "Nephalim," as in Genesis 6. These guys were indeed huge—from seven to ten feet tall. Og, King of Bashan, was one of them. "His bedstead was of iron 4 cubits wide and 9 cubits long—a cubit being from 18 to 24 inches." (Deuteronomy 3:11) Goliath was also one of them.

Of course, Joshua and Caleb were the straight walls who trusted God, but it doesn't mean that Joshua wasn't apprehensive if not flat-out fearful when he stood near the land that God had told him to conquer. Why else would God tell him not to be afraid or dismayed? We, too, face a battlefield of fierce and gigantic enemies. When all you see in the news is people as caviar, when disaster and the deterioration of values and humanity itself are what fill the eyes and ears from almost every medium available, we can feel alone and helpless, and even hopeless. In the next chapters are examples of real-life people and circumstances where agency and the consequences of free-will choices are a matter of historical record. It helps to know there are straight walls and ways God provides to deal with overwhelming situations.

Like Enoch and Noah, we are living in a time of increasing wickedness, but God can turn the worst to the best, and it strengthens us when we know there is history that shows us God's faithfulness, both in biblical accounts, and in human history. I've picked a few people from recent centuries that particularly speak to me about the reality of free will and the freedom we have to make choices when it seems we really don't have any options. It's not a box. It only looks like a box. We always have options. There are always opportunities to experience the faithfulness of God and, in doing so, we bring Him glory.

The Donner Party

When I first heard about the Donner Party, someone said, "You never know what you'll do if a situation gets bad enough." Having been exposed to the lifeboat exercise of situational ethics and not being a Christian at the time, I began to worry. What would I do in the face of that extreme suffering? The PBS documentary with words from diaries and reports from others left me with horrific images of decent, respectable folks reduced to fighting over the body parts of their fallen companions and friends. Really? Is that the inevitable end if you get hungry enough? For years it troubled me. But years later, when I happened to stop at Donner Pass, I found in their gift shop some books and diaries. It's surprising when you look into things instead of hearing only the general circumstances and the ugliest parts. What did I find? The family of James Reed did not eat human flesh. In her diary, nine-year-old Virginia Reed states theirs was the only one that didn't. And every member of their family survived, including all four of the children. They are the straight wall.

Sometimes children can be more effective than adults in difficult situations. Seven year-old Patty Reed distracted the adults from their miseries by amusing them with her dolly. *Patty Reed's Doll* is one of the books I bought at the gift shop. I was so astonished that a little girl would think to do that, and I can see those starving adults smiling in spite of their suffering as they enjoyed Patty's entertaining presentations with her doll.

One of the greatest tragedies of the Donner Party is there was food everywhere. The woods were full of game. The lake was full of fish. I also seem to remember that Virginia Reed said there was still leather available at the time they were rescued. They could have continued eating it, but they chose not to.

Certainly the best straight wall when it comes to hunger is Jesus. After His baptism, the Holy Spirit led Him into the desert where He fasted and prayed forty days and nights. Scripture says after that, He hungered. You think? Luke 4:4 says the devil tempted Him to turn the stones into bread, whereupon Jesus sliced through the deceitful words with Deuteronomy 8:3. I think the context of that passage is helpful to see the plight of hunger from God's perspective. Reminding the Israelites of their time in the Wilderness far from food and water, Moses said, "So He humbled you, allowed you to hunger, and fed you with manna which you did not know nor did your fathers know, that He might make you know that man shall not live by bread alone; but man lives by every word that proceeds from the mouth of the Lord." (Deuteronomy 8:3 NKJV) Sometimes God allows us to lack things we legitimately need. In my forty-five years of belonging to Jesus, I have learned it is when there is no hope on the horizon and nothing I can do to help myself, He provides manna from heaven and water from Rock. Has this happened to you? Share it with your friends. Show them God's faithfulness even if it feels small. God provides much more often than we realize, and we don't necessarily think to mention it to other people. Scripture says, "Do not despise the day of small things." Any time we thank the Lord and give Him credit for the blessing, it builds the faith of all of us.

The Endurance

Another straight wall, Earnest Shackleton, was in a similar situation as the Donner Party. He had taken twenty-seven men to attempt to cross the Antarctic. When their ship became trapped in the ice, they had to leave its protection. At that point, Shackleton changed his goals from the possible glory and adventure of a successful trans-Arctic expedition to one thing only—getting all of his men home. They had to live in extreme cold without adequate shelter or supplies, and they were there for sixteen months. The story of the Endurance (an apropos name for the ship) is one of those astonishing survival stories in history, one that inspires us still, and miracles happened that confound our understanding. This was 1914-1917 and there was no way to get help or let anyone know where they were. And yet all of them survived. And nobody ate anybody (though one journal entry said they thought about it).

My God Shall Supply

The problem with the Donner Party was they were city folk who knew nothing of how to supply for themselves from the land. They brought flour, sugar, salt, and other staples, but they didn't know how to fish or hunt or look for nourishing plants. I think of the children of Israel in the Wilderness crying out to Moses, blaming him for their lack, complaining about their hunger and thirst. They did not cry out to God, who turned out to be the One who could sweeten bitter water, provide manna every day for forty years, and bring thousands of gallons of water out of a rock for nearly two years.

God knows what we're going to need and can show us surprising ways to deal with it (example: five loaves and two fishes to feed thousands). I think members of the Donner Party could have been inspired to find what they needed, and so can we if we cry out to Him, and don't thrash around blaming the people we think are responsible for our lack of necessities. Just a thought. Deuteronomy 8 specifies that sometimes God causes us to hunger to teach us something hugely significant about what really matters so we can keep the Main Thing the main thing and not try to satisfy our hunger by eating our friends.

Cynthia Leal Massey

As a small publishing house, we at Earthen Vessel Productions have encountered a bunch of eager authors clamoring to have their book in print. Even poets can have that lust for public readings and a book of their own. It's a sign of legitimacy and merit. One of the writers whose essays and poetry we published said his book gave him credibility. So it's a big deal to have a real publisher want your story.

I met Cindy at a Women Writing the West conference shortly after she had been offered publication in a textbook that would be read by thousands of kids. It was quite an honor and a significant opportunity, but she turned it down. I asked her to share her story with you because most writers would have killed to have that honor, but she did not compromise. She is a straight wall in a field where situational ethics suggests one little change of your story for a chance for success. What Cindy faced is a right-now dilemma with serious consequences. Big publishing houses have now sunk to focusing on the bottom line; it's no longer about truly original and enriching material. Now it's about appealing to the widest audience and selling the most copies. If you expect to have the endorsement that comes only from having your words published by a big name house, you will have to bow down to their gods. But we have choices. It's not survival of the fittest, doing whatever you have to do to stay alive. We never have to compromise or hide our faith. Success is not measured by the standards of Earth. We are citizens of the Kingdom of God and our rewards are everlasting.

Language of the Heart
by Cynthia Leal Massey

My short story, "Language of the Heart," appeared in the May 2000 issue of *Cricket,* a magazine for children ages nine to twelve. Set in the Rio Grande Valley of Texas, the story is about a twelve-year-old Mexican-

American girl who can't speak Spanish who, for the first time, meets her Mexican great-grandmother who can't speak English. The young girl discovers that there is a language that transcends spoken word, a language of the heart.

Four years after publication, I received a request for reprint and audio rights from the publisher of the Scott Foresman Reader, Grade 6, for permission to republish the story for national and state-specific books in their elementary reading program. I was very excited; however, my excitement was short-lived. With the request was a copy of my story with deletions that involved references to my character's Catholicism—a porcelain figurine of Mary and the baby Jesus on a coffee table (which the illustrator depicted as a figurine of a flamenco dancer!)—and the blessing given to Teresa (the main character) by her great-grandmother.

I was troubled by these deletion requests. I sent a letter to the publisher explaining my concerns. In the Hispanic culture, religious icons are pervasive. If you were to walk into the home of an average Hispanic family in Texas, not only would there be figurines of the Madonna and child, but also of Jesus, as well as crucifixes and religious paintings depicting representations of Jesus and Our Lady of Guadalupe.

The benediction from the elderly matriarch is an integral and essential part of the Hispanic experience. In fact, I was prompted to write the story because of my vivid recollection of my great-grandmother's blessing when I was Teresa's age. This is the phrase in the story that was scheduled for deletion: "'But first, she is going to bless you.' Doña Alicia wakened from her reverie and made the sign of the cross over Teresa's face, then pressed the palm of her hand against her great-granddaughter's forehead. '*Que Dios la bendiga y te proteja siempre, mi hija.*'(May God bless you and protect you always, my daughter.)" The blessing is the heart of the story and the impetus that propels Teresa's actions at the end.

The references to Christianity and Catholicism in the story were minimal, but necessary and indispensable. If someone were writing a story about a Buddhist child, I would expect to see some references to the appropriate icons and beliefs of that faith and would not be offended. I knew the story was meant for a diverse population of children in the public school system and the publisher was leery of offending anyone with dissimilar beliefs. However, I felt it was just as important that the Hispanic cultural experience be depicted accurately and truthfully. To separate Hispanic culture from its religious roots is to inaccurately reflect our history and experience.

The goal of fiction is to foster understanding and tolerance; this cannot be done by obliterating religious symbolism from stories, particularly from the story of a culture that is intricately woven in its religion. I told the publisher that I would gladly give my permission for publication so long as the work was reprinted as I originally wrote it.

Off my letter went. About a week later, I was told that the story would be "dropped from the book." The illustrator of the story, who was also Hispanic, sent me an email saying that the "story was flagged (at the eleventh hour) because of some 'overly religious' aspect that Scott Foresman could not associate themselves with." She too was disturbed by their reason and told the publisher's designer, "Most ethnic stories about Latinas/os (Hispanics) would have religious overtones. This 'is' the culture."

What I didn't know at the time was that the removal of references to religious experience—especially Judeo-Christian religions—in public school literature had already been going on for a long time. The first phrase of the First Amendment states: "Congress shall make no law respecting an establishment of religion, or prohibiting the free exercise thereof"; nevertheless, our public school system, bolstered by secular authorities, has taken this to mean that public schools should show no interest in religion at all.

As Neil Postman wrote in The End of Education in 1996, "One consequence of this … is that public schools are barely able to refer to religion in almost any context." Postman goes on to say, "… there are few better ways to inculcate a sense of tolerance and even affection for difference than to teach about the varieties of religious experience."

Our public schools, aided and abetted by government and special interest groups, abdicated their responsibility to our children many years ago. While they have clearly become anti-God—the Christian God—they do teach "religion." Their curriculum includes seminars and special programs on acceptance of diversity of lifestyles and inequities because of race. Those who "teach" these classes—a new industry—make thousands of dollars polluting our children's minds with secular religion.

What happened to me sixteen years ago was an eye-opening experience at just how far our country has gone in the wrong direction and explains a lot about the rioting and mayhem today in the name of "justice." It also explains the rise in charter, private, and home-schooling.

I have no regrets about withholding my permission for the story to be published. I could not in good conscience allow it, as a Christian and as an author. It does grieve me that so many children were denied the opportunity to read an authentic story about the Hispanic culture, a culture that now comprises almost 18% of the population of the United States.

Email from Cindy:

"I'm so glad you asked for the story and like what I wrote. It was a pivotal point in my life as a Christian and as a writer. It was my first published story and having it picked up by a national textbook publishing company would have propelled my career, but I knew even then that I could not compromise my faith or my integrity as a writer. I hope it gives others support for the hard decisions we often have to make to be followers of Christ."

12

Hard Choices

Cindy's decision had short and long term consequences on her career as a writer. It took courage and conviction coming from the deepest part of her. But what if you're just driving along and someone cuts you off? What you say when you're alone, triggered suddenly by something that annoys and offends you, also comes out of the deepest part of you. Scripture says what fills a man's heart comes out his mouth. What you say inside your car is private. Nobody hears it but you...and God...and whoever else is listening in the invisible realm.

My son John drives an hour and fifteen minutes to work, rain or shine, and in Oregon, there's a lot of rain. Last night he was heading home when a big truck passed him in a hurry to get around another car that was, like John, going the speed limit. It wasn't safe. Did John spew a few choice explicatives his way? No. He prayed. He said, "So I just called out to God as if He were sitting right next to me in the car because that's where He is when I'm driving. I said, 'Lord, I don't know who that man is or why he has to drive so angrily and irresponsibly. I ask that you will heal whatever it is that makes him impatient or angry. Please show him that there's a better, happier way to live. That person really needs to be safe. That person needs Your help.'"

There in the privacy of his car, John gave God glory. He exhibited the image and character of God, who created that driver and has a divine and fulfilling destiny for him to discover in partnership with the Savior of his soul. Who knows if anyone has ever prayed for that man? Who knows what went into his childhood to make him reckless enough to risk his life and those of others on the road, to get where he wants a few minutes sooner? It doesn't matter. What counts is John did not curse him, but blessed him with the goodness of God. And though no other humans heard or saw, God saw, and so did others in the invisible realms—on both sides. I love that we can give God glory like this. It's a small matter, sort of…

Scripture says not to despise the day of small things. He who is faithful in the little things will be faithful in the big ones. I think this story illustrates this principle. It touches me because I'm becoming increasingly aware of how worldly-minded I am, how easily I react out of my flesh when it comes to these little things. But Scripture says good water and bad water cannot come out of the same fountain, and if I want God's healing words to have power when I speak them into the dark places of the world around me, then I need to be mindful in all of my words, not as a muzzle, but from a change of heart. In this matter, John shows me how to be a straight wall.

What has this to do with you? When you have been wronged, abused, cursed, insulted, robbed, raped, or any other violation, you have legal access to the offender. They made the unwelcomed connection, but now that connection is a fact, and you have a spiritual legal right to them. You may ask for retribution, answer in kind, call for the destruction of those who have wronged you, or you may pray for them—as Jesus did from the cross, as He told His disciples to do, as my son John did in the rain on the road home after a long day at work. We get to give God glory.

But what if it's much more serious than a rude and reckless driver? What if it's a predator who strangles children for fun? How can you forgive? How can you pray for anyone that depraved? How can you love? There, my friend, is the supernatural power that comes with aligning with Jesus in the true Christian life.

The depraved person described above is theoretical, but I know the insides of some tragedies, entrusted to me by friends, and they were willing to let me share them with you. The next stories show me what's possible because these Christians did what seems impossible, though sometimes it took many years and many tears.

LILLER

Liller's husband Weedz was murdered by Mike Silka, a drifter who was picking off people with his rifle as they arrived at the Manley boat landing on the Tanana River, 3 miles from the village of Manley Hot Springs, Alaska. It was in the spring and the river ice had just gone out. Several people from Manley had gone to look at the river, and Weedz arrived by boat. Silka shot them all.

I met Liller in the 1990s and worked with her for several years, bringing what was journal entries, letters, and newspaper clippings into a book of her thoughts during the first year living in their cabin alone with God. *On the River of Grace* chronicles her journey to wholeness after the loss of her beloved husband. Recently I asked her if she had anything she wanted to share about that time, now several decades past. This is what she sent:

> "May, 1984
>
> Was it totally unexpected? YES.
>
> Did God remove the hedge of protection that was around me? YES.
>
> And when it happened, and Weedz was murdered, how did I react? Respond?"God's grace poured out on me because I never hated Mike Silka, I never harbored unforgiveness; I reached up and took hold of the Father, I trusted Him and His sovereignty, His control in

everything that happened. I praised Him in the midst of my pain, I believed there was a blessing in even this experience, and that one day I would also feel the blessing.

"And how did I do this? I always knew it wasn't me. That it wasn't my strength. It was God's grace bestowed on me. I was so totally emptied and He was able to perform His sovereign will. Psalm 50:15 was my lifeline. And He indeed was glorified. I am in awe at how God works and deeply humbled that He chose me. He would not let me go. We are to glorify God with our lives and His Holy Spirit works within us to do just that."

May you never have to deal with anything as heinous as a serial killer, but may you experience for yourself the amazing life that Jesus opens to us as we believe His Word and do things His way.

I told the rather small story of my son John's drive home specifically because it *is* small. David didn't start out slinging stones at giants; he aimed at targets on the hillside—a bush, a twig. He practiced his aim and learned the range of velocity at which a stone could leave a sling. It became so familiar that, when it came time to face the giant, he had more confidence in that one tool than in the armor of the king. Knowing, understanding, and living the heart of Father God is not natural to us. We're far more apt to walk after the flesh than in the Spirit. But it can be learned, practiced, and implemented little by little every day of our lives.

Nikki

But what if it's a predator who molested your toddler, terrorizing him at family gatherings with threatening looks, twisting his arm to hurt him while bullying him with words that dismantled his sense of safety and worth? What if you find out years later that it was your sister's boy? How can you forgive the one who hurt your son? How can you pray for anyone that depraved? How can you love?

It was years before "Joey" told his mother what his cousin had done to him. My friend "Nikki" was horrified and angry—mama bear angry. She wrestled with it before the Lord. And here is the supernatural part. God enabled her to forgive.

Today Nikki's nephew is clean, washed in the blood of the Lamb, no longer a predator or twisted. And he is graciously able to help others in their destructions and addictions. As Nikki told me her story, the Holy Spirit spoke to me gently, saying that the opening of the door to her nephew's heart was made more possible because she forgave.

This is the supernatural power that comes from letting Jesus take the mess of our human free will and work it together with His love into something that is good. It takes a miracle to release a grieving parent from bitterness and hatred. It seems impossible, but Jesus did it on the cross. He told us to follow Him and do like Him and be like Him. We are able because the Holy Spirit lives inside us and the same power that raised Christ from the dead is working in us today.

After my son John read Nikki's story, he sent me these thoughts.

"I knew a family who found out their daughter had been molested by a family friend. For years. He told the child he would kill her parents if she told them. It came out and he went to prison. The parents had it leaked into the prison about his crime. His fellow prisoners killed him. It makes me think about the young potter who watched as his beautiful creations were shattered on the floor in front of him. Yes. A predator is off of the streets. The family had their revenge. But what could God have done with that man if he had found Jesus in prison? Puts a whole different spin on it."

This morning I asked the Lord what happened to the parents of that girl. Did their revenge give them closure? peace? release? He showed me their hearts were still clenched tight as fists. Revenge cannot release you. Only forgiveness can.

Is this too hard? If it were, it would be unjust of God to require it. Is it impossibly hard? Yes. That's why the normal Christian life is supernatural. It takes transcendent power from God to be a straight wall in a crooked world. But any time any of us manages to forgive, to bless and not curse, to love our enemies, we are living the life of Christ on Earth, *and* the power of God is released here in ways that resonate *with* the heart of God and shift the spiritual atmosphere more than we can understand. The harmonies of heaven from our choices to honor Him go on and on and on. Who knows? Like Nikki's nephew, the predator can be saved. So can the ones who put Christians to death, thinking they're doing God a service. Just ask Paul.

Majed

This story is from a man I don't personally know. I listened to a lengthy interview and felt the Lord wanted me to share it because we can sometimes go through situations that seem impossible to come through intact, much less be a straight wall aligned with the will of God.

Majed was born into a prominent Muslim family. His uncle was a supreme court judge, and he himself, even as a little boy, had a large library in his bedroom. It was full of books on justice, human rights, and high ideals. He read them all, believed them completely, and knew, by age five, that he wanted to be an attorney when he grew up.

Majed's best friend was a Christian, born into a Christian family, and they were as close as brothers. They went together all the way from elementary school through university. One day Majed noticed that the law said it was legal to build places of worship—mosques, temples, synagogues, but not Christian churches. He began to notice the persecution that was being directed at Christians and wondered why. "You don't persecute somebody unless you're scared from the life they carry," he said. So he asked his friend what was so threatening about the Christian religion. His friend said he didn't know, and handed him a Bible saying he would find the answers to all his questions in it.

Majed began comparing the Koran to the Bible, and that led him to Jesus. He saw it was "not just judgment and rules, but sacrifice, forgiveness, and love. Now I know what's Christ," he said. "He's a flower in the middle of the desert, a mighty Light in the middle of the darkness, a warm hug in the middle of cold night."

Majed started an underground human rights organization, built two churches in mountains and caves, one Bible school, one medical clinic, and founded a newsletter to send to the Egyptian government to ask for equal rights to the Christian minorities. "And I started to write a book about the differences between Islam and Christianity." That, of course, started attracting attention. Majed said for them as followers of Christ in Egypt, life is perilous. "Every day when we say good-bye to our families we don't know if we will see them at the end of the day." Majed's group went from 7 members to 24,000 in two years.

Early in the morning on Aug 15, 1990, five soldiers broke into Majed's office in Cairo, arrested him, and took every piece of paper, every computer. The officer at the police station said, "I know who you are. I know about the organization that you built. I know everything about you. But one thing I don't know. I don't know who is the rest of your group. Who is working with you?"

Majed told him, "I don't know which group, and what organization, and if you know everything about me, why are you asking me?"

The next day they transferred him to a special jail. Twenty-five percent of that jail is underground. "There are many rooms down there," Majed said, "They call it the torture section and very few people come out alive. I was prisoner of this section for 7 days. For me it was like 700 years."

They told Majed he would undergo seven days of torture, each day's more severe than the last. Here is the account of the first three days in Majed's own words.

"Day #1: They shave my head. They hold you from your neck. Your hands are tied behind your back. They put your head in very cold water for one minute (there is ice in the water) and immediately after that they take you and they put your head in very hot water. They torture for two or three hours, they give you rest for ten to fifteen minutes, and then they carry on until the end of the day. At the end of the night, they will tell you what you will face the next day if you do not speak. All night long you're sitting down thinking about it. It's part of the psychology.

"They put me back in my cell and they said tell us the name of your friends that are working with you. I told then, 'To be honest with you I did not take a shower for a long time and I enjoyed the cold and hot water and I'm very handsome without hair.' When you're facing your enemy, you never show them your pain or your fear. Never.

"Day #2: They hang me upside-down, 90 degree position. The lower part of your body is hanging, the top part is on the ground. They burned me with cigarettes, they beat me with what they had in their hands. They grabbed the toenails on my right foot. The only thing I remember of Day #2 is the taste and smell of my blood. It was everywhere. I couldn't walk, so they carried me back to my cell. They told me what would be the torture the next day if I did not speak. They release three dogs to attack you. These are usually German shepherds or Doberman.

"If you were in my place, what would you think? You're underground. No windows. No doors. There is no light. And to be honest with you, in this moment you even doubt if there is a God or if there is a Father. If anybody told you, 'No, I didn't doubt that,' they are lying.

"What do you do if you're in my place? Pray. It's the only thing that you can do. Even in the middle of a doubt, pray. This was my prayer. I told Him, 'Lord, thank You for Your gift on the cross. Thank You that You died for our sin and our pain and our disease. And I thank You Lord that You rose again to give us the way, the truth, and the life.' I told Him, 'Lord, it's an honor to be tortured for You. You drank the whole cup and it's an honor just to have a small sip of it. But, God, You created me. You know my weakness. You know that I am made of flesh and blood. Lord, if it carries on like this, I am scared'—because you don't know how much you can handle before you speak. My friend, I will tell you something and remember it as long as you live. Christians are like bag of tea. You don't know how strong they are until you throw them in hot water.

"I told Him, 'Lord, I don't know how much I can handle it, so I will make with You a deal. Just kill me before tomorrow morning. Just take me home—from ash to ash, dust to dust.' In His name I prayed and I lied down in my bunk.

"Next day, Day #3: My cell is very dark. When you open the door there is a light in the corridor. It's a red light. When they open the door, the light will come into your room. Whoever is walking in the corridor, you can see their shadow. So the door opened and another door opened at the end of the corridor and you can hear the sound of the voices of the dogs. When you have three big dogs, all of them chained, they have a voice I cannot describe. The way that they're breathing, and they always breathe very heavy. You can hear the chain. You can hear their feet. And I can see their shadow getting closer and closer and closer to my room. I stood up and went to the corner of my room. I put my back to the corner so my back was protected by the corner. I sat down so my knees were on my chest and my hands were on my face. What you're doing is protecting yourself from the dogs' attack. Just trying to make the damage from outside to the best of your ability. The dogs are getting closer and closer and closer to my room and I can hear them. I can't see anymore because I covered my face by my own hands. I can hear them step by step getting closer and closer and closer to my room until I know that they are there. I know that they're in my room. I start to prepare myself for pain. I start to prepare myself for agony. I couldn't feel anything. I know that they're there because I can hear them breathing in my ear. I took my hand away from my face and that's what I saw—three dogs sitting around me. Not one of them moved one single step.

"Officers and soldiers start to beat the dogs to attack. The dogs didn't move. One of the dogs, the middle one, they hit him so hard, they slapped him so hard on his body with a belt that it pushed his body forward and I can see the muscle in his leg trying to hold not to fall. And he didn't attack. I have secular friends in the media who would say, 'Well, what is the scientific explanation for that?'

I tell them, 'You want scientific explanation for that? I'll tell you. These dogs have been trained to listen to their master but there is no higher Master than Jesus Christ, and here is your scientific explanation.'

"I can hear the soldiers and the officers telling maybe there is something wrong with these dogs. 'Take the three dogs. Get me another set of three dogs.' Another set of three dogs sit in the same position with one little difference—the middle one took a step forward and licked my face. These are dogs trained to attack flesh. Officers and soldiers didn't know what's happening. They took the three dogs. They closed the door and I didn't hear from them the whole day."

Animals, you see, obey the Lord. Even these "vicious dogs" trained to rend and tear, would not because the Lord was telling them not to. Humans, however, can shut off the voice of God, especially if they believe they are actually doing God's business by finding every Christian rat and destroying them. The next four days were much much worse than the days before. I will not describe what was done to this man in their attempt to make him divulge the names of the others. I'll just say there comes a point at which the pain is so intense that your entire nervous system blows out, and that's what happened to Majed. He could not move for three months. They put him in the police hospital until he was strong enough to be under house arrest for eight months. During that time they did a medical assessment and reported that he was mentally ill.

Why don't they kill you or leave you in prison to die? Majed said "If they did this, they would make out of you a hero, a martyr. So the Middle East system with human rights activists is to ruin their reputation first before they kill them. Then no one will care about them.

"At the end of eight months, they present me to military court for Court Martial. You have no lawyer. You don't have any defense. They made three charges against me. Number one charge is I tried to make revolution against the Egyptian government. Number two, that I tried to change the official religion of Egypt from Islam to Christianity. Number three, believe it or not, that I worship and I love Christ. In the end, the judge asked if I had one last thing I wanted to say before they gave me my sentence. I told him, 'I'm guilty as charged.' I told him, 'If loving Christ is wrong, if loving the Father is wrong, I don't want to be right anymore. And if it's a crime, I'm guilty as charged.' I received the death penalty."

In four days, Majed would be hanged. He was taken back to the place he was being kept under house arrest. The day before Execution Day, Majed's team attacked the house which was protected by five soldiers—two outside, two inside, and one on the roof. The story of Majed's escape is worthy of a James Bond movie, but I'll just say his friends rescued him from where he was being held, he hid for months, and finally made his way to Canada.

You'd think the hard part would be in not renouncing Jesus or divulging the names of your friends, but it is more difficult than that. It was hard for Majed to forgive those who had tortured him. Even knowing it was what God wanted from him, he refused.

"It took me three years to forgive," Majed said. "During the three years, I couldn't preach because of this. Forgiveness is a choice. It's not an option; it's a choice. The Lord was wise enough to understand that there's no society that can live an eye for an eye, a tooth for a tooth. The whole society will end blind and toothless. You forgive, not just for the benefit of your enemy, but for your own benefit.

"In the old ancient history, if somebody killed other person, your punishment wouldn't be death. They take the dead body that you killed and they hang it on your shoulders forever. After three days the dead body on your shoulders starts to decompose and the bacteria from the dead one starts to kill the live one slowly. In a matter of weeks you die. That's what happens when you carry revenge in your heart. It kills you slowly. And one day after three years of carrying this dead body on my shoulders, I said, 'Enough is enough,' and I threw it. I said, 'Lord, this is not mine anymore. That's Yours.'

"Forgiveness is very hard in this case, but it's not impossible. You forgive when you know that it's not about if they deserve forgiveness or not. But you forgive when you know that you, yourself, are forgiven by the Father, and you forgive when you know that you have to forgive to let go of this pain and to close this page in your heart."

Majed now lives in safety, and helps other Christians escape persecution and torture. In one of Darren Wilson's documentaries, Majed asked one of the rescued Egyptians to remove his shirt so Darren could film the scars from multiple cigarette burn on his back. The man said he had been a normal, casual church-going Christian until this happened. There were numerous tortures, and the man said every time he passed out from the pain, he felt Jesus hug him. He is no longer casual about his life in Christ. Now it's everything, and he says he's happy even though he left all his riches in Egypt and is living in a refugee camp with nothing.

That man's testimony touches me because he wasn't, as Majed, a fierce activist whose conversion was based on biblical truth that ignited fire in his bones. The other man wasn't all that serious about his relationship with Jesus until he was persecuted. I'm not saying this is what usually happens; I'm citing it to show that it *can* happen, including his joy.

Let all bitterness and indignation and wrath (passion, rage, bad temper) and resentment (anger, animosity) and quarreling (brawling, clamor, contention) and slander (evil-speaking, abusive or blasphemous language) be banished from you, with all malice (spite, ill will, or baseness of any kind). And become useful and helpful and kind to one another, tenderhearted (compassionate, understanding, loving-hearted), forgiving one another [readily and freely], as God in Christ forgave you. (Ephesians 4:31-32 AMPC)

13

Choosing Where To Stand

Who shall separate us from the love of Christ? Shall tribulation, or distress, or persecution, or famine, or nakedness, or peril, or sword? (Romans 8:35 KJV)

The Little Girl and the Candle

My son Thomas was telling his Sunday school class of teenaged boys a story from *Foxe's Book of Martyrs*. A little girl had been captured by soldiers who said, "We know you're a Christian. You need to deny Jesus!" The girl refused. One of the soldiers had a candle. He lit it and held the girl's hand over it. He demanded, "Deny Jesus!' As her hand was beginning to smoke and the pain intensified, she still refused. "Deny Jesus and we'll remove your hand from the flame." It doesn't say more except she didn't deny Jesus.

Listening to the story and imagining the agony the little girl was feeling, the teenaged boys were wondering if they could make it through something like that. Thomas asked, "Where do you think that little girl is today?"

They all said, "Heaven."

Thomas said, "So was it that big a choice? If you could step back a moment. Don't think about 'my hand hurts right now.' It suddenly becomes a really easy choice. And that's God's perspective. Time doesn't matter. He sees the beginning from the end. And we get too hung up with right here, right now: I'm hungry. I'm thirsty. I need something. If I'm worried about this thing my boss wants or whatever—are those pressures? Absolutely they are. And they're real things. If I don't pay my rent, they're gonna throw me out. That's a real thing. I also know that God loves me and that even if I don't make rent and get thrown out, it does not change my relationship with God in the slightest. Somehow things will be okay even while they're awful. I don't know how that works, but I know that on the cross must have been pretty awful. Getting crucified upside-down must have been pretty awful. *Foxe's Book of Martyrs*—every bit of that is as awful and horrific as you could ask for. And not a one of them would change any of that today."

Choosing Where To Stand

It's a luxury to have this time of relative quiet. There's also a hazard in relative quiet. There's no urgency to decide what really matters most. What we have is working well enough. Along those lines, I want to tell you a story. I had a friend who was high up in designing weapons for the government. He was also a dipper into the dark side, even though he was a devout Catholic. When I told him it wasn't safe to do that, and recommended giving his entire allegiance to Jesus, he said he needed the power that came from the dark side for the designing of those weapons. I told him God knows how to blow things up. Just look at Mt. St. Helens. But he insisted it wasn't the same. No, it's not the same; it's better, and a lot safer too—especially for his soul.

Not long after that conversation, in my mind's eye I saw him standing on the flat, dry ground of a vast, desolate plain. A thin crack ran through the land and my friend was straddling it, one foot on each side. The sun was shining. The sky was blue. Suddenly the crack opened into a yawning abyss. My friend had to quickly leap to one side. He didn't have time to think. Recently the Lord has reminded me of that picture. We still have time to decide, and help our families decide, where we'll stand.

I remember hearing about some Chinese Christians who were caught. You remember the Chinese are big on filial piety—devotion of children to their parents. That's how I was reared and I'm so blessed to have two wonderful, godly sons who love me very much. So I heard about these captured Christians—a woman and her son. One of the soldiers was torturing the woman in front of her son. He said, "I'll stop torturing your mother if you deny Jesus." How cruel is that! I don't remember the end of the story, but immediately I told John and Thomas, "If that ever happens to us, do not deny Jesus. If you do, you will hurt me much more than any torture ever could. If you deny Jesus, you are not my son." I wasn't leaving anything to chance.

One more story. My friend Stephanie told me this one. I think it's from *Foxe's Book of Martyrs*. She said there was a family with two children. The soldiers captured all of them, but somehow the little boy got away and escaped into the woods. As the soldiers prepared to hunt the boy in the forest, the father stopped them saying, "Let me talk to him." They gave permission so the dad called into the trees, "Son, if you hide in there, they will hunt you down and you will be killed anyway, but if you come back, you can be with us and we can all enter heaven together as a family." The little boy came back.

I'm telling you these stories because we have never in recent history had to give the slightest thought to this kind of persecution, not in our country whose mottos ring with words of tolerance, equality, and freedom of speech. Freedom to worship as each one chooses. I grew up with that security. I don't feel the same anymore. Things are going on we couldn't have imagined. Scripture said it would happen. Things would be totally upside-down, good would be called evil and evil would be called good. Forty-five years ago when I first heard that, I couldn't imagine how it could be like that, but now I know.

In the Olivet Discourse, Jesus tells His disciples they will be persecuted. They were, and have been ever since. In other countries, Christians are being arrested, imprisoned, tortured, murdered, and it very well may happen here. We are certainly seeing odd edicts from officials placing heavy restrictions on churches while other establishments are not restricted at all. I'm surprised—and also not. If you look at what's happening as an outpouring from a worldview that believes God doesn't exist and religion is the enemy of science and progress, it makes perfect sense. And also, Jesus said we would be persecuted.

There may come a time in the near future that pastors will be arrested and put in prison for violation of human rights regarding issues of gender and lifestyle. Each of us has to decide where we will stand. And we still have time. It's not happening yet. We have the luxury of lots of information from wonderful teachers such as John Lennox and Chuck Missler, and preachers such as Chuck Smith and the Calvary Chapel shepherds who go verse by verse through the whole counsel of God. We have resources galore and the Bible itself. We have plenty of evidence for the reality of the spiritual realm, God's involvement in human lives, and even some insight into the details of other people's sufferings—how God has transformed them through the horrors we probably won't ever have to face. Ever since I heard about the martyrs, I've worried that I might crack under torture, but these real people telling their verifiable stories, show me what God can do in overwhelming situations, even providing intimacy with Jesus in supernatural gifts and enablements not possible under any other circumstances. We have time to dive into deep relationship with the Lover of our souls, fill ourselves with His truth that makes us free no matter what it looks like, and we can talk to our children about it. It's not true what I was told—that you never know what you'll do if circumstances are bad enough. This is not situational ethics. There is no sliding scale. There are eternal absolutes and a supernatural Helper to counsel, strengthen, and guide us through the labyrinth of lies and deceptions. There are only two sides, two views of reality, and we have time now to decide where we will stand.

The Sower and the Seeds

In Matthew 13:4-8, Jesus told the people about the sower and the seed that fell on four different types of ground. Just to refresh your memory, here it is in the NKJV. "And as he sowed, some seed fell by the wayside; and the birds came and devoured them. Some fell on stony places, where they did not have much earth; and they immediately sprang up because they had no depth of earth. But when the sun was up they were scorched, and because they had no root they withered away. And some fell among thorns, and the thorns sprang up and choked them. But others fell on good ground and yielded a crop: some a hundredfold, some sixty, some thirty.

This Scripture worried me more than the lifeboat exercise. When I was in the legalistic church, I had no trouble believing I was a hundred-fold person, but when I began to live the real Christian life, no longer measuring my performance by being able to assiduously keep the Law and obey, I realized what dangers lay before me. Of all the types of soil, I worried I would be the one so caught up in the cares of this life that I'd lose track of what matters most and end up in futility. I think that's why I'm so concerned about my fellow Christians in the coming days. There's unbelief, roots that don't go deep, and the cares of this life. I'm so glad the disciples asked Jesus to explain, because He described precisely what can keep us from having fruitful, fulfilling lives, especially now. Here is His explanation with the overtones of the words.

"Listen then to the [meaning of the] parable of the sower: While anyone is hearing the Word of the kingdom and does not grasp and comprehend it, the evil one comes and snatches away what was sown in his heart. This is what was sown along the roadside. As for what was sown on thin (rocky) soil, this is he who hears the Word and at once welcomes and accepts it with joy; yet it has no real root in him, but is temporary (inconstant, lasts but a little while); and when affliction or trouble or persecution comes on account of the Word, at once he is caused to stumble [he is repelled and begins to distrust and desert Him Whom he ought to trust and obey] and he falls away. As for what was sown among thorns, this is he who hears the Word, but the cares of the world and the pleasure and delight and glamour and deceitfulness of riches choke and suffocate the Word, and it yields no fruit. As for what was sown on good soil, this is he who hears the Word and grasps and comprehends it; he indeed bears fruit and yields in one case a hundred times as much as was sown, in another sixty times as much, and in another thirty." (Matt 13 :18-23 AMPC)

I used to think the biggest danger was in being distracted by the cares of life and its deceitful pleasures, but reading this version shows me a greater danger: when affliction or trouble or persecution comes on account of the Word, at once he is caused to stumble [he is repelled and begins to distrust and desert Him Whom he ought to trust and obey] and he falls away." It's because he doesn't understand the Word. He doesn't know it has treasures to give him, riches that will keep him strong and steady no matter what comes. Does that sound familiar? The night He was going to be arrested in the garden, Jesus said to His disciples, "You will all be offended and stumble and fall away because of Me this night [distrusting and deserting Me], for it is written, I will strike the Shepherd, and the sheep of the flock will be scattered." (Matt 26:31 AMPC) There's a strong correlation between offense and falling away. Here's what Jesus thought about these sheep. "When He saw the throngs, He was moved with pity and sympathy for them, because they were bewildered (harassed and distressed and dejected and helpless), like sheep without a shepherd." (Matt 9:36 AMPC)

When Jesus told His disciples they would all desert Him on the night of His arrest, that's what was going to happen. Why? They expected Him to take over, defeat Rome with God-power, and give them peace and freedom with Him as King. Instead, when the soldiers showed up with swords and torches, He didn't resist or fight back. He gave Himself up. Jesus was doing something much more important than freeing them from tyranny, but they didn't understand. They scattered, bewildered, confused, distressed, disappointed. "Wait! This isn't what we expected! You're not who we thought you were. You're not doing what we thought You'd do. Why aren't you protecting Yourself and us? Why are You letting this happen?" Jesus said they will be offended. They will distrust and desert Him.

When affliction happens, when persecution comes, there will be a falling away. Harassed, the sheep will wonder where their Leader is. Scripture connects this lack of understanding to a lack of depth of soil, a lack of roots deep in the Word. There was excitement at first hearing of the Word, but no real rooting and grounding in it. I apply this to both a lack of nourishment from the written Word of God and a weak connection with the Living Word Himself. In the Amplified Bible, the overtones of the word "faith" are described as, "The leaning of the entire human personality on God in absolute confidence and trust in His power, wisdom, and goodness." When Jesus doesn't do what we think He should, those are the three things we doubt. Did He really tell us to do it this way? We don't want to turn the other cheek, concentrate on getting the log out of our own eye instead of obsessing on the speck in our brother's eye. We don't want to endure patiently the abuse of others or overcome evil with good. We want to do what seems right in our own eyes. Hence the falling away.

According to Strong's, "falling away" is from the Greek word "*apostasia*," from which we get our word "apostasy." It includes defection from truth. I always thought there would be distorted doctrine in the last days, and that is certainly true, but Spiros Zodhiates says *apostasia* has to do with standing away. He says some have associated themselves with Christ because of advantage, social favor, but when it becomes dangerous or unpopular, they move away, disassociate, no longer aligning themselves with Jesus.

It has certainly become unpopular to be Christian (which many equate with "Conservative," though I have lots of dear Christian friends who are not Conservatives). In some people's minds, Christian means "Hater," "Racist," and a number of other ridiculous associations. But Jesus *did* say things would be upside-down…

There's danger to us when we don't really understand God, His nature, His wisdom, His goodness no matter what it looks like to us. Disappointment leads to distrust, offense, stumbling, falling away. That's why I've written so much about God's nature and intentions. That's why I want very much for all of us to commune with Him in a profoundly beautiful way. That's why I encourage reading the Word—all of it, and praying using every weapon available to us. We need to make sure our soil is deep, that the Word doesn't lie inert by the side of the road where it can be snatched away by the devil, that we remain free from distractions and thorns that snare us, because Jesus made sure we would know about the dangers and gave us the Holy Spirit to convict us so we can produce a harvest 30-, 60-, 100-fold.

More Falling Away

Here's the really scary part about falling away. "Let no one deceive you by any means; for that Day will not come unless the falling away comes first, and the man of sin is revealed, the son of perdition, who opposes and exalts himself above all that is called God or that is worshiped, so that he sits as God in the temple of God, showing himself that he is God." (2 Thessalonians 2:3, 4 NKJV) "The day" Paul is talking about is the real End Times. It's "The Day of the Lord" so often mentioned in prophecy. He's talking about the one we commonly call "anti-Christ." Before the man of sin reveals himself to be as wicked as he really is, he makes a good showing of being the great peacemaker, bringing all peoples into unity, harmonizing all religions and becoming the leader of the entire world. During that time, a lot of people who call themselves Christians will be disappointed in Jesus and, in their offendedness, stumble, distrust, desert Him and give their devotion to this other guy who has all the answers and fits their specifications for a real leader worth following.

Why am I telling you this? Because I've heard it said we're not responsible for the condition of the soil, only for sowing the seed, the Word of God, hoping it will happen to land on good ground and be transformative of the lives that take it to heart. I thought Jesus was describing how things are—categories of mind and receptivity to the Word. These guys bring forth fruit. These don't, and here's why. But He's not. It's a parable. It's an illustration of how things are, not how it will always be. If you're born into a family of alcoholics and drug addicts, sorry. You won't have deep enough soil to set your roots down, and when hard times come, you'll wither and blow away. If you're a fun-loving person who wants parties and pleasure, you will turn a deaf ear to the Word and have no fruit when you come before the King. Or your heart is too hard and the Word just bounces off your head. You can't even comprehend it. Sorry about that.

Do you see the fatalism in this interpretation? What the Lord showed me is it's a description of how things happen, not a prophecy of what must happen. He showed me we can pray into each kind of soil. If there's a Christian friend without much depth, you can pray for more soil, broken up, fertilized, enriched, watered. If there are weeds and thorns distracting, enticing, choking out the truth of the Word, ask the Lord to send in celestial weed-eaters...These are just thoughts off the top of my head. He said you'd be able to figure it out, and your inspirations, breathed by the Holy Spirit through your personality and understandings, would be deeper and more effective than anything I could suggest. So I leave that to you. Just know there are multitudes of Christians who don't believe in the supernatural, in the goodness of the nature and character of God, in the power of prayer, in the transforming power of the Word of God, in the reality of the cosmic war and the wiles of the devil, or the potential in their own lives to change the world around them. They don't read the Bible. Their communication with God is shallow. When the scorching heat comes, when persecution arises, when "normal" is less and less reliable, they will need help to stand their ground. Some of them attend your church. Some are members of your family. You can help them not be deceived, disappointed because things aren't going well according to their expectations, concluding there's nothing special or precious about following Jesus, scattered, bewildered, harassed, distressed, discouraged, feeling helpless, falling away.

But wait! I see lights in the distance. Is that a city on a hill? I see lights in the houses. I'm so on Empty. My friends say they're praying for me. And there's this odd peace that comes upon me. Maybe I'll keep driving towards the light. Maybe I'll find help and a hug.

Obdurate

Obdurate. That's the word He gave me. Obdurate. Over and over till I asked, "Who's obdurate, Lord? Me? Your church?"

"No," came the answer. "Some people in the world." I thought of stiff-necked, hard-headed people—both God's chosen ones and Pharaoh, who hardened his own heart against the Lord and then got worse as plagues went on.

According to my Dashboard dictionary, "obdurate" means "stubbornly refusing to change one's opinion or course of action." Well, that fits some people, both that belong to God and some who don't. But why bring that up when I'm writing about persecution? Because the invisible realm is not the only one watching. I think of something I heard about martyrs in the Russian persecutions. One soldier said, "As we tortured them and killed them, they loved us with their eyes." How do we know the soldier said that? Because later he became a Christian and wanted others to know the reason why.

When Moses announced the coming plague of hailstones, some of the Egyptians took their livestock and workers out of the fields. Why? Because they believed Moses. They were starting to see his God was mightier than their gods and were willing to change their opinion about Him and acted accordingly. So none of them died from the hailstones. And I think the reason we know about the little girl and the candle is because someone who was there, someone who believed he was doing right in persecuting believers in God, saw she had something he didn't have. And he wanted it. And now he has it, and has joined the cloud of witnesses that has seen and can testify first-hand that God is real, and He's something worth dying for.

I've thought about that a lot, since martyrdom is a real possibility in the Christian life. I think of the girl standing up in her classroom, acknowledging her Savior though it cost her her life. I think of Christians being beheaded with machetes by religious fanatics here in the twenty-first century. I think of all the pressure of normal life to compromise, fudge, fib, minimize, fit in, agree, bow the knee just once.

Sometimes it's easier to die for Christ than to live for Him. But this passage from Philippians helps put a different face on it. And Paul should know. He's in prison in Rome, writing his last letter, knowing his time is short. What will he tell these beloved brothers and sisters in Christ? Sixteen times he uses words relating to joy. How can that be? The walk he proposes is pretty demanding, though he, himself, has shown it can be done. The key is in the last part: It's God's power. He doesn't ask us to do anything He didn't do, or that we can't do. He gives us supernatural enablement, and the result is we shine like stars, like beacons, like candles in the darkness—the life of the Word that is the Light of the world. And the Light shines in the darkness, and the darkness cannot overcome it. Ever.

"So then, my dear ones...continue to work out your salvation [that is, cultivate it, bring it to full effect, actively pursue spiritual maturity] with awe-inspired fear and trembling [using serious caution and critical self-evaluation to avoid anything that might offend God or discredit the name of Christ]. For it is [not your strength, but it is] God who is effectively at work in you, both to will and to work [that is, strengthening, energizing, and creating in you the longing and the ability to fulfill your purpose] for His good pleasure. Do everything without murmuring or questioning [the providence of God], so that you may prove yourselves to be blameless and guileless, innocent and uncontaminated, children of God without blemish in the midst of a [morally] crooked and [spiritually] perverted generation, among whom you are seen as bright lights [beacons shining out clearly] in the world [of darkness], holding out and offering to everyone the word of life." (Phil :12-16 AMP)

One Who Took a Stand

Eric Liddell (like "little" with a "D") had an unusual running style, knees pumping high up to his chest, his arms rotating like a windmill. As he neared the finish line, he would throw his head back, mouth open, and, looking at the sky, finish the race. It was an odd sight, but he was fast.

When Eric chose not to run on Sunday, entering the 400 meter race instead, people who had favored him to win gold in the 100 now thought he hadn't a chance to win anything. Looking at the schedule, it certainly didn't look promising in any way. Everything was against him. It wasn't just that he was running in a race four times the length of his specialty. He was inexperienced, never having run internationally before. He was in the outside lane, a distinct disadvantage. Then there were the number of races he had to run one shortly after another—first and second rounds within a few hours on Thursday, and semi-final and final within four hours on Friday. He had never run back-to-back 400 meter races until he went to Paris. Surprisingly, he improved his time in every race. In the final 400 meter race, when Eric passed the 100 meter mark, his speed actually increased. Then, when he reached that moment he was known for—his arms windmilling, his head thrown back, mouth open wide, eyes on the sky—Eric crossed the finish line five meters ahead of the other runners and broke a world record.

After that astonishing performance, Eric was a national hero, yet, at 22 years of age, he gave up all the fame and celebrity and sailed for China to serve as a missionary. He felt his accomplishments were small compared to what the missionaries had been doing for many hard years. Eventually he married Florence and had started a family when the war threatened their safety. Eric and Florence made the hard decision to separate. Florence and the girls left for Canada and Eric stayed behind with "his people." He didn't believe he should abandon them for the sake of his own safety. So it was that, when the Japanese rounded up all the foreign nationals (now termed "enemy nationals"), Eric and 1799 others were confined to a prisoner of war camp. Three hundred of those prisoners were children and teenagers who had been at the China Inland Mission boarding school, children of missionaries who were serving elsewhere.

Eric had grown up in such a boarding school, seeing his parents every seven years. He understood the issues of children being without their parents, especially in such harsh conditions. So he tutored them, held Bible studies, refereed games, organized sporting events, helped others with chores when they weren't strong enough to carry out their assigned tasks, and encouraged everyone. He loved them as Jesus loved them. That was hard enough in a camp with nearly two thousand people of varying backgrounds and ways of life—international business executives, opium addicts, babies and the aged, entertainers, tourists, missionaries, and atheists. Eric loved and served them all. To me, that took supernatural help from God.

But there was something else unusual Eric did. He took the Bible seriously and helped others do the same. One of the teenagers who studied the Bible with Eric was Stephen Metcalf. Stephen recalled talking with Eric about the Sermon on the Mount. He said, "He was discussing whether you really could love the Japanese guards. We discussed it. Was it really practical? I remember it was Matthew 5, and the last verse was 'Be ye perfect as your Father in heaven is perfect,' and we decided it was a goal to be aimed at. Love your enemy. Eric smiled and said, 'I thought so too.' Then I realized that it says, 'Love your enemy. Pray for those who despitefully use you.' He said, 'We spend a lot of time praying for the people we like but we spend no time at all praying for the people we don't like.' He said, 'I get up every day and pray for the Japanese.' And he challenged us. I started praying for the Japanese from that time."

After Eric Liddell's death, Stephen Metcalf said, "I told God if I survived in the prison camp I'd go to Japan as a missionary." and he did. That change of heart is more impressive to me than Eric's surprising win in the 400 at the 1924 Olympics. It was a metamorphosis, a transformation, a surrender to the will of God, taking Him seriously and aligning with His values, and His power flowed through Stephen Metcalf to minister in love to the people he had previously so intensely hated.

Of all the teenagers in the camp, one of the closest to Eric was Joyce Stranks. When he was hospitalized with a brain tumor, she visited him daily, bringing him news of what was happening in the camp, and talking with him on the things of God. One day when she went to see him, something happened no one expected. Joyce said, "I was sitting beside his bed and we were talking about the third chapter in his book about the surrender of our will to the will of God, so that, in everything we did, in our attitude it was not what we wanted to do and what we felt like doing, but what God wanted us to do, and to surrender that will that we all have to Him. He started to say surrender. He said, 'srurren... surren...' and then his head went back."

It struck me, as I listened to Joyce's account, that God had given His faithful servant, the one who surrendered his will to Him, a special gift—a look into heaven as he crossed the final finish line.

It's easy to point out the supernatural nature of Eric's spectacular win in Paris—Eric always prayed that every athletic event would bring glory to God—but it takes more than talent and training to survive in a Japanese prison camp for an unspecified time, bunched together in crowded conditions with 1800 strangers with no privacy and only bread and water to eat for years. There's no way to hide who you are. Eric had sent his wife and children to safety in Canada, and had no way to communicate with them, much less see them, but those who interviewed surviving internees said they never heard a word spoken against him. More than one said he was the most Christ-like individual they'd ever met. They said he was a friend to everyone and lived each day encouraging them, loving them, and helping any way he could. Eric's eldest daughter, Patricia, was six years old the last time she saw her father, and she wondered why God would take her daddy away when they needed him so much, but after the war she was able to speak to many of the internees who had been incarcerated in the camp as teenagers. She said her father gave them stability and spiritual grounding that helped them come through the ordeal whole and able to live their lives well.

Wherever he was, Eric lived for the glory of God—*doxa*—in the image and character of God. He was salt and light, a city on a hill, a light on a lamp stand that shed the life and love of God to everyone around. After Eric died, one man, who did not believe in God, is reported to have said, "Jesus Christ used to live in our camp." Scripture says we become like the God we worship. Eric's was Jesus.

Ebed-Melech

This is a story about being a slave in circumstances that don't seem to offer many options for a fruitful life. This story predates the Babylonian Captivity during the time Jeremiah was speaking a very unpopular message.

Ebed-Melech the Ethiopian was one of the eunuchs in King Zedekiah's house during the time that Nebuchadnezzar was besieging Jerusalem. He heard the prophet Jeremiah had been lowered by ropes into what most translations call the dungeon, but it says it wasn't full of water; it just had muck at the bottom, so I tend to think it was, as the Amplified Version suggests, a cistern. It's also called a pit. It was probably cold and dark and yucky. To me, one of the saddest lines in the Bible is, "Jeremiah sank into the mire."

Ebed-Melech was alarmed. He went to the king and said Jeremiah would starve down there, so the king, who had allowed the princes to do what they wanted to Jeremiah, told Ebed-Melech to take thirty men and get Jeremiah out. Ebed-Melech got old clothes and rags and told Jeremiah to put them under the ropes under his armpits and they pulled him out.

What I love about this story is Ebed-Melech thought to cushion the pressure of the ropes, a kindness that is not mentioned when Jeremiah is lowered into the pit. Ebed-Melech obviously wasn't as high ranking as the four princes who talked King Zedekiah into this wrong doing, and yet the king listened to him and Jeremiah's life was saved.

I'm sharing this little incident because I am so impressed with Ebed-Melech, who was a nobody, especially compared to kings and princes and those who had the power to put you in a pit and leave you there. "Ebed" was not his first name; it was a title meaning "servant of the king." He was a slave, castrated to keep him incapable of messing with the palace women, and he could have been bitter, resentful, despondent, or disinterested in the troubles of others. My friend Kathy has in the signature line at the end of each of her emails a little saying, "If you can be anything, be kind." What a concept! In an era when society declares, "Follow your heart. You can be anything you want if you just try hard enough," I don't hear many urging us to make our goal a lifetime of being extraordinarily kind. Along those lines, I don't think Ebed-Melech tried to better his position or increase his political power. I think he spent his life being kind as he went about his duties, whatever they were, and Jeremiah, whose life was fraught with miseries and humiliations, remembered it gratefully, and included it in his book (Jeremiah 38). I believe this kindness helped Jeremiah in more ways than the comfort it gave him as he was being hauled out of the dark pit of mire and despair. I think it flooded Jeremiah's heart with gratitude, and gratitude, the Lord told me this morning, changes everything.

I'm reading in Exodus right now. Just came across the first murmurings in the wilderness. No water. Two million people with flocks and herds in a place so hot it sucks the moisture right out of your body. That would make you thirsty. Exodus 17 says they tested God at the waters of Marah. "Is God going to show up or not?" But, in actuality, who was doing the testing? God was letting them demonstrate their inability to apply what they had just seen, repeatedly and spectacularly, of His provision. Ten plagues, deliverance from Egypt with neighbors loading them with precious things, not to mention the crossing of the Red Sea on dry land and the destruction of Pharaoh's entire army. But at the next serious need, they didn't see anything but bitter water they couldn't drink. That would be hard. "Yeah, He rescued us all those other times, but this is different. We're probably just going to die of thirst."

I have to admit I've been there. "Yeah, God, You've gotten me through a lot of hard things, but this is different. I don't see how I'm going to survive this one." This morning, I got the words "wood in the water." Exodus 15:25 says," So he cried out to the Lord, and the Lord showed him a tree. When he cast it into the waters, the waters were made sweet." (NKJV) There was more to it than that. The tree is a symbol of the cross, the means through which God would transform the bitter things of life into sweet. Then God says, "If you diligently heed the voice of the Lord your God and do what is right in His sight, give ear to His commandments and keep all His statutes, I will put none of the diseases on you which I have brought on the Egyptians. For I am the Lord who heals you." (Ex 15:25 NKJV) Hmmm... Sounds like a plan. Instead of complaining and sinking into the mire of my bitter attitude, I paraded all of my issues before God—resentment, fear, worry—well, you don't need to know. What I found was, in every case, gratitude neutralized the poison. Bitter was made sweet. I could see clearly God's presence and provision in each circumstance. There was wood in the water. The cross has broken down the wall between Creator God and me, and now I can freely and joyfully call Him Abba, and that reminds me my daddy can fix anything.

Jeremiah's life was full of woes. He's not called "the weeping prophet" for nothing. There's a whole book called "Lamentations" where Jeremiah sings the blues. But I think there were gifts from God that helped him endure the hardships all along the way. One was this kindness from an insignificant slave. We can do the same. We can help each other keep going through hard things by the kindness we show. Kindness can raise us out of the pit and bring about gratitude that changes our focus and gives us the courage to go on and finish the work God has given us to do in these difficult times.

Daniel in Babylon

The prophet Jeremiah had been telling the people of Judah God was going to judge them for their idolatry. The instrument of that judgment would be Babylon, a powerful kingdom in the ancient world. The people rejected this message, saying the other prophets were telling the truth and Jeremiah was a traitor, demoralizing the people, saying if they stayed in Jerusalem they would die in the siege from famine, pestilence, and the sword. That's how Jeremiah ended up in the pit. The other prophets were saying Yahweh was their God and He was on their side. He would protect them from the enemy. They were convinced they were doing just fine. Sound familiar?

Through Jeremiah, the Lord told the people to go with their captors and settle down there, building houses, planting gardens, raising their families, but not being assimilated, blending in, adopting the values and ways of the culture around them. They were to be examples of life lived connected with Yahweh, the one true God. It happened as God said, and

Daniel was carried off along with other gifted, good-looking young men, including the three we know as Shadrach, Meshack, and Abednego, to be trained for service in the court of King Nebuchadnezzar. What is not mentioned is they were probably castrated. They were also given new names, ones that identified them with Babylonian gods instead of their own. We read immediately that those four teenagers chose not to eat the king's dainties, which probably included meat offer to idols. The head eunuch was worried it would cost him his head, but, after the 10-day trial run, the youngsters looked better than all the others. It doesn't say who the others were. Perhaps they were promising Jewish young people being groomed for service. We do know that, after the seventy year captivity was over, many chose to remain in that foreign land rather than return to the land God had promised to give them forever. It shows me we always have a choice where we will live and whom we will serve.

Dream interpretation was a big part of Daniel's influence and reputation in Babylon. It began with Nebuchadnezzar's dream—the statue with head of gold all the way to the feet with toes of iron and clay. King and slave became close, and there's very good evidence that Daniel took care of the king as he spent several years eating grass. God did not kill Nebuchadnezzar for his overweening pride; He showed him he was not God after all, and the once proud king wrote an outburst of worship and praise that made it into the book of Daniel, the only words written by a pagan to be included in the Holy Scriptures. Some scholars surmise that, when we get to heaven, we might see Nebuchadnezzar there. I agree. I think that's why God humbled him with behavior like an ox and didn't kill him. I think He saw Nebuchadnezzar's heart under all that pride and gave him a chance to turn around. Would the king have experienced the grace of the Living God had Daniel not been there, uncompromising and full of God's wisdom and truth? I don't think so.

The Magi

Who were the Magi? Herodotus, a writer who is credited with being the first historian, said they were a hereditary priesthood among the Medes. He said their chief skill was not astrology, but dream interpretation. They were not originally followers of Zororaster, though many scholars who don't go back far enough say they were. Darius the Great recognized their skills. They were attached to the court, and they became the king-makers. They were a combination of priest and magistrate. That's where we get the word "magistrate," from Magi.

Daniel 6 says, "Darius decided to appoint 120 satraps over the kingdom, stationed throughout the realm, and over them three administrators, including Daniel. These satraps would be accountable to them so that the king would not be defrauded." In verse 3, it says, "Daniel distinguished himself above the administrators and satraps because he had an extraordinary spirit, so the king planned to set him over the whole realm."

Daniel was honored for his wisdom and good counsel. He was respected for his integrity and he made no secret of his allegiance to Yahweh, praying three times a day towards Jerusalem as was his habit, even after it was forbidden by the jealous officials who figured out a way to get him thrown into the lions' den because of it. He didn't even bother to close the windows. Everyone could see him worshiping his God.

Darius was fond of Daniel, and very upset when he realized his officials had tricked him into agreeing to an edict that made praying to anyone or anything besides himself a capital crime. Into the den went Daniel, much to the king's dismay. Scripture says Darius spent a sleepless night fasting. At the first light of dawn he hurried to the lions' den and cried out in anguish, "Daniel, servant of the living God, has your God, whom you continually serve, been able to rescue you from the lions?"

Daniel answered, "May the king live forever. My God sent his angel and shut the lions' mouths; and they haven't harmed me, for I was found innocent before him." (Daniel 6:18-22) I love what Darius said, "Daniel, servant of the living God, has your God, whom you continually serve, been able to rescue you from the lions?" Daniel was faithful to God, and it brought God glory. You can be sure Darius was really impressed.

Darius made Daniel one of the chief administrators, and that included overseeing the Magi, the learned ones earnestly seeking truth. Around 500 years after, later generations of Daniel-trained Magi were still seeking the Truth. They were the ones who followed His star, and, when they found the King of kings, they rejoiced with exceeding joy. If Daniel hadn't been in Babylon, do you think any of the court officials or administrators would have taught the Magi about Messiah? I think God wanted Daniel there for that purpose, to teach them a special star would point to the King of the Jews half a millennium later.

As a side note, did you ever wonder why Herod and everybody else in Jerusalem was so upset when the wise men came? Three guys on camels would not have created much of a stir, but a group of powerful Persian priests with the authority to crown kings accompanied by a military presence—well, I guess that could have been rather alarming.

Daniel was in Babylon through other notable reigns, including the infamous banquet with the handwriting on the wall. But the last one I want to mention is when King Cyrus was riding in after the brilliant, surprise conquest that happened so quietly it took awhile before the people realized they were now under the rule of a different king.

So King Cyrus was riding in, and Missler says he was met by the aged Daniel who handed him a scroll of Isaiah in which Cyrus is called by name.

When I look back over these significant events I can't help thinking God wants us to know there are times we may feel captive in a society whose values are diametrically opposed to ours. We may even feel castrated, impotent and powerless to bring about new life, be fruitful, or make a difference. In this hostile place, how can we live free to follow God? It seems impossible, yet the Lord told His people to establish their lives in Babylon. In the midst of those circumstances, He had reasons for them to be there. All through the Bible you see this: He wants to show there is a difference between those who align themselves with Him and those who do not. Noah, Abraham, Moses, Joshua and Caleb, and on. When darkness covered Egypt with a darkness so thick they couldn't see their hand in front of their face, there was light in the homes in Goshen. The Amplified Bible specifies it was natural light. It wasn't oil lamps or candles. When disease attacked the livestock of the Egyptians, not one animal in the flocks and herds of the Hebrews was ill, and when boils afflicted the Egyptians, the Hebrews were free from that plague. And how about this? Big hailstones and fire beat down on all the land of Egypt, but not one piece of ice or fire fell in Goshen. God wants to make a distinction between His people and the world. It's not to show off; it's to show it's better. And it's not exclusive. Anyone who wants to may come along. You also see that frequently in the Bible.

We are in a unique time, unprecedented and uncertain. We will have opportunities we would never have at any other time or in any other circumstances. And we may very well come in contact with earnest seekers who will be excited to find the One they've longed for, and in whose presence they will have exceeding, overwhelming joy.

Worldviews

The Lever

Many years ago, researchers did an experiment that really stuck with me. I've always wanted to share it, and now I get to. I don't remember the exact details, but I trust you'll see the point.

There were two rooms, each with a table and four chairs. One group of four volunteers was put in Room A and another in Room B, and both groups were given the same difficult problem that they were to solve together as quickly as they could. At the same time, a very loud, obnoxious noise was going to be blasted through the speakers in the room. They were told to signal to the researchers as soon as they completed the task. The rooms were identical except for one thing. In Room B, there was a lever. That group was told if the noise became too unbearable, they could push the lever and the experiment would stop. And so the experiment began. Soon the group in Room A became agitated, irritated, and conflicts broke out among them. They couldn't concentrate and they certainly couldn't work together. Finally they signaled to the researchers that they had to stop. They couldn't bear the noise or each other anymore. Meanwhile, in Room B, the volunteers worked steadily, cooperating with each other, quickly solving the problem with no difficulty. What was the difference? Room B had the lever. But here's the surprising part: They never touched it.

I've pondered this for years. Why didn't they touch the lever? Apparently the difference in their ability to concentrate, cooperate, and solve something together had to do with the fact that they had an option.

David Hume said miracles cannot happen because they violate the laws of nature. That seems reasonable as long as you think of life as a closed system. If what you see is all you get, you have to make things work out according to your human reasoning and whatever resources you have available to you. I picture it as being in a prison cell. Nobody wants to be trapped. Not many creatures can bear being locked in a cage.

But what if it's not a closed system? What if God can come in and dance with you? What if He could rise up from within you and give you and Silas songs in the night? What if you can bear the cacophony around you in a hostile society because you know there is much More going on than just what's in front of you and on the news? And you never have to touch the lever because Jesus already gave you His own indwelling in your innermost being, His own supernatural presence and guidance here on Earth, and an Eternity without tears in your life to come. It's not a box. It only looks like a box. You always have options. You have Jesus indwelling, abiding, strengthening you, and all that He has is now available to you. He is mighty to save, to *sozo*, to make whole, hardy, wholesome, healthy, and holy. And we can carry that Life into the world to bring the hope that never disappoints and the love of God which gives us vision and perspective from a very High Place.

For I the Lord your God hold your right hand; I am the Lord, Who says to you, Fear not; I will help you! (Isaiah 41:13 AMPC)

14

Trials

Trials. Ugh. My first reaction is definitely not, "Oh joy! Oh joy!" Yet, James 1:2-4 says, "My brethren, count it all joy when you fall into various trials, knowing that the testing of your faith produces patience. But let patience have its perfect work, that you may be perfect and complete, lacking nothing." (NKJV)

The Greek word for "patience" is *hupomeno*. It's made up of two words—

hupó = under, + *méno* = to abide. Literally, it means to abide or remain under. A more accurate translation for *hupomeno* is "endurance" or "perseverance." Patience, especially as we use it in English, is too passive. *Hupomeno* does not mean sitting around twiddling our thumbs while waiting for something to happen. It means "fortitude," "the capacity to bear up in the face of difficulty," steadfastness," "holding up under pressure." One word study site says it means "abide, not recede or flee. To preserve: under misfortunes and trials to hold fast to one's faith in Christ. To endure, bear bravely and calmly: ill treatments." NAS Word usage) It's a quality that makes progress against a trial, rather than merely waiting for a difficulty to pass. It refers to that quality that does not surrender to circumstances or succumb under trial.

Interestingly, one of the word studies says this abiding under is "as in under the rule of someone." As Americans, that gets our hackles up. Isn't that what the War for Independence was about? No monarchs. No rulers. Nobody telling us what we can and cannot do. Or, worse, what we *must* do. But people in authority are forcing things upon us we don't agree with. How do we follow Jesus in such times as these?

First, it helps to remember that God says He puts people in power, even if we don't like them. It's His sovereign choice and He has His reasons. Sometimes, as with Pharaoh, it's so He can show ruler and people who is God and who is not. In view of lice and boils and locusts and plagues, do you still think your gods are worth serving? Maybe you should reconsider… Sometimes God raises up kings who make edicts that say you can't pray, with lions awaiting you if you do. In normal life, we don't have to make a choice. We're free to worship as we please. It costs us nothing. But what will we do if following Jesus will cost us something? Is there anything worth clinging to no matter what? What's real? What has lasting value?

Powerful kingdoms with their powerful leaders do not endure. In Isaiah 40, God says they're like a drop in a bucket, like dust on a scale. Hitler, Nero, Ahasuerus, Sennacharib—they're all dead. Their kingdoms are gone, dissipated in the dust of ancient history. Yahweh alone lives forever.

Scripture says to pray for those in authority—all of them, not just the ones we like. Then, remembering our God, not those other guys, is King of everything, we realize we are not trapped. We have options. Nothing they do surprises, thwarts, or baffles Him. Look for the face of God in the middle of the muddle and what He would have you do to make a difference. Daniel did immense good in four kingdoms with their idolatry, intrigue, and deceit. Rome was even worse, and just look at what Jesus was able to do. We can too, without folding, whimpering, or being squashed.

James says trials increase our stamina to bear up under pressure, to endure. Where do we get this strength? It comes from our Father because He, of all others, endures—forever. His mercy endures forever. His goodness, His throne, His righteousness, His love, power, authority…everything about Him endures forever because *He* endures forever. We get it from our Dad.

Hupomeno is always about enduring circumstances as opposed to being long-suffering with people. It's dealing with hard things as Jesus did, even when it includes the rule of someone else, such as Rome with its culture based on power and might. *Hupomeno* does not mean we endure passively, forced by overwhelming pressures to conform to the shape current rulers find acceptable. Instead, with this ability to persevere, we flourish, maintaining our integrity, character, and values while what we have is tested and proven to us, and to those around us, to be better than any of the plethora of alternative ways of living that are exhibited in society today. Like Daniel and his three friends in Babylon, we maintain our commitment to God without being absorbed in the lifestyle of a wicked culture. Trials are a good thing. They develop our ability to stay strong till the end—mature, complete, lacking nothing. What's the quickest way to reach that place of endurance? Find God in the morass and let Him show you His way through it. Or, you can go your own way, based on what seems best to you. It's your choice. There's supernatural help available for the asking, or flesh, *sarx*. You get to choose.

Scripture says to walk not after the flesh, but after the Spirit. To help clarify our two choices, here's what the Bible says about them: "Now the mind of the flesh [which is sense and reason without the Holy Spirit] is death [death that comprises all the miseries arising from sin, both here and hereafter]. But the mind of the [Holy] Spirit is life and [soul] peace [both now and forever]."

Romans 8:6 AMPC

You've got to find God in the difficulties. If you have true heart peace, chances are you're in cooperation with Him. If you're missing the mark, there's probably some thrashing going on. Trials have a way of exposing our flesh. If you're rights-oriented, if you're dead set on doing it your way, you might get very angry when things don't go the way you think they should. Trials show whether you're operating in opposition to Jesus or in harmony with Him, the One you call "Lord." Is He really? Are you taking up your cross and following? Are you dying to yourself and living in His resurrection, transforming Life? If you are, you will find peace, release, and even joy from surrendering to Him. Notice, I didn't say "in surrendering to whatever is causing you distress." It's not about externals. It's about internals—alignment with the One whose way is perfect. It's letting Him lead you through the fire and through the flood. He knows the way. Bible teacher Graham Cooke says there's always something good promised at the end of the trial. Yep. That's what James 1 says. I guess that means a reasonable question we may ask during a trial is, "What do You have for me in this, Lord Jesus?"

When Eric Liddell went to China, he intended to spend the rest of his life there as a missionary. Instead, after he married and started a family and was getting established in that work, he was rounded up with other foreign nationals and locked in a Japanese prisoner of war camp. He had already sent his wife and daughters to Canada for safety, and now he was trapped, one of eighteen hundred people under very difficult conditions. It was definitely a trial for all of them.

In college, Eric had begun a daily practice of quiet time with the Lord. He would get up before dawn, read his Bible, talk to the Lord about it, and then wait in silence for Jesus to speak to him about the day ahead. In the camp, Eric continued that practice. Every morning he waited on the Lord, received His download, and then went out into the camp to help in any way he could. To Eric, being a Christian meant surrender—following the way of the Spirit, avoiding the thrashings of the flesh. It meant doing what needed to be done as the Lord opened new opportunities before him. I don't think he wasted much time bemoaning the loss of his chosen life's work. "But," you say, "he was a missionary. The Japanese simply provided a different mission field." Yes, that's true. And He's doing the same for us in these present days. He called us to be lights. What better time to shine than when it's dark and getting darker still? While we go through whatever happens to be the trials *du jour*, people are watching. God says, "Let them see Me."

Testing

James says the trying of your faith produces patience. In other translations it says "testing." But God does not do Pass/Fail tests. Spiros Zodhiates says "God tests to prove our progress." In that case, you can see why James wrote that we are to count it all joy because God is going to show you something about Himself and yourself and give you experience that will verify that what you trust in will hold up in the crisis.

When young David was about to face Goliath, King Saul wanted him to wear his armor. David put it on, and then took it off. Scripture says he had not tested it. He didn't know what it could do. But he had tested his slingshot and knew exactly what stones would fly best and how fast and far they would go. They had already proven their effectiveness against the lion and the bear. Goliath was simply a bigger target. Most of all, David had spent countless hours worshiping God and fellowshipping with Him. He understood the Lord does not save with sword and spear, for the battle is the Lord's. (I Samuel 17)

Graham Cooke puts it this way: "It's impossible for me to have a situation where God is not present. Christ is in me, therefore He's in the situation." Somewhere He is present no matter what it looks like. This is the question we can ask God, "What is it You want to be for me now that You couldn't be at any other time?" When I ask that question, the focus goes from the horror before me, the unknown, the insurmountable, to God, who is mighty, able, quite sufficient for each thing. Lord, what do You want to be for me in this cancer? this pandemic? this unemployment? this fractured relationship? this debt? this prison? this impending death? Show me how to see it with Your eyes. Lead me through my fears and catastrophic thinking. Somehow You will work all these things together for my good. You said You would. I'm so discouraged I can't see how, but I trust You, Lord." Really? Will our beliefs in His ways hold up? If not, it's better we know now and get a course-correction than have something really big come along and be totally unprepared.

I'm reminded of Captain Edward J. Smith with his perfect record of many years of taking ships safely across the seas. He was proud of his spotless record which did not include a single emergency of any sort. It had been smooth sailing all his years. Because of this, for his last voyage before retirement, he was given the prestigious privilege of taking the luxury liner *Titanic* on its maiden voyage. When the ship struck the icebergs, Smith had no idea what to do. Contrast that with Jim Lovell, a former test pilot and fighter pilot who had to land in adverse situations, including trying to find the deck of an aircraft carrier which, to avoid enemy detection, had no lights on. Suddenly his instrument panel went black. You probably know the story. When Jim Lovell looked down at the dark sea, he saw a trail of green phosphorescence. It was algae being churned up by the wake of a large ship. Had his instrument panel been lighted, he would not have seen the glow. You also probably remember he was Commander of Apollo 13, a flight that would require everything he knew, a deep ability to bear up under pressure, and his prayers and the prayers of millions of people around the world, to bring the astronauts safely home.

Then there is Captain Sully Sullenberger. He had also landed disabled fighter planes in extremely dangerous situations. After retiring from the Air Force, he became a pilot for

U.S. Airways. He had a really good record—forty-two years of uneventful flights with a million passengers safely delivered to their destinations, but on January 15, 2009, the passenger jet he was flying collided with a flock of Canada geese not long after take off from LaGuardia. Both engines were destroyed. There was no way he could make it to any airport, so he made the decision to land the plane in the Hudson River. To that point, such attempts of water landings had always ended in disaster. But Sully had studied accident reports, memorizing what the pilots did right and what they did wrong. He had experience with risks and dangers from a thousand hours flying fighter planes in the Air Force, and he knew what he had to do—fly the airplane and fly it well. He landed the huge passenger jet on the Hudson River in the only place he calculated would have the ferry boats who could rescue the passengers from the sinking plane and carry them to safety. Not one life was lost.

These men had dealt with multiple emergencies. They had experience. They knew how to stay calm when things were going crazy around them. "So Let patience have her perfect work that ye may be perfect and entire, lacking nothing." Experience. Preparation. Testing and proving. It helps us meet the next difficult thing, having faced emergencies before.

Most of us would prefer smooth sailing. God loves us too much not to build our confidence that we can make it through whatever trials come, and if we have to land on the Hudson River, we won't panic because we know what to do, and where the best help comes from.

Always Be Certain of This - a prophecy

"Always be certain of this: I go before you.

I encircle you. I AM your rear guard.

Never will your answers have to be your answers.

Never will your reaching out to others have to be you reaching out.

The willing vessel is the one that will go forth with Me.
Remember, I AM ever with you.
Remember this always: You are not alone.
Learn through the times that are coming to rest in Me.
There is a rest even now.
Let the turmoil rage. Let the world come.
Let the world wash against the rocks.
You stand firm in Me and stand quietly.
Walk peacefully through all these things,
Through everything that comes against you walk peacefully.
That is what will draw the world.
They will stand in awe and wonder as they watch you.
Watching you. Watching you. Watching you.
There are many eyes upon you even now.
There are those who speak against you.
There are those who have many, many thoughts against you.
They're but thoughts. They're but words.
Even as they speak the words, they are watching you.
They are watching you.
Let them see Me. Let them see Me, Little Ones,
Because I dwell within you. I can bring life to them too.
I can bring life to them if they will but hear.
So let us go together, and ever know:
You are not alone. You are not alone."

The Wisdom of Struggle

When I was a child, I spent hours and hours in my parents' colorful backyard studying all the living creatures, especially butterflies. We had a wealth of different kinds, from little yellow Skippers to huge striped Tiger Swallowtails. But my favorites were Mourning Cloaks—velvety black wings edged with a pale narrow border. Their caterpillars were fuzzy and black, and their chrysalises were little works of art hanging like lavender sculptures till they were ready to hatch.

It was easy to catch the caterpillars and keep them content in jars, feeding them their favorite leaves until they attached themselves to the transparent glass. I'd seen many emerge, the small split in the casing widening as they struggled their way to freedom. They'd push, then rest, push, rest. I don't know how long it actually took, but it felt like forever. Finally the butterfly would struggle free and rest wet and rumpled, its thorax swollen with the fluid that would be pumped into the veins of its wings. That, too, took forever.

One day I had three Mourning Cloak chrysalises on the back porch in jars. The lids were off, and I knew it was about time. One of them had begun to split. I could see the dark shape inside struggling. The split widened. The creature pushed against the tight transparent shell. Then I had a bright idea. Why not give it some help? Gently I pulled the chrysalis open. The butterfly lay, crumpled and wet, completely free from its casing. I knew it would still take a long, tedious time to finish its unfolding, so I left, satisfied I had given at least one butterfly a head start in life.

About an hour later, I returned. The other chrysalises were empty. But the butterfly I had "helped" lay exactly as I left it, except now it was dry and dead. I did not know that the repetitions of struggle and rest were necessary to give the butterfly the strength it would need to pump the fluid through its wings. Same thing with chicks and ducklings. There's something in the effort, the rhythms of exertion and rest, that build the strength the newborn needs to move in the new environment. We see it as struggle, and even as suffering, but it's blessing built in by Creator God, provision for endurance for the life to come.

When my boys were little, I could stop their tears just by picking them up and holding them close. Now they're in their fifties and much too big for me to pick up. But I still want to. As John goes through his trials, I want to solve the problems and rescue him from his distresses, but the Lord reminded me this morning of the butterfly. He said John has been going through the soup stage in his metamorphosis—the time when he has no strength at all. Everything he knew before is nothing but formless former caterpillar within the shell of his new confinement. But transformation is mysteriously taking place, organized by the perfect activation of imaginal cells, the ones that will become a new body plan with extraordinary capabilities meant to enable life in a whole different realm, one that includes flight.

John must go through the process of transformation and then face even more grueling things—struggle, rest, push, rest. Like birthing. There's a time, John told me, where your wife looks at you and says, "I can't do this," whereupon you respond, "You're doing it." It happens at the end of Transition when she's thoroughly exhausted from hours of contractions and frantically resisting the overwhelming urge to push. But all of it is necessary for the health of the new baby who needs the squeezing through the narrow canal to activate lungs and provide the start of a healthy microbiome. It's all planned, and the outcome will be better because of it.

God intends the trials He ordains for us to be beneficial for our growth. He designs them for our good. Trials are not meant to prove us guilty or not guilty, with the guilty ones locked up in jail until they learn their lesson. It's more about discovering that what we have is tried and true. It's where we discover "no word from God will be without power." (Luke 1:37 AMPC)

Opportunities

I want to share another prophecy with you. This one parallels James 1.

"Opportunities are what I'm going to give, opportunities for you to put into practice what you've been taught, opportunities for you to praise Me in situations that the world would call difficult. I remind you trials are but opportunities. Opportunities you shall have. As you depend upon Me, you will come out singing My praises."

John is at the point he's saying, "I can't do this," but God keeps saying, "You're doing it." God tells me it's necessary. I am not to pull the chrysalis apart to free my son from the pressure of process. He reminded me of this Scripture, which shows the pattern God intends, one that is much better grasped when the person is in the midst of the hard thing.

"But we all, with open face, beholding as in a mirror the glory of the Lord, are being transformed into the same image from glory to glory, just as by the Spirit of the Lord." (2 Cor 3:18)

If it weren't for the intensity of the pain, I doubt John would be going to God with such an open face—totally honest and vulnerable, wrecked and undone. He's hanging onto His mighty hand, keeping his eyes on his Father's face, listening for directions, instructions, evidence that where he is is where God wants him to be. And it is transforming John and giving God glory. Even though we humans can see only a reflection of God's full Being, it has an astonishing effect upon us. It transforms us (metamorphosis) from glory to glory. The Spirit does it. He builds into us the image and character of God.

I prayed quite a lot for my son this morning. God assures me He's doing magnificent things in his life, things that could not happen under any other circumstances. John is developing tensile strength—flexibility and resilience. He is gaining endurance and the ability to bear up under pressure. And there will come a time when he will find himself aloft.

"Therefore we do not become discouraged (utterly spiritless, exhausted, and wearied out through fear). Though our outer man is [progressively] decaying and wasting away, yet our inner self is being [progressively] renewed day after day. For our light, momentary affliction (this slight distress of the passing hour) is ever more and more abundantly preparing and producing and achieving for us an everlasting weight of glory [beyond all measure, excessively surpassing all comparisons and all calculations, a vast and transcendent glory and blessedness never to cease!], Since we consider and look not to the things that are seen but to the things that are unseen; for the things that are visible are temporal (brief and fleeting), but the things that are invisible are deathless and everlasting." (2 Cor 4:16-18 AMPC)

Notice that this transformation happens as we look not at the things which are seen, but consider the unseen gifts and workings of God—His presence, His wisdom, power and goodness, His loving and specifically directed care for us in every circumstance. New opportunities open up in the midst of difficulties if we let God show us what they are. It makes me think of the cattle farmer whose entire property was smothered in ash after Mount St. Helens erupted. All the cattle died. But the man was also a glass blower. He scooped up the ash and started making wonderful objects with it. I visited the mountain about six months after the eruption. In the gift store were exquisite balls of blown glass in wonderful colors. Their tags said "Made from Mount St. Helens' ash." I bought one for me and one for my mother. Told her the story so she could remember what God can do when it seems all your hopes lie buried because of a catastrophe you didn't cause and couldn't avoid. From that can come something else more wonderful than before. My friend Debra says the difficulties often bring great blessings because of, not in spite of, the circumstances. Beauty for ashes. It's His specialty.

Why Do We Have To Fight?

Why does the Bible use words such as "weapons of warfare," "the battle belongs to the Lord," "fight the good fight of faith"? Because we need to. There's something about the process that is essential in refining us, especially in our ability to trust God. Through humility and obedience, we find ourselves triumphant. I think of the children of Israel, about to cross over into years of battles against powerful, wicked cities. God tells them He will drive their enemies out little by little, not all at once. And then they are to occupy. He could have sent an angel or two and wiped out all the cities in the land, but He didn't. Why? Because we have to own it. Victories that are handed to us with no effort on our part aren't meaningful. We already know God is powerful. What we *don't* know is, in Him, we are too.

God leads us through our conflicts bit by bit, not all at once. Just as we can't have it handed to us without any effort on our part, we can't be facing the totality of giants all at once either. God knows us. Bit by bit we learn God is faithful and what He has provided in Christ enables us to be faithful to Him through the hardships and uncertainties. Many of us have areas of severe, unreasoning fears that so terrify us that we're paralyzed by even the thought of them. Trials take us through those very things bit by bit until they lose their power over us. Fears make us vulnerable to triggers that can blind us in a crisis to the point we endanger other people. When

Captain Smith heard Titanic was starting to sink, he froze. He actually made things worse for the crew that looked to him for leadership in the crisis.

The Chinese word "crisis" is made of two other words, "danger" and "opportunity." As we face each crisis, God gives us opportunities to discover the trustworthy realities of His Kingdom ways, and it equips us for whatever comes next as nothing else can. We have to use the weapons of our warfare to gain confidence that they will hold up in battle. We need to know that what we've been taught is true. There is joy in the victory that comes from trusting Him to get us where we need to go. Trials are a big part of that preparation. Oh joy. Oh joy.

Night Route

There was tension in the dining room as we ate our dinners. Under the tables, our guide dogs snoozed at our feet, unaware that we would soon be facing the hardest challenge of our training—the night route. We would be given instructions, then released at thirty second intervals so we couldn't help each other. Each guide dog partnership had to finish on its own. My classmates jostled for position in line, each wanting to be first so they could get it over with as quickly as possible. One of them was a young man, let's call him Barry, who had confided in me his fears. Barry was a black Rapper from Detroit, gold chains, dreadlocks, who had carried a gold-tipped cane rather than admit to anyone on the street he was blind. He told me any sign of weakness was an open invitation to muggers. He lived in a rough neighborhood. One night when he was in a crosswalk, a big truck ignored the red light and nearly ran over him. Obviously he needed help. That's why he'd come to guide dog school. But he wasn't happy about it.

It was pitch black when we arrived at downtown San Rafael. Street lights and store windows barely illuminated the sidewalks we would have to travel. I stood in line, repeating the instructions. In my left pocket were three pieces of kibble. In my right pocket, there were four. After each street crossing, I would reward Hedy, and I would also know how many crossings I had yet to complete and which direction I was to turn. Hidden in dark doorways were our instructors, watching to make sure we were safe, and also evaluating our confidence and ability to manage our dogs. But even knowing we would have help if we needed it, we were nervous. Most important were the street crossings. We would be reading traffic with our ears. If we couldn't safely cross every street and successfully complete the route, we would not graduate.

"Go," the timer said.

I commanded, "Hedy, forward," Immediately she leaned into her harness and the handle pulled me quickly forward. We passed shop windows full of Christmas decorations. The night air was chilly. Hedy pulled steadily at a rapid pace. My heartbeat quickened. I was no longer cold. As we strode down the sidewalk, I could hardly believe how good it felt. I was enjoying the movement, the freedom, the speed. I wanted it to go on forever.

Abruptly Hedy stopped and would not go on, signaling to me that there was a change of elevation or a hazard. I put my foot out and felt around. We were on the curb of the first stop light.

San Rafael has audible traffic signal indicators that let you know your direction has permission to go, but we were also taught not to trust the electronics, since human drivers didn't always pay attention and could easily run over a blind person in a cross walk. I listened and heard no cars. But there were electric cars back then too, and I had to trust Hedy to let me know if there were any obstacles of that sort. I gave the command, "Hedy, forward." She did not hesitate. She pulled ahead and I stepped off the curb after her.

When we were safely on the sidewalk again, I put a kibble in her expectant mouth and felt a rush of relief. One down.

I won't take you on the entire route. I'll just say my confidence grew each time we made a successful crossing. I could practically feel the approval from the instructors as they watched, vigilant and attentive, from their hiding places. They wanted us to succeed. In a way, it wasn't just about whether we could do the work; it was proof they had done their job well.

When Hedy and I turned at last into the brightly lit Downtown Lounge, I could hear loud sounds of relief and triumph coming from my classmates. Ours was a talkative group, but this night the room was especially noisy. One voice caught my attention—not loud, but significant. It was Barry's.

I followed his voice to where he sat on the floor, his arms wrapped tightly around the broad chest of his sturdy yellow Lab. He was rocking and weeping and saying, "I love this dog! I love this dog!" When I could get the story out of him, he told me he had started into a crossing when he sensed an approaching truck and totally froze. He couldn't go on. He was stuck in the intersection. But his guide wasn't having any of that. When she sensed his plight, she leaned into her harness and surged forward, practically dragging him across to the other side. Together they crossed street after street till they swung triumphantly into the Downtown Lounge.

After that night, Barry changed. He was sweet and talkative and happy. He told me he could return to Detroit unafraid of being jumped by thugs because he had this awesome dog that would guide him and make sure he was safe.

Just before graduation day, I told the head instructor this is the accomplishment I'm most proud of in my life. She was surprised and asked me why. I said, "Everything else I've done was easy because I did them myself. But for this I had to become partners with a very stubborn, hard-headed little black Lab, and deal with many intimidating situations I have never faced before."

It was probably the hardest twenty-eight days of my life, and often I felt I was flat-out failing, but there we were, graduating as an official guide dog team. I couldn't be more proud.

You see? I had to own it. I had to know I could do it. I followed what I'd been taught—all the signals, all the procedures—and they worked.

Hedy changed my heart rate, the length of my stride. She ended the isolation of blindness. She gave me freedom—not only to walk without running into things or falling into holes, she changed my beliefs about myself. I was no longer the incompetent indecisive second daughter of the Confucian scholar. I could walk with confidence at night in an unfamiliar city and celebrate at the end with all of my classmates, who also found new freedom in life because they acted on what they'd been taught and it worked.

We are surrounded by so great a cloud of witnesses. And we know we can trust God to be watching out for us, even if we don't see Him in the shadows, and we can be sure He, too, is cheering us on.

15

Miracles with a Message

There are times God does things that confound the understanding because we need hope. He intervenes to stop what the enemy wants to use to defeat us—big things that have a lasting effect on human history and mind. I can't help noticing how He raises up very unlikely beings in times of immense distress. During the Great Depression, a small, unimpressive West Coast race horse won a match race against the blue-blooded Triple Crown Winner, War Admiral. Then he came back from a crippling leg injury to win the "Hundred Grander" at Santa Anita. He was seven years old at the time, running against three-year-olds in their prime. To the people who were discouraged and ready to give up, Seabiscuit represented hope against all odds. In the news, he was the most written about public figure in 1938, ahead of Roosevelt and Hitler.

Then there was the Cinderella Man, Jimmy Braddock, a boxer who broke his right hand and lost his powerful right punch and his ability to fight. With his hand in a cast he began working as a stevedore at the docks. He went from an affluent contender for the light heavyweight championship title to shoveling coal all night and laboring on the docks (when he could get the work). Bread lines and soup kitchens kept his family of five from starvation, but finally he had to go on welfare just to survive. You might know him as the man who returned the relief money with interest. He gave it back after a surprising upset win against a favored contender for the heavyweight championship of the world. Jimmy had been a right-handed hitter with a weak left. After having to do heavy work using his left hand, he was now a two-handed fighter with a powerful left jab. God was raising him up to bring hope to people who were broke and broken. His victories were their victories. Like Seabiscuit, if someone so old and beat-up could come back and win, maybe they could too.

Through shocking comeback victories, Jimmy found himself facing Max Baer, whose powerful right hand had killed two men in the ring. One little boy's father thought the match was so important that he drove him the sixteen miles from the farm in Oklahoma to the pool hall where he listened and prayed that Braddock would prevail, that this underdog hero would be able to withstand the fury of Max Baer. Many others were also praying, both for the victory, and that Jimmy would not be killed. In the 15th round, when everyone thought Jimmy, by all accounts, had won the fight, they were telling him to stay away from Max's lethal right hand, but he held nothing back. Jimmy's endurance, that strength of character, was what the little boy remembered. Later he would tell it to his own son, who would make the movie "Cinderella Man." Ron Howard said, "My father had used him as kind of a morality tale or a story of strong character." The part that Ron's father wanted him to take as his own was Jimmy kept going at Max and didn't back up. For the despairing human beings beaten down by the Depression, Jimmy's courageous endurance was something they needed to see. It gave them vision, something to keep them steady when they were tempted to cast off restraint and run amuck.

Something in us responds to the story of the underdog who triumphs over overwhelming adversities. We wonder—could we do that too? Maybe hidden inside us is someone who can rise up and do extraordinary things during the worst of times if only we have a chance. If only someone believes in us. If only we have the right kind of help.

Hidden inside mild-mannered Clark Kent is Superman. An ordinary man steps into a phone booth and out comes a being from a different world with superhuman powers. You know why that captures us? It's true. Hidden inside each one of us is a divinely designed being, born not from the will of the flesh, but born of the Spirit, created to function within a different reality with superhuman powers. God positioned each one of us for a special purpose in this time. People around us need to see what God can do in an ordinary life, even if it's beaten up. My son John has been doing that at his job. His co-workers have wondered how he could be so calm considering the impending expulsion from his home with no prospects in sight and the days rushing rapidly to the deadline. John tells them He trusts God. It isn't that he's putting on a brave face. They see his situation and watch him searching for a place to move. They know it's a struggle. They also see *hupomeno*, bearing up under pressure. John operates in a different reality, one that includes a different energy. It's not a closed universe. He can feel Papa walking with him. Because John is trusting God, he is able to endure without falling apart. We are praying. He is praying. He has the right kind of help. It's supernatural. It's light in the darkness. It shows others there's something else. Something transcendent. Something More.

Apollo 13

In recent history, the most dramatic crisis happened on April 13, 1970. We had landed a man on the moon and were continuing exploration with additional scheduled flights. Jim Lovell was named commander of Apollo 13. You may be old enough to remember what happened. If not, I recommend another superb Ron Howard movie, "Apollo 13." But for this book, I'll give you the short version. A damaged coil built inside an oxygen tank caused a spark that ignited an explosion that blew out the side of the control module. After that, all efforts were directed at getting the astronauts safely home.

They had to shut off all the power in the command module, including the computers with their guidance system, and the astronauts had to survive in the fragile LEM (Lunar Exploration Module) which was designed for two men to land on the moon, not keep three alive for days. The walls of the LEM were the thickness of three sheets of Reynold's Wrap.

Thousands of people worked on figuring out how to meet every crisis, and there were many. They were able to get the ship back on a trajectory to Earth, but there was no way to know if the command module could be powered up again. In spite of everything that could have gone wrong, the data came back up on the computer. Then all that remained was to get through Earth's atmosphere without burning up. Was the heat shield cracked? Would the parachutes open or be three blocks of ice? A typhoon warning came in for a possible storm in the recovery area. So many unknowns, crucial ones, any one of which could prove fatal. The news carried continuous coverage of the re-entry. Walter Cronkite reported, "In New York City, thousands of people have gathered to watch updates on the mission in Times Square. Many countries have offered help and the State Department said it would ask for it if it were needed. The House and Senate passed resolutions calling on the American people to pray tonight for the astronauts. In Rome, Pope Paul led 50,000 in prayer for the safe return of the astronauts. In Jerusalem, prayers at the Wailing Wall."

In her house crowded with family and friends, Jim Lovell's wife Marilyn watched the coverage of reentry. She said she had never prayed so hard in her life. My mother, listening to the radio in her back office in Pomona, prayed the entire time until the module landed safely in the ocean and the men were retrieved. I didn't even know she believed in God, let alone that she ever prayed. I wonder how many others turned to implore God for their safe return. Crisis can do that. What else can you do? Worry doesn't touch it. In times of intense need, prayer, like poetry, is the only thing that can carry our hearts' cries beyond ourselves and this prosaic mortal life. Somehow we know we have to reach beyond, hoping hoping hoping Someone is there to listen and respond.

In all of these accounts, the circumstances were dire, suffering was immense, and multitudes came together to help, and the comeback or the winning or the rescue lifted the hearts of countless others who found it inspired them with the hope and strength they needed to continue on. I also find it interesting that Seabiscuit's owners, Charles and Marcella Howard, Jimmy and Mae Braddock, and Jim and Marilyn Lovell all had a strong faith in Jesus Christ as Savior God. You can bet they prayed through their ordeals, and a lot of prayers from a lot of other people were also going up for the horse, the boxer, the astronaut—prayers for a miracle.

By the way, I believe the devil wanted to attach something horrible to the moon and the number 13—an association with disaster with accompanying terrors of images and imaginations. Generations would look up at the sky and picture three brave men incinerated in the plunge through Earth's atmosphere. Instead, the crisis became a time of global unity and millions praying with one heart for one purpose. What the enemy meant for harm God used for good. When the enemy comes in like a flood, the Lord raises up a standard against him. God not only thwarted the evil, He turned it into a triumph that the whole world shared.

Endurance and the Penguins

Here's an unexplainable mystery, one of my favorites. This one was recorded in the diaries of men who were on the expedition with Earnest Shackleton when their ship became trapped in the freezing Antarctic sea. As ice began to crush the vessel, about half a dozen Emperor penguins walked up to the side of the ship, and started keening. George Butler, Director of the documentary, "The Endurance," said, "It must have been a mystical moment to end all mystical moments because the ship was literally whistled by penguins into its grave. There was no explanation for this kind of out of the ordinary, unworldly behavior of the penguins and the doomed ship."

How did the penguins know the ship was dying? What would make them come to mourn its death? For that matter, how did the animals know when to go to the ark, two by two? Or the ravens know where to deliver food to Elijah? Why would Balaam's donkey turn aside in the path? We know the answer to that one. She saw the Angel of the Lord standing in front of her with a sword in His hand. I think there's a clue here. Animals seem much more aware of spiritual realms than we are. My dog, Hedy, and the dogs of my friends, signal us when there are angels around—and other things. Two sets of three big dogs sat around Majed, the man they were supposed to attack, and one stepped forward and licked his face. And let's not forget the big sea creature that swallowed Jonah or the one that picked up the coin and impaled itself on Peter's hook so he could pay the taxes. In all the examples above, the human beings were facing impossible situations. God used animals to demonstrate to them He was watching, and there was more going on than they knew.

Personally, I think God sent the penguins to demonstrate something unexplainable to the men who would need to hope in miracles in order to survive the months ahead. If I had been there watching my ship being destroyed, a group of penguins keening its demise would give me something to think about. Supernatural things always remind us this is not all there is. It did indeed take miracles to rescue those men, and some of the most spectacular miracles of all time were part of their adventure.

In our normal Christian lives, there are supernatural realities happening all around us, but we don't often see them. It takes attention, desire, and a certain kind of vision. In his "Conversion Song," my friend Dale Enstrom sang it this way:

"I can see the things unseen,
for I've got spiritual eyes.
I've got You inside
and You've made me alive.
Darkness has fled away,
overcome by Your marvelous light.
You took the veil from my heart."

The next group of stories helps us see the supernatural workings of God in different ways. They remind me God is not limited, and, because we are His, neither are we.

Don Piper

I did not meet him myself. My good friend Carol did. It was 2007, and she was on the prayer team that was designated to pray for people at the altar after their guest speaker, Don Piper, had finished his message. You may recognize that name from the book, and now the movie, *90 Minutes in Heaven.* On January 18, 1989, Don Piper was leaving a pastors' conference and headed home to his church. On a narrow bridge in the rain, an eighteen-wheeler swerved to avoid hitting a car and collided head-on with the little red Escort Don was driving. Nine wheels rolled directly over the car, crushing it. Don was killed instantly.

Traffic on the bridge was completely blocked and a line of cars was backed up for miles. Dick and his wife Anita were in one of those cars. They got out and asked the policeman if there was anyone for whom they could pray. The policeman said no. The man was dead. Dick had no theology for praying for dead men, but he distinctly heard the Lord say, "Pray for the man in the red car." The officer said the car was a crushed wreck of sharp pieces of metal and broken glass. Furthermore, the interior of the car was a gory mess, which is why there was a tarp over the man. But Dick felt compelled. He insisted, saying he had been a medic in Vietnam. And so he was given permission. Dick crawled in through the back and located the man in the dark under the tarp. The only thing Dick could reach was the man's right shoulder, so he put his hand on it and prayed. And prayed. He asked that there be no damage to the brain or internal organs. He asked that the man would have a meaningful life. He prayed for over an hour without stopping. More prayers were going up as churches were called to pray. Word spread quickly and soon there were thousands of people all over the world praying for the pastor who'd been in a terrible accident. They didn't tell the churches the pastor was dead.

You may have heard the story. After a long time, his hand still on the man's shoulder, Dick began to sing hymns and, while he was singing, 'What a Friend We Have In Jesus" the dead man also began to sing.

I think that's a lovely detail, but it didn't change the way I do things. This is the detail that made the change for me. Don was taken to three different hospitals. Each one evaluated him. In the second one, they reported his head had been crushed and he had severe brain damage. His chest had been impaled by the steering wheel, causing multiple internal injuries. But by the time they arrived at the third hospital, tests showed there was no brain trauma and no internal injuries. Since then, whenever I'm asked to pray for something like this, I always pray for God to protect the person's brain and internal organs, and I've actually heard of that being reported back through the prayer chains. Dick's prayers and Don's testimony showed me something I didn't know could be asked or done. As Don says, "Ye receive not because ye ask not." Sometimes we believe what we see, not what God is telling us to do. That may include being compelled to pray for the dead man in the red car.

"Let us therefore come boldly unto the throne of grace, that we may obtain mercy, and find grace to help in time of need." (Hebrews 4:16 KJV)

I want to add that Don was so shattered that he didn't want to continue to live. He had seen heaven and wanted to go back there, and the pain was so intense that he had no strength left to fight. When he told his best friend, his friend said they were going to pray for him all night. He said Don didn't have to fight; they would fight for him. At the front of Don's book, it says, "You prayed. I lived." That's another important concept. Sometimes people are too devastated to pray. That's when we can come alongside and bear one another's burdens. As I was writing the stories for this book, I noticed that prayer was often a key factor in the outcome. I have no doubt a lot of people were praying for Majed, and that helped him endure unimaginable suffering without divulging the names of the other Christians.

It's not empty words in the air. There's Someone mighty at the other end of those prayers. There's more. God not only hears our prayers, He has built into His universe surprising capabilities for our spiritual work. Remember I said something is transmitted in the invisible realm when we pray—something tangible? Mark 16:18 says "and they shall lay hands on the sick and they shall recover." There's an impartation when there's touch. People are ordained for service by the laying on of hands. There's anointing from supernatural realms, empowerment to do the work. Jesus said, "Again I say unto you, that if two of you shall agree on earth as touching any thing that they shall ask, it shall be done for them of my Father which is in heaven." (Matthew 18:19 KJV) There's immense power in agreement, people praying fervently as one. It's as if they're close enough to the need they're actually touching it.

Don also spoke about having to find a new normal. That term is now so common that people are tired of it, but my association with that concept will always be tied to Don, because God didn't miraculously restore him to perfect health. He didn't speed up the process of reconstruction and rehabilitation. Don had to find a new way to see himself and let God redefine his life. He had skin grafts and bone grafts and excruciating procedures that left him so depressed he wanted to die. But God has chosen to have him stay here on Earth. Though Don miraculously survived the injuries, was brought back from death by God Himself, and the arm and leg that had been completely severed now function surprisingly well, he is still in a lot of pain. He commented at the meeting that he really wants to go Home because the pain is still there every day. He will never again be the healthy, thirty-nine-year-old he once was. After you've been broken to pieces, you can't be.

God doesn't always remove evidence of the trauma. Jesus still has scars. Bethany Hamilton still has only one arm, though she was able to return to championship-level surfing after the shark bit off her left arm up to the shoulder. Nick Vujicic still has no arms or legs. He was born without them and travels the world, a head with torso standing on one small left foot, and when he speaks to inmates at maximum security prisons about the reality of being able to have a living, vibrant hope in Jesus, they believe him. Joni Eareckson Tada is still a quadriplegic in a wheelchair, and has been since she was seventeen and broke her neck in a diving accident. She paints with a brush between her teeth and inspires others by what she understands of suffering and the goodness of God. I was a young Christian when I first heard her story and I envied her. I wanted what she had, something more desirable than being able to walk or use her hands. Sometimes God leaves us in our broken state so others can see we're not doing positive thinking, cheery affirmations, or platitudes. No, it hurts. It still hurts. But this is not all there is, and something is given supernaturally in the dark moments alone in the night that you can't have any other way. And it can be felt and perceived by others who believe you because that extraordinary divine presence is there.

I know it too. I remember standing by my mailbox one clear night. I looked into the black sky and said, "I wish I could see the stars."

God said, "In heaven you won't miss a thing." Then He added, "Will you do this for Me?"

What? I thought. *Be blind?*

"Yes. Be blind. Will you be blind without focusing on what you don't have, what you've lost, what ways it makes you feel helpless, small, disabled? Will you be open to opportunities to touch people with encouragement in ways you could never reach their losses, fears, and griefs except by being blind yourself? Will you live your life for My glory instead of mourning for what you can no longer do?"

This is not all there is. When Paul talks about looking not at the things which are seen but the things that are unseen, he's reminding us not to put all our focus on the physical world. Anyone into quantum physics knows about the illusion of solidity. What looks like solid physical reality is really a lot of space with forces holding it together. To give some perspective, if you imagine the nucleus of an atom the size of a golf ball, the nearest electron would be a football field away. That's a lot of space.

Years ago my friend Sophie and her sister Tina were taking care of their father in his last days of life. One day when they drove up to his house, Sophie saw a man pacing back and forth out in front. She assumed he was from hospice, but when she pulled into the driveway, he was gone. She described him to her sister, a tall man in a white shirt, light blue slacks. Couldn't see his face because of the trees.

Sophie said, "The next day, we were all sitting in the living room, Tina, my dad and I.

He asked, 'Who are all these people? Be careful! Don't step on Babe!" Babe was an old family dog. She died many years ago.

I asked him, 'What people?'

He said, 'All these people here.'

I asked, 'What are they doing?' He said they were busy around the house. One was cleaning his bone marrow.

"Hmmm... I asked, 'Who are they and how does that make you feel, Dad?'

He said, 'A little put-out because there are so many. It seems like I should know them, like they're family.' Then he said there was a man standing right in front of him. He described the same man I saw outside, and he too couldn't see his face due to the light from the ceiling fan. He said he was peaceful. He then said, 'I keep thinking you girls are all going with me.'

I prayed and God showed me the Angel was like the angel from Lot. He was dressed in the clothes of their day. He also showed me the more my dad's earthly body was fading, the more his spiritual body was alive, and he can see more of the spiritual realm.

He said, 'I can't wait for you girls to be where I am so you can be solid.' To him, Tina and I looked transparent. Then he said, 'I'm excited to go see everyone!'

I said, 'Like your mom and dad?'

He said, 'No. Moses, and Abraham, and, of course, Jesus.'"

1 John says when He appears, we'll see Him as He really is and we will be able to see Him because we'll be like Him. We won't be temporal, transparent, and transitory anymore. No more "through a glass darkly." We'll see true Reality, solid, enduring, everlasting.

I love what John Lennox said, so I'm going to repeat it because I think it puts things in a very right perspective for us Earth-dwellers awfully inclined to believe this current life is what's real and what really matters. Asked what he will say to Jesus when he sees Him, Lennox answered, "I think I'll say, 'If I had known it would be like this, I'd have invested far more in it.' And then I think I'll fall at His feet and say, 'Thank You!'"

Heaven Is Real

The one thing I've heard from people who have been to heaven is how real it is compared to this world. Carol's daughter Stephanie told me this detail from the Piper talks at their church. She said everything is so alive in heaven. The grass is conscious. The flowers turn to watch you as you go past. Best of all, people will meet us at the Gate—people who have helped us get to heaven. Don Piper saw two kids from his high school. They had picked him up to make sure he made it to Sunday School. Before they graduated from high school, one was killed in a car crash and one drowned. But both were there at the Gate to greet him with big smiles on their faces. Don said everyone there looked good. He said if you want to look good, heaven is the place to go.

I have thought about that at times when I'm having trouble getting to sleep. I picture the Gate and the people coming to meet me. Myrtle and Marge will be there. They loved me to Jesus when I was hostile to Him and sinking horribly into the occult. I begin to picture each one I love, no longer infirm, their faces free from the pain of advancing cancer or crippled from knotted bones or disintegrating spines. My mom and dad will be walking—something they couldn't do at the end. Dennis will be his best, energetic self. And the Gideons! I'm going to give them great big hugs. I'll get to thank them in person for their prayers for me at a crucial time in my life. I'll get to see Diana again. And Tina and Jeremy. Bea Cull will meet me, for sure. She was my very special mentor. When I saw her last, she was in her late nineties and had lost her hearing, then her sight. She told me she couldn't understand why Jesus didn't take her home. At her memorial service, her son Greg told me I would be comforted to know that when the doctor said, "Mrs. Cull, I'm afraid I have bad news. There's nothing we can do for you," whereupon Bea said with a radiant smile and an enthusiastic pump of her fist, "Finally!"

"And God shall wipe away all tears from their eyes; and there shall be no more death, neither sorrow, nor crying, neither shall there be any more pain: for the former things are passed away. (Revelation 21:4 KJV)

One more thing. Don Piper asked God why He showed him heaven and then took it away. Now after years of ministry, no longer to a tiny church near Houston Texas, but internationally wherever God wants him to go, he understands. People need to know heaven is real, and it can be theirs. There is no Saint Peter with a big ledger book counting the good deeds against the bad. It's not God who keeps us out. It's our own decision where we will spend Eternity.

These days, much of the population in Earth thinks there's either nothing after death or and endless repetition of chances to get it perfect so you don't have to suffer another lifetime to try to get it right. My dad was so afraid he'd never see my mom again that he forbade me from giving her Communion (he thought it was Last Rites) or talking to her about heaven. He said it would make her want to go there, and he wasn't sure there even was such a place. After her death, she'd be lost to him, so he had to keep her alive no matter how much her illness took from her. That's why I was so shocked when he asked me what I thought happened after we die. I told him about heaven and why we can have it. At the end, I said, "Daddy, when you die, if Jesus invites you to go with Him, don't tell Him no."

Six years later, I got the call. He had simply gone to sleep. He was 95 and he had told me it was coming. I was glad for him, because that was the way he wanted to "go," but I started worrying. Three days later, I was still worrying. "Lord,"I said, "I can't settle down. I'm worried about my daddy. I need to know where he is. But if he's not with You, don't tell me." Right then I saw a picture of my mom and dad together. They were young and smiling. Suddenly I remembered that picture. For three nights in a row, I had dreamed that image. With a start I realized what it meant. I knew where my mom was. If he was with her, then he was there too. Relief and joy poured over me. Only in Jesus can there be overwhelming joy in the midst of sadness and grief.

There's a difference between holding someone's memory in your heart, and knowing you're going to be together with them forever someday. However, if heaven were the whole thing, the goal of the human life, then as soon as a person decides to give their heart to Jesus, that would be it. Suddenly they're whisked away to the Gate and the happy reunion. But there's more. God intended us to bring Kingdom power into the heartbreaks and dead ends of the lives of others, it's the Energy of God that we invite in to stop the devouring, the devastation. Our prayers matter in huge ways because the weapons of our warfare are not human ones, but supernatural, mighty through God. We can direct long-range missiles at the works of the enemy. We can love bomb places controlled by darkness. We can pray for a dead man who has severe brain damage and internal injuries, and God can give him reconstructive miracles by the time he gets to the third hospital. When our hearts are tuned to God's, we may ask in accordance with His will, in the fullness of His character. Jesus said to pray in agreement as touching. When we are in agreement so close that our prayers are touching, miracles can happen.

16

Some Lives Saved

Kevin and Amanda

It just happened again—another Christian family shattered by the suicide of a son. Third in the past year. The families are still in shock, still grieving, still wondering if they could have done something, feeling guilt and lost and wondering what went wrong.

There are many reasons people decide not to live anymore. After I came out of ten years in a legalistic church, I was so depressed I had to make the decision every day to continue to live. That went on a year and a half. People who aren't suicidal can become so when they suddenly go blind and everything changes including their sense of themselves. I mention those two because I lived them. I've also prayed with a number of people dealing with the aftermath of a loved one's last desperate act.

I want to share some things with you—things I hope will help.

1. There's this belief that all those who kill themselves go to hell. It's even a doctrine in some churches. Why? Because they say the person doesn't have time to repent, confess, and be forgiven. Others say it's an unforgivable sin. I've talked to the Lord a lot about that. First, God is just *and* He is merciful. He will do what's right. He will do what's best. Second, nobody but the person knows what went on in the last moments of life. Survivors of attempts have mentioned the stretching of time. Things are in slow motion. Jesus paid the full price for every human life. Don't you think it likely He would do

everything possible to save that loved one before it's too late? The Word through Whom all things were made knows how to extend time. And there's that unobstructed perception that comes when the spirit leaves the body and can perceive, reason, and remember with clarity uncharacteristic of how humans think when they're in their mortal body. Think of those reports of people who have been on the operating table and watched the procedures from a high corner of the operating room. They can recount all the conversations, describe the instruments on the tray, and remember everything that went on in the room. I've heard more than one suicide survivor tell of leaving the earthly sheath only to suddenly understand the true nature of the entirety of the situation that seemed impossible before. I heard one young woman say when she saw the issues clearly, she decided she really didn't want to die, and returned to her body a changed person with a revised view of the importance and significance of her life.

Of course, many suicides succeed, but the point is we don't know what happened as they died. Having talked to God about this at length, I believe many of those desperate human beings were taken into heaven. I'm not saying this in order to make it more attractive to people to take "the easy way out," because it won't be over when it's over and there are no guarantees where they will end up. But for those left behind, it's important to know the loved one did not automatically and inexorably end up in hell.

2. Many serious suicide people discover they really don't want to die after all. How do I know? I went to a suicide prevention seminar and heard them talk about it. I want to share with you just two.

Kevin was seventeen when he decided life was too painful and jumped off the Golden Gate Bridge. Part-way down he cried, "Oh God! I don't want to die!" He hit the water so hard it broke his lower back. There in the icy waters of San Francisco Bay, Kevin tried to swim, but his legs would not respond. Then a large marine creature rose up underneath him. A shark? Kevin waited for the grip of razor teeth that would rip him down to his death. Instead, it supported him in the water until the Coast Guard was able to reach him. Kevin asked his rescuer how many people he'd pulled out of the bay. "Twenty-seven," was the reply.

"How many lived?"

The Coast Guard man said, "One."

Five years later, Kevin was giving a talk on suicide prevention and a man came up afterwards to speak to him. "I was five feet from you when you jumped off the bridge," the man said. "I never could find out if you lived." Then he told him the animal that saved his life was not a shark, it was a sea lion.

Kevin made a film on his attempt to kill himself, his miraculous rescue, and interviews with others who have attempted suicide. All have found how precious and significant their lives really are, and all have said how glad they are to be alive.

I came home pondering that evening's events, which included a panel of local suicide prevention workers with similar stories of discovering after they had done the fatal deed that they really did not want to die. The next day I was doing some music with a young woman named Amanda. Just before we began the vocal warm-ups, I blurted out about the people who had tried to kill themselves and were glad they had been given more time. To my surprise, Amanda said, "Oh, I did that too."

I was shocked. Amanda is talented, naturally funny, a delight to be around. Why would this lovely young woman think her life was worthless? She said it was boyfriend problems, college was too hard, and everything felt as if it were crashing around her. Too much stress. Too much anxiety.

Amanda said, "The thing about anxiety and stress is sometimes you get really really overwhelmed and instead of turning to someone to help you with situations and problems, you go to the extremes.

"One day when it was too much for me, I opened up a drawer and took every single pill in that drawer. I thought, *Wow, this is going to be an easy, quick way out and I'll be done. I won't have to deal with any more pain.* Even as a Christian you can get to the point you think, *No one can help me except for myself.* I thought, *God'll understand.* It was too bad. It was too much. I had to do it. I had to take control. It was an extreme moment for me. Instead of turning to God or anybody to talk to, I took the pills. And then not five minutes later, I thought, *I don't want this. I don't know what to do.*

I thought of my mom. That was hard for me. I thought, *How selfish! My mom has been a rock in my life and she has gone through so much. She alone should be the reason I want to live.*

When you're sick, you want your mom. When I was getting sick that day, I wanted my mom. That's really what started turning my whole thought process around and I reached out to God. "I don't want to die!"

I've always viewed God as my best friend So it wasn't like a formal prayer. It was like, "God, help me! God, You know what's going on. I don't even need to tell You what's going on. I need help." I got sick, but I did not die. I ended up on the bathroom floor throwing up for days, but I did not die. And I'm very very happy I did not die because it really really taught me that I'm here for a reason. If I was supposed to be gone, I would have been gone. There was no reason for me to still be alive after everything that happened.

"I always have strange medical conditions that no one can figure out. I'm always sick. There were a lot of pills in that drawer—things like opioids from teeth issues. I had every sinus thing in the book—allergy pills, Nyquil. It was a small side table but the top drawer was pills. So, for me to take all of those…Like I said, it's a miracle that I'm alive. And I didn't have major medical conditions afterwards, which is a miracle because that could have destroyed my organs. I just got ill. For three days. It was more like having the stomach flu instead of completely crashing out. If that's not a miracle, I don't know what is."

Amanda got married and eventually adopted a fifteen-year-old foster daughter with Asberger's. That surprised me. I know a few adults with that syndrome, and it's not easy to communicate with them. Yet, this daughter is the light of Amanda's life. I think of the blessing Amanda is to that former unwanted teenager who could have spent her life never belonging or being so thoroughly loved. I think of Kevin, who travels the world encouraging the discouraged and defeated to find purpose in their lives. It reminds me how precious each human life really is, and how God sovereignly stopped the death that was about to swallow two young people so they could find meaning and purpose where they thought there was none, and inspire them to reach out, giving fresh vision to others who are struggling with despair. There's amazing hope. It's not a box. It only looks like a box. It's not a closed system. God can reach in and introduce a new energy powered by His love. And maybe even send a huge sea lion to keep you from going under.

Greg's Bus Story

If all you see are headlines in the news, you'd seriously wonder about the goodness of God. Why would He allow disasters to happen to children? I'd pondered that issue for years. Why would God allow nice Christian kids to be hurt or killed on their way to church camp? I'll tell you, it looks different from the perspective of someone who was in one.

I'm not telling you this will settle your mind forever; it's just a chance for you to see one from the inside.

It was Christmas break. My son Thomas had brought his college roommate home with him to spend the holidays with our family. Since it was more than thirty years ago, and since Thomas has no idea where Greg is now, I cannot get the exact words to this story, but it made a big impression on me and I remember the most important parts. Here's the gist of it.

Greg's youth group was in a bus on its way to a camp in the high mountains where other youth groups were converging with the host church of the area. The road had steep grades and sharp turns. Seated directly behind the driver, Greg could see the scary twists and turns of the narrow, two-lane road as it snaked its way up the mountainside. Tall evergreen trees screened the alarming drop on the right, but Greg could catch glimpses of it through gaps between trees. They were on the outside lane. Carefully the driver eased the long bus around each hairpin turn, airbrakes hissing to reduce momentum as the driver guided the heavy vehicle. At last they reached the crest. Now they had to go down the other side.

There were yellow signs with black symbols warning drivers of the hazards with posted safe speeds, but Greg said he thought one had been mis-marked because the angle of that outside curve was much more severe than the others and the grade was very, very steep. As the driver started into the curve, it was clear he would not be able to make it, and the weight of the bus was making it speed up. Airbrakes pumping, the driver cut across the line into the oncoming lane, but suddenly he saw a car coming toward them in that lane. Quickly the driver turned the bus back to its own side, frantically pumping the airbrakes as the bus sheared off the trees and plunged over the cliff straight into the river. Everyone went flying forward and was knocked out.

Following in a car behind the bus was the mom of one of the kids on the bus and her two other kids. She pulled over on a wide shoulder, jumped out and looked down. Meanwhile, the driver of the other car had turned around and parked behind her. He had a CB radio in his car ("Citizen's Band" radio for all of you who know nothing about how people communicated on the road before cell phones). He called for help. When the first policeman arrived and looked at the bus, he said simply, "Bring body bags." It took awhile for rescuers to make it down to the bus and get a door open, but the amazing thing was everyone was able to climb out. One girl had lost some teeth from colliding with a front pole when the bus hit, but there were no other injuries. Another bus arrived, but none of the kids would get into it. They chose to go in the cars of people from the church who took them safely away.

Greg said the mom had been talking with the man with the CB radio, bent down to say something to her children, and when she stood up, the man and his car were gone. Vanished without a sound. "He was an angel," Greg said.

"Don't be silly!" I snapped. "Angels don't cause accidents."

"You don't understand," Greg said. "If the driver had cut across the lane, he still wouldn't have made the turn and the bus would have rolled all the way to the bottom. We would have all been killed. This way, we went straight over the edge into the river. We were knocked out for a minute or so, but that was all."

Right then the Lord spoke to me very clearly, "When it looks like I'm trying to kill you, I might have just saved your life."

I asked Greg, "Did you learn anything from the bus accident?" He said, "Yes. Any time I start to stray from God, I hear the sound of airbrakes pumping."

I think it's interesting that God knew I was wondering specifically about those bus accidents with Christian kids and sent me Greg to tell me his story. He volunteered. How else would I have known he'd been in one? To me, that's supernatural. God knows what we struggle with and finds ways to help us understand.

I'm not citing this story as a template of how God works, because plenty of Christian kids have died in tragic accidents. None of the stories in this book is meant to be a template of what we should expect from God. I simply want to show a number of situations from their insides, not from the distant generalization of headlines in the news. The news can never tell you what God would have you know. For that, you have to have revelation from the Holy Spirit. It's never something you can guess, but this you gotta know: God is good all the time even when we don't understand.

17

Hope and Trust

Hope

My kitty Hope was the cat of my dreams. I was her favorite lap. She would sit bolt upright on it while I worked at the computer. She always faced the screen, as if she were checking what I was writing. She liked to sit next to me on the piano bench and extend one smoky paw to hit a key, always in the right rhythm to whatever I was playing. It was hilarious.

When she was fourteen, Hopie began to fail. She stopped eating and drinking and let me know she was ready to be done with this life. One day my friend Carol was visiting, and Hopie came out, staggering a little, then flopped on her side right in the middle of the floor. It was time. Carol and her husband Randy had owned mortuaries, so she was not afraid of death. She said she would stay with me until it was over. I sat on the floor near Hopie and Carol sat on a chair watching. Suddenly Hope's legs began moving rhythmically. Carol said, "It looks like she's already running in heaven." I thought so too, and asked the Lord if that's what we were seeing. He said yes. Her spirit was already with Him, bounding across the tender green grass. That went on several minutes and then it stopped. Hopie lay very still except for small twitches here and there, less and less often. Interestingly, the sadness I had been feeling was completely gone. Hope was no longer in that emaciated body, elderly and infirm. She had finished her purpose on Earth and Jesus had welcomed her Home.

I have heard pastors say animals do not go to heaven. I agree to this extent: *some* animals don't go to heaven. I have talked to the Lord at length about this issue and studied

Scriptures and its words. I'll tell you what I've found. In the Hebrew text of Genesis and other Old Testament writings, the word for spirit is *nephesch*. There are other words too, but that's the one used for animals and humans, and it can be translated "spirit" or "soul," though they don't actually mean the same thing. Sometimes translators are not sensitive to nuance; they're after one-to-one word translation.

In the Hebrew Lexicon by Bible Scholar Spiros Zodhiates, I noticed it says the *nephesch* is what leaves the body upon death, and it can be killed. That means it is not always killed. With humans that is certainly true. Every human being is eternal. When I read those words, the Holy Spirit nudged me, saying, "It applies to animals as well." The Lord and I had quite a talk about this. What qualifies an animal to go to heaven? C.S. Lewis wrote about this already, so I won't repeat what he said. He certainly had a better brain than I, and was fluent in the original languages. I'll give you the short version.

The basic qualification has to do with connection. If there's a deep bond between human and animal, something transpires that transcends normal mechanisms of life and death. Because animals were designed for relationship with humans, and were put by God's will under our dominion, we are to care for them and make sure they are able to fulfill their purpose. In the Garden, it's likely the animals could talk. Why do I think that? When the serpent spoke, Eve was not surprised.

God created domestic animals to help us. In Genesis 2, there is a distinction between wild animals and domestic. If there wasn't a difference in relationship and purpose, why would God bother to mention it? Jesus came to restore what Adam lost in the Garden—fellowship with Almighty God. And we, the redeemed sons of Adam and born again sons of God, have the privilege of restoring what Adam lost of connection with animals, especially the ones God has chosen and designed with purpose to be in our lives.

But it takes deep, loving relationship. And it takes *nephesch*. Who will not be there? My black widow spider Gwendowyn. I spent hours feeding her flies and talking to her, but she didn't care about me. And also, insects do not have a *nephesch*. Reptiles don't have *nephesch*. I think warm blood is a requirement for you to get one. I've had other dogs and cats, some I didn't love or that didn't love me. It has to be both ways, and it has to be deep. So I know my Hopie will be there, and Joshie, and Alexander, and Velvet.

I was very surprised when the Lord told me He wanted me to write about this subject. It's not like situational ethics or Darwinian atheism that can undermine and dismantle the faith and identity of human beings. No, but there is an underlying misunderstanding of the heart of God when we say animals do not go to heaven. I believe pastors and parents who say that are trying not to perpetuate false hope or fantasy in their attempts to make the children feel better. So they may say something like, "Well, sweetie, Strawberry has gone to goat heaven now, and she's happy." Okay, so Strawberry gets to live forever with the good goats in a special place God made just for them. But you're still separated from that one you loved.

I believe the vast extent to which the sacrifice of Jesus has redeemed all that He created would be less complete without our reunion with those we love. I still miss my mom and dad so much, and sometimes I picture seeing them meeting me at the Gate—them and my beloved animals. Jesus came to reclaim and redeem *all* that was lost. I believe there is much more to that than we can imagine, and I don't ever want to think less of God than He really is. He is God—the only One. And He is good. And He is unlimited. And He is Limitless Love.

"Now may the God of hope fill you with all joy and peace in believing, that you may abound in hope by the power of the Holy Spirit." (Romans 15:13 NKJV)

ESPERANZA

I've always admired people who lived completely by faith. Brother Andrew is one of my heroes. In his biography, *God's Smuggler*, there are jaw-dropping stories of God's provision and protection. Books abound like that. George Mueller supported his entire orphanage for decades never asking anyone for a penny, God supplying always exactly what he needed to keep it going. Heidi and Rolland Baker experience that in Mozambique today with thousands of orphans they've adopted (it was 8,000 when I saw the documentary, "Finger of God," and that was about ten years ago. It's probably 10,000 by now). However, I never met anyone who lived like that... until Darda.

Darda Burkhart had a story to tell. *Splendour from the Sea,* the book that W. Phillip Keller had written about her dad's ministry, was out of print, and people had been after her to retell it. My friend Dale Billester lent me the book and told me some of the stories about his grandfather's ministry. Dale knew I wrote books and suggested that his mom talk to me about how to get a new book written and published. That's how Darda and I came to attend two conferences for Women Writing the West, going to lectures and rooming together. We didn't get much sleep! But soon Darda produced Forging Ahead For God in her own careful, precise prose.

While we were together, Darda told me many of the stories, which astonished me, but she kept saying, "That's the normal Christian life." Notice she didn't say "average" or "usual." It's normal because God intends that level of trust in Him to be the norm. I asked Darda to retell some of these accounts for you. She sent me two. But before you read this one,

I want to say something about what happens when a person lives by faith following the call of God.

Dale knew his grandpas, his mom's and dad's dads. They were both pastors. When I asked him what it meant to him to be descended from them, he said, "I can only hope I will be one-tenth as good a man as they were." Dale is a locksmith. In a community as small as Lake County, reputation, for good or for ill, is quickly known. Dale is respected as a man of deep integrity, and he is thoughtful, kind, and gently funny. In the thirty years I've known him, he has always been a trustworthy and faithful friend. But there's more. Dale's son Jason is one of those radiant young men who carries the light of Christ into every second of his daily life. God gives him favor with others, and words, visions, and prophetic dreams. God's energy crackles out of him, and boy! can he pray! But wait! There's more. Jason's son Joshua is ten years old. He began having visions, words of knowledge, and spiritual insights when he was six. I have been privileged to see five generations of this blessing demonstrated in Darda's family, and it all began with her dad, who believed Jesus who said, "Ask Father that He will give it to you that He might be glorified." (John 14:13, 14) To this day, miracles continue to flow through this family, showing what God can do through ordinary people who give their lives to Him.

THE STORY OF *ESPERANZA* BY DARDA BURKHART

"My father, Percy Wills, was the pioneer missionary to the very isolated West Coast of Vancouver Island, Canada, in the early 1930's. God called him from a thriving pastorate to this spiritually deprived outpost, lashed by the Pacific Ocean waves. When he first began to view the coastline with two others via an Indian canoe, he was struck by the isolation of the people. There was every kind of need one could think of—physical, medical, relational, and most of all, spiritual. The population was about 4,000 people of several ethnicities, stretched over 300 miles of coastline. The people could be reached only by boat, or by hiking the trails, as the only roads were for logging trucks. Those living there could be a few in a protected bay, some lighthouse keepers on a lonely rocky shore, or a small village. Most men worked as miners, loggers, or fishermen.

"Along with the spiritual needs, the lack of medical help was of great concern to my father. While traveling along the coastline he searched for an ideal plot of flat land on which a hospital could be built. One day he found that perfect place at Esperanza in the Nootka area. It had a southern exposure to catch all the sunshine there would be, a creek of pure fresh water. He and a doctor God had also sent to minister with him, went across the bay to a lumber mill. When the manager asked what they were building, my father told him, a hospital. He said if they would take the lumber at that time, they could have it free. With great eagerness and joy, the two men got the lumber, tied it into bundles and towed them back to the building site. By the end of that summer, the small hospital, 14 by 32 feet, was open and the first patient was treated. A similar small building was erected for the doctor and his family.

"The hospital at Esperanza was built hastily, but well, because summer was so short and a lot of work was needed. The government had said the mission could lay claim to the parcel of land, but in case something went wrong, the hospital was built on skids. Once opened the doctor and staff were seeing patients as they arrived.

"At this time, Dad was in Port Alberni. B.C., and he went down to visit the ship that was on its routine stop with mail, supplies, and passengers. A friend of Dad's saw him and told him that the land inspector was on board with instructions to sell the government lands at Esperanza. The hospital was built on one of them. Dad wrote a quick note to the doctor to meet the ship at Zeballos and buy the land. This friend of Dad's took him to a lawyer, who listened to the story and told Dad to go back to what he had been doing and the matter would be taken care of. That same day a wire came to Dad from the Minister of Lands in Victoria reading that the inspector was to withdraw the sale of Lot 2 where the hospital was.

"At the next port of call when the Doctor read Dad's note, he was really troubled, for there was no money in the bank. However, quite a bit of mail was addressed to him. As he opened letter after letter, there were a number of checks enclosed, totaling $310.00. The Doctor rushed over to the inspector waving the money and saying he would buy the land. The inspector was dumbfounded, for now the hospital was untouchable, due to the hand of God protecting it. He had a change of mind and arranged that the land be leased for 21 years at the price of $1.00 per year.

"Without putting out ads for nurses, God sent the ones He wanted to give loving care to this new building of ministry to those injured, or where pregnant women could safely give birth to their babies.

"As the work grew, the early canoe became a 32-foot boat, named Messenger II, followed several years later, the Messenger III, a larger 50-foot boat was required. Both were built with the highest standards of wood, engines, and fittings, to withstand the rough waters through which they would sail. Winter storms could cause high winds and 30-foot waves. Also both were built strictly on God's promises to provide every need for the work He called my father to. I recall time after time money coming in, even from other nations, just as the bills became due. The missionaries themselves, lived by these promises, as their monthly stipend was small, and paid only after all other bills were paid.

"I remember a little boy who learned about the boat and put his whole allowance of 2 cents into a jar that he labeled "Mission Boat." One day his mother found the jar where her son had hidden it in his closet. She told a neighbor and word got out. Even though this was during the Depression, people added to the little boy's jar and soon his 2 cents increased to $300, then $400.

"The boat was fully free of debt when it was launched. The same thing happened to the next boat, and for all the provisions, fuel, and maintenance of them.

"Over the more than forty years of Dad's ministry, and many others also called to that field, the area and importance of the work grew to include three campsites, other, smaller boats, many more qualified men and women, and a bigger outreach throughout the length of the Island. It is still a vital mission today, although smaller. All through those years, a faithful band of Christians gathered weekly to pray for the mission and its needs They were so faithful, that for many decades, only slippery winter days kept them at home."

"*Esperanza*" is the Spanish word for "hope" certainly the people who lived in that desolate region needed someone to care for them and bring comfort and loving encouragement in their isolation and difficult circumstances. The hospital Darda's father built was tangible evidence of God's provision, but the dangers Percy and the others braved just to visit the people brought them hope in a very personal way, and showed them God loved them individually. They were not forgotten.

Sophie's Story

I met Sophie and her husband Jim in the 1990s, and through them I met Dan, Jim's boyhood friend, who became Earthen Vessel's recording engineer, and then an integral part of my life in a partnership of creativity that has lasted for nearly thirty years. Since we lived only a few miles away, I visited them often, and I watched their little boys Jeremy, Dustin, and Corey, grow up until the family moved to Texas.

In 2010, Jim went to heaven. That same year, 30-year-old Jeremy began a battery of treatments for cancer. We were so relieved when he recovered. But just two years later, it was back, worse. We prayed as Jeremy endured an extremely risky surgery, amazed and relieved when he made it through and took up life again with zeal.

Then, in 2020, Sophie called to ask for prayer. There had been a terrible motorcycle accident. Jeremy didn't survive. His wife was in critical condition. Sophie said his Harley hit the side of a ramp, catapulting them over an overpass. They dropped twenty-five feet onto a grassy strip. Rescuers tried to resuscitate him, both there and at the hospital, but to no avail. He was thirty-nine years old.

Through the difficult months that followed, things began to come out—things that could not be anything but God's doing. A year later when Sophie told me everything that happened, I said I wanted to include her story in my book and she sent me her recollections. Sophie is currently writing a couple of books herself, and Jeremy's story in its entirety will be in one, but certain miraculous things stood out to me, and that's what I'm going to share.

Sophie and her second husband Ed live in Houston, usually just the two of them, but COVID-19 had shut down the school in Huntsville, Texas, where Dustin was studying, so he returned to Houston and was staying with them. This first detail isn't miraculous, unless you're a mom getting a disturbing phone call at night, hearing alarming things, wondering what happened, then having to drive thirty minutes through unfamiliar city streets, trying to find your way though your eyes don't work well in the dark. Then you have to leave your car in a parking garage distant from the ER so you must walk, a woman alone at night, across the hospital parking lot. Then you have to hear dreadful news and see your eldest son for the last time. If you were that mom, wouldn't you recognize in this gracious provision of the presence of your second son the fingerprints of God? Dustin is a calm, steady person, a thoughtful young man who brings stability and strength wherever he is. Sophie told me over and over how grateful she is that he was there.

It was 10:30 at night when Sophie got the call telling her there had been a motorcycle accident. Would she be coming to see her daughter-in-law? Because of COVID-19, no one would be allowed to see her after she was admitted. Sophie asked, "Is my son there?"

The voice hesitated, then said, "Yes, he's here."

Sophie had thoughts that she quickly pushed away. She called to Dustin and Ed and they prayed together. The supernatural peace of God descended on her. She felt her spirit responding with, "I trust God."

They drove the dark streets to the hospital, Dustin and his mom. There they heard the terrible news that Jeremy was gone. When they went to tell Jeremy good-bye, Dustin was a calm presence that Sophie said gave her strength. Later, Dustin told me he is able to be at peace in the face of death because he knows this is not all there is. Especially in the midst of sudden tragedy, such knowledge gives stability and peace that nothing else can. Sophie had it too. She said, "Before I left Jeremy, I remember having an almost out-of-body supernatural peace; I had no anxiety, no fear, total peace. I kept hearing loudly in my mind and spirit, *I TRUST GOD!* I even said out loud, 'Lord, If You felt it was best for him to come home now, I trust You. I don't like that he beat me there. But I trust You, God.'"

Then they went to see Jeremy's wife. She was bruised, swollen, and sobbing. "Mom," she told Sophie, "something happened to Jeremy. Something happened while we were riding." They had a code when they rode the motorcycle. If she felt unsafe, she would pat him on his thigh, and he would pat her back and make adjustments. She told Sophie he was driving a little weird, so she patted him and he patted her back.

He straightened up, then slumped forward, his hands still on the gas throttle. They sped up and hit the side of a railing. She didn't remember being hurled through the air or landing on the grassy place. She only remembered looking over and seeing her phone, picking it up, and dialing 911.

Sophie worked in the medical field. When she heard about the erratic driving, she suspected something was going on with Jeremy. He was a careful driver. He would not have done anything reckless. Right then a doctor entered the room. Sophie introduced herself and asked if they could do an autopsy on her son. He said yes. I couldn't help noticing the timing.

Sophie's youngest son lived in L.A. She had called him to tell him about Jeremy. Corey immediately called his pastor to pray with him though it was one in the morning. Not long after, Corey told his mom the church was buying him a ticket to Houston and he'd be there later that evening. Like the timing with the doctor and Dustin's presence, it's a small thing, but I see on it such obvious fingerprints of God.

Other things were not so small. Houston is a huge city. Jeremy and his wife could have been hurled into a lane of fast traffic. Instead, God had them land on one of the few places in the complex of freeways that had grass. This looks like supernatural intervention to me. And what are the chances that the cell phone would land right next to her head?

The next day, Friday, within 12 hours of this tragedy, Sophie got a call from Pastor Jerry, her pastor. He knew Jeremy from church, and had asked him to share his testimony one Sunday service. He called and said, "I heard a rumor and wanted to see if it was true." She told him it was. He cried. Then he said, "Let me pray for you." At the end of the prayer, he prayed in tongues, then interpreted it, and Sophie heard God say, "My daughter! My daughter! Have I ever let you down? Haven't I always been there for you? Haven't I always been here for you? I will not leave you now. I will carry you. I will show you things in the days ahead, and more will unfold as the days go by. My daughter, I love you. I will carry you."

Sophie said, "My heart was broken, but God was so close at this moment, I could hear him loud and clear in my heart of hearts."

As the days went by God showed Sophie other things. Within a week, her daughter-in-law received a call from the doctor who did the autopsy. The report said the cause of death was blunt head injury, but the autopsy doctor said, "You need to know that his heart was so full of scar tissue it was imminent that he would have a heart attack any minute."

Sophie said, "When I heard this I knew Jeremy died from a heart attack and then hit the railing. God put my daughter-in-law on the bike with Jeremy so that we would know he collapsed before hitting the rail. God knew we would have never known what exactly happened had she not been on the bike that day."

One day Sophie and Dustin were sitting with Tim, Jeremy's boss, talking and trying to process their loss when Tim said, "You do know Jeremy's cancer was back, didn't you?" They were surprised and said no, they didn't know. Tim said Jeremy had gotten a call a week or two ago. When he got off the phone he told Tim, "It's back."

Tim asked, "What's back?"

Jeremy said, "The cancer." He immediately made three appointments for Monday and one for Wednesday. On Tuesday, Dustin stopped by to see Jeremy. COVID-19 was escalating and people were nervous. The brothers laughed about not dying from COVID-19, but going out in style, riding their Harleys, dying exciting and spectacularly like Evel Knievel.

Sophie said, "I was surprised to hear Dustin had stopped to see his brother the same day I did. God had prompted me several times on the way home from work to stop and see him. This day it was late, I called to see if he was still working because it was right at their closing time. Jeremy answered and asked if I had the corona virus, I said, 'No, I have the Bud Lite virus.' He laughed and said okay, I could come in. I am so thankful I listened to God's prompting. God knew this would be the last time I would see him this side of the veil."

Because of COVID-19, the staff at the dealership decided Jeremy should not be put at risk, so Wednesday they had a meeting and told everyone he would be working from home. Then they sent him home. If he had been working on Thursday, he would not have been out running errands with his wife. He could have had the heart attack at work. Or in his car on the freeway and caused a huge pileup. It could have been so much worse, causing more pain and injury, or leaving terrible memories for other people, especially for those who loved him.

Sophie said, "I was thinking back on my last visit with Jeremy. He had his face covered due to COVID-19, and he said, 'In my condition, I shouldn't be working.' I questioned 'condition.' He calmly said, 'You know, Mom, my half of lung and all'… I think he wanted to tell me more but didn't. I believe Jeremy didn't have time to tell his wife or myself because he didn't have all the facts yet about the returning of cancer. God is faithful to show me things I didn't know. I have great peace, I know now, God was having mercy on my son, bringing him home before a 3rd time of cancer and the battle he would have gone through.

"Approximately two weeks later I hear God say in my spirit to go for a walk. 'I want to tell you something,' He said. So I went for a walk, processing in my mind the loss of my son. It was still so overwhelming. I hear God remind me of the story of Isaiah going to King Hezekiah and telling him he would die this night. The king pleaded with God for more time, God had compassion and gave him fifteen more years (Isaiah 38:1-5).

God impressed on my heart that my son should have died seven years ago when he had the cancerous tumor removed from his heart. This was after his 8 months battle with second-time cancer. At the end of this battle, he had half his lung removed and a tumor removed from his heart. The surgeon had explained prior to surgery that this was a very dangerous surgery removing the tumor from his heart and that he hoped it would stay intact. Apparently, Jeremy had pleaded with God for more time; my son was 32 years young. God honored his prayer and gave him seven years.

"Jeremy had been living in South Carolina, but at the end of the cancer battle in 2012, he moved back to Houston to marry the woman he met during his cancer treatment. He lived and worked close to me. I was able to see him here and there, stop by his job, and bring him lunch or Starbucks. He was here for all the holidays. This was a special gift from God. You see, Jeremy joined the Air Force when he was eighteen and hadn't lived by me since then. I realized during my walk with God that He had given me a gift of seven more years with my son. My heart leaped with joy, and my perspective changed. I am so grateful for the years. Instead of me being sad that he died at thirty-nine, now I'm so grateful that he didn't die at thirty-two. Thank You, Father God, for walking with me and showing me these things I could have never known."

"God impressed upon my heart that Jeremy's harvest would come in during his Celebration of Life. I immediately started praying for his harvest and told as many prayer warriors as I could to pray for it too."

Because of COVID-19, it took four months before the celebration could take place. Finally, through the heroic efforts of a lot of people, everything was ready. In the parking lot of the Harley-Davidson dealership where Jeremy had worked, people had gathered, riding up on 185 motorcycles. Sophie stood on a huge flatbed and prayed for their ride. Dustin and Sophie were the first to lead behind the police escort on the fifty-mile trip to the beautiful country church with its huge outside arena. More than 325 people showed up to honor Jeremy. Sophie was overwhelmed that they would come to this outside event since it was in the miserable heat and high humidity of summer.

Towards the end of the celebration, Sophie stood on the platform and said to them, "I love each and every one of you. I don't know you, but because you loved my son, I will always love you. Please come and let me hug you." Then she told them, "There's Someone else that I know. If you know His Son, you can come to Him with anything. That's God. If you know and love His Son Jesus, He will welcome you and love you always and forever." Sophie told me, "I could feel the Spirit pouring through me to them. It was another amazing supernatural experience. I told this amazing crowd, 'I know I will spend forever with my son one day. If you too want to spend forever where he is, please talk to me or anyone here volunteering if you don't know God's Son Jesus.'"

Sophie told me she didn't know what she was going to say when she got up to speak at the end of the celebration, and then all the words tumbled out.

Here's what God showed me. This is from Matthew 10:19 and 20, Jesus speaking to His disciples about what they would be facing because they follow Him. They would be beaten and arrested, witnesses of Him through their testimony both to Jews and gentiles, "But when they deliver you up, do not be anxious about how or what you are to speak; for what you are to say will be given you in that very hour and moment, for it is not you who are speaking, but the Spirit of your Father speaking through you." I've always accepted that enablement in the context of defense and witness, but now I also see it as what happened to Sophie on that day. She could feel the Spirit of God pouring through her. It was no longer her words. The love of God came out, living water on the thirsty crowd.

I listened to Sophie's story, moved by the ways God had comforted her. He revealed things that changed her perspective on what would otherwise look like a tragic, senseless death. Instead, God was sparing Jeremy another horrible battle with cancer, one he would not have won. But I still had a question. Why a motorcycle accident? Even though Jeremy's wife has recovered and is able to live without crippling, permanent injuries, she was still badly hurt. Sophie said there's something among motorcycle people. It's like cowboys dying with their boots on. It's going out in style, not old and decrepit, weak and sick and unable to get out of bed. Jeremy was flung over an overpass, flying through the air like Evel Knievel. It increased the power of his death, and raised his status in the eyes of his special community, many with whom he had shared Christ. Sophie had prayed for Jeremy's harvest. God had already given it extra supernatural power, bringing out more than three hundred people in the heat of summer to hear the message of His love. I can picture the Holy Spirit standing behind Sophie, empowering her, speaking His words of love through His beloved daughter with His own, sweet breath, His inspiration.

Sophie added, "I know God. He is faithful. He has been faithful to show me the things I didn't know. I was immediately comforted by my Father God. He didn't have to show me anything, but he chose to, I am forever thankful. God said, 'I knew you would hear Me.'

"He said, 'I desire to speak to all My children this way, but so many don't hear Me or see the things I want to show them. They are distracted by so many things.'

"I'm forever grateful for the ears to hear and the eyes to see. God is faithful. He is a loving Father. I am in awe every day of Him. I am not any more special than you are. You also can hear and see God. If you desire to have a relationship with Him, like He so desires to have one with you. Then you too can have a relationship like I have with my Father God, and Jesus, my Hero."

18

Timing

Sometimes you have to endure the humiliation of barrenness for decades because God wants to bring about something extraordinary and it takes a miracle birth to signal the significance of the child. Sometimes you have to be in prison on false charges and then be forgotten by the only one who can help you get out because things have to be learned of language, courtly behavior, etiquette, and matters of state, not to mention deepening your relationship with God, before you have what you need to become Ruler of Egypt. Sometimes you have to be in prison, beaten and manacled so your songs of praise to God in the night can shake the ground and cause the locked, impassable doors to fly open. Or you're chained to a member of the elite Roman guard for two hours at a time so they can't get away from you as you share the truth of God's love for them and the new life that is available for the asking.

God doesn't automatically free His children. But He always has reasons, and they're always very good.

God also doesn't automatically heal His children. Sometimes you spend decades in a wheelchair painting with a brush between your teeth, inspiring people with the wholeness of your heart and the wisdom you learned in the fullness of your suffering. Sometimes you stay crippled and in pain from being beaten by soldiers or run over by an 18-wheeler, because your story is so remarkable it would be much harder to believe without the physical proof. And, of course God didn't spare Jesus a lifetime of ridicule and humiliation concerning the circumstances of his birth, or the rejection even from within his own family, or the torture and mocking that went on after the betrayal by one of His own chosen disciples. And He still has the scars. What we see in this non-deliverance is that most horrific thirty-three years any human being has ever experienced, and it shows us how God can take the worst and transform it into the best—the most astonishing best, a best whose ramifications changed human destiny for all time. God did not spare His Son, and because of that, He can now give us all things, including zoe life on Earth and opportunities to transform the world around us in the same eternal ways that Jesus did.

The Long Wait To Heart's Desires

When Dan and I co-authored our musical, *Even In Shadow* (*EIS*), we knew it had value. In fact, for me, I said then, and I still say, it's the best thing I've ever done. For nearly two decades I fervently wished it could be brought back to the stage. Finally, three years ago, I decided to tackle the daunting task of rewriting it. We had written the script in such a hurry that both Dan and I felt it needed a lot of cleaning up, but I'd never had the energy and then I did. I wanted to do it. Dan said to go for it, so I spent six months on it. Then he revised my revisions, we did a read-through with actors, started recording the music and auditioning voices so we could record the songs in preparation for making it available for licensing for schools, community theater groups, anyone looking for something meaningful to perform. We had just begun recording when COVID-19 shut us down.

That was a disappointment, to say the least. For a year, nobody could go anywhere, especially not to our studio to sing. So we let that dream go. We had been so hopeful. The message was timely (dealing with life and death and the meaning of both). The need for community and connection. The potential for deep, enduring love. But, no. We were stopped cold. It went to the back burner, but, in my heart, I still felt God wanted it to be available, and I still hoped…

Nearly six months later, I happened to be working with my friend Sophie on her story for my new book (this book, as a matter of fact), and we started talking about her son Dustin. She said he had gotten his degree in performance and was an actor and had been in operas, among other things. His advanced degree was in dance. Hmmmm… I started wondering if he might be interested in helping Dan and me with ideas on how to bring our musical to the public in ways that would meet COVID-19 regulations, and possibly have more power than if it were done the usual way. She thought he might. She said she'd ask. She did. He and I talked. Dan sent him the script and some songs. Then we talked again.

I'll give you the short version. There are dance numbers in "Even In Shadow." Dustin is a choreographer as well as a dancer. Dan and I are lousy at blocking and movement. Dustin has directed shows and movement is his specialty. We have no actors. Since Dustin is one and has worked with a community of them, he knows a lot of talent. He also knows singers. He's made films. He's written scripts. He knew what was wrong with ours (all the really wordy parts are dialogue I'd written). I loved talking with him. Not only does he have training and experience in all the areas required to bring *EIS* to performance, he has the depth and sensitivity to handle the subject matter of our show.

Okay, so he is perfectly suited to help us with the ideas and resources we need to take this production to the next levels. That's pretty amazing in itself. But to me, the most obvious God-thing about this whole thing is God's timing. When we first wanted to bring *EIS* back to the stage, it was eighteen years ago. At that time, Dustin had no training, no experience, and no extraordinary maturity. He was a little kid. That just makes me laugh. God knows what He's doing and

He knows what it will take to bring your heart's desire to full fruition, even if that means you have to wait a couple of decades first. I guess there's biblical precedent for that...Abraham, Joseph, Joshua and Caleb...

One last thing to share, because it highlights how special this collaboration is. When Sophie asked her son if he'd be willing to help us with our project, Dustin said, "Dan and Carolyn? Sure. Anything they want. They're family."

Seeking Miss Cora's House

Stephen and Alex Kendricks believe in prayer. They grew up seeing their parents pour prayers over every aspect of their lives, and they witnessed frequent miraculous answers to those prayers. When they decided to make movies that honor God, they prayed over them too. They waited on Him for inspiration for the concept, asking Him what was on His heart. Then they prayed over the script, the characters, the plot, God's choice of actors, locations, and crew. One of the main characters in "War Room" is Miss Cora, a serious prayer warrior whose expression of worship and praise was scheduled to be the first scene shot.

Two weeks before shooting began, the Kendricks brothers still hadn't found a house for Miss Cora. They were prayer walking the streets of Charlotte, asking the Lord to help them find it. They said they were walking and praying, turned a corner, and found the perfect place. It belonged to a pastor who had been trying to sell it for nine months with little to no interest. He agreed to let the brothers rent it for a month to shoot all of Miss Cora's scenes.

As they did with each of their movies, Stephen and Alex prayed with the actors and crew over each scene before filming it. They also asked the Lord to sell the house for the gentleman who had so graciously allowed them to film there. They said, "The day we finished shooting, a couple shows up, falls in love with the house, makes an offer, and it sells."

What I love most about this story is not just that the Lord sent the couple to buy it right after filming there was completed, it's that it didn't sell for the nine months before that. I think it might have been discouraging for the pastor, who undoubtedly prayed for God to sell his house, to have no one want it, lovely as it was. Perhaps he was praying, as I have in my own circumstances, that God would send just the right people He chose to be blessed there. He did, but He saved the home for Miss Cora's scenes first, and the new owners could move into a house that had been saturated in prayers, both those of the pastor, and those of everyone who participated in "War Room," which is all about the power of prayer.

God's timing is always perfect. He is never late, but neither is He early. And when a house doesn't sell or a woman is barren all her life into her elder years, it may be that God wants to do a miracle that is much more obvious because of, not in spite of, the delay. Ask Sarah, Hannah and Elizabeth. Sometimes the delay is to highlight a spectacular presence for a transcendent purpose. Just ask Isaac, Samuel, and John the Baptist.

Watkin Roberts

One of my very favorite stories is in the film *Beyond the Next Mountain.* It opens with a young Welshman, Watkin Roberts, who was so stirred by the Spirit of God that he went to India to bring the Good News to the Hmar tribes. The established missionary officials told him to go home. He didn't. He said, "The Bible charges us to go and tell. The increase is not ours to give." He set off on his own on foot, bringing the love of God into the hills of Manipur. But the missions board discovered him and expelled him from the country before he had time to do more than sow some seeds.

Fast-forward one generation. Young Rochunga is saying, "In the years before I was born, my father told me of a white-skinned missionary who came to the Hmar people. He was called by our tribe Mr. Youngman, and the stories he told changed our ways forever. My father gave his name to Jesus in the time of Mr. Youngman. He was fifteen years old. Now I am his son and he is the preacher on this mountain." Rochunga grew up hearing about the courageous white man who lived with them and loved them, teaching them God's ways from His Book. It had transformed the violent headhunters into a God-loving, peaceful people, but Chawnga, Rochunga's father, told him the people needed God's Book in their language. Some were beginning to question the teachings. God's Book would stop their doubts.

Young Rochunga took up the charge. He learned English, Hebrew, and Greek, crossing two oceans to receive all the learning needed to translate the New Testament into the Hmar language.

While Rochunga was in Chicago, a letter came to the university where he was studying New Testament theology. It was from a man who had heard there was a student there from India and he very much wanted to know if he could do anything to help him. It was signed "Watkin Roberts."

Amazed, Rochunga made his way to Robert's apartment and introduced himself to him as Chawnga's son. Roberts was stunned speechless.

Rochunga looked into the face of the one he had only heard about and said, "When I was a boy, you were a giant that once walked our hills. Every leaf of the forest trembled with your name. When I was older, you were a dream that would not go away."

Roberts replied, "The Lord has given me this moment to go back. I see you, Rochunga, and I see your father."

"You could go back now," Rochunga said eagerly. Laws had changed about religious freedoms. He would not be expelled for doing his work.

Ruefully Roberts answered, "The Hills of Manipur demand strong legs. Mine seldom obey me anymore."

"Then we would carry you, Mr. Youngman, with honor from village to village. There are more than a hundred churches in our mountains, and your early converts are now our elders and leaders."

At Roberts' request, Rochunga sang for him a hymn written in Hmar by one of his former students. Fighting back tears, the aged missionary said, "Please try to understand my difficulty. I went back to my trade, a chemist, perhaps 40 years ago now. And I've always questioned. What an amazing Christ! He never seeks for our approval, only for faith to believe that He is at work. All is mystery. To put one's life in His hands is not to be led astray. I was allowed to carry the seed, and you, Rochunga, are the first fruits of the harvest.

Rochunga returned to India and married his childhood sweetheart, Mawii, who waited for him all the years of his studies abroad. They established eighty schools, a hospital, and a vocational training center for the people of Northeastern India. They also founded Bibles for the World and have sent a Bible to every name in the phonebook in such countries as Afghanistan, Pakistan, and Russia. They consider themselves seed planters, and the film said the sowing of the Word continues to this day.

I was watching the movie on a big screen in the gymnasium of a university where students had gathered from all over the world to compete at the international ACE (Accelerated Christian Education) convention that was in Illinois that year. Quite a few of my students from our Christian school had qualified to be there, and I got to go along as one of the staff members. On the last night, we watched *Beyond the Next Mountain.* As we applauded, the screen was pulled up into the ceiling, revealing a man and a woman, brown-skinned, black-haired, dressed in the oranges and yellows of the Hmar people. It was Rochunga and Mawii. Rochunga told us he had now translated the Old Testament as well, and Mr. Youngman had returned to India. Joyfully they carried him from village to village where he preached to new generations of Christians who had found eternal life through the words of his first converts when he followed in faith the call of God.

Watkin Roberts had no idea the seeds he'd planted were bringing forth such abundant, wonderful fruit. What a blessing for him to meet Rochunga and return to the people he loved! I take this to heart, because many times I expend a lot of energy sowing seeds without ever seeing the fruit. God reminds me all I have to do is obey. The rest is up to Him. God told me, "You are here to change what would be without you." Our lives matter. What we do for Jesus matters. Nothing is ever wasted when it's done for the love of our God. Keep reading the Word. Keep speaking the Word. Keep praying the Word. It will never return empty. It will always accomplish something supernatural because the life of God is in it, breathed by the Holy Spirit afresh when we speak it for Him on behalf of His astonishing sacred work.

Asking Dad for Help

My son John does not usually ask for help, not even from his mom. But he got so desperate that he called me. Before that, he thought I was too busy to talk. He didn't know I was missing him, but figured he was too busy to talk. Then came the crises, one after another, and the phone calls on the way home became a lifeline between us. But it's one thing to talk to your mom, who has kept in contact, and another to reach out to your dad, whom you haven't been close to in years. The housing problem finally drove John to do it. He called his dad and his dad said, "Let me help." He was sincere and energetic, immediately calling rentals, agencies, lending institutions, real estate places, things John didn't have time to do because of his 12-hour days. John saw that his dad really wanted to help, but he had to *call* him first. Hint hint. Our Papa God waits for us to ask for help. It isn't that He doesn't know, but He's waiting for us to get to the point that we turn to Him and say, "I need help. Will You please?" And then we get the response. He doesn't just drop it on us without our asking. For one, we wouldn't know He had responded to us. It would have been sort of out of the sky. But when we're in desperate need and ask for the help and then it comes, there's a connection made, there's an association. "Oh. I asked. He responded. There's Someone at the other end who cares." That's what this did for John, another amazing, important connection that Papa God would respond and come through. And his earthly father would also respond and come through, giving the help and emotional support he needed.

Bibles in China

Smuggling Bibles behind the Iron Curtain, Brother Andrew told of approaching the border where guards were inspecting the luggage and vehicles of people seeking entry into the country. He told the Lord, "You made blind eyes to see. Now please make seeing eyes blind." The guards looked in the vehicle and waved it through, apparently not noticing the hundreds of Bibles that were there.

That actually happened to me too, in 1980, when I went to Mainland China as one of the first tourists to enter the newly opened Communist country. Having heard that it was very difficult to get Bibles in China, I had brought 200 little blue Gideon New Testaments, and even though the guard put his hands directly on them as he searched my suitcase for contraband (and Bibles were certainly contraband!), he closed my suitcase and waved me through. Two hundred little blue New Testaments traveled safely with me into Communist China.

For reasons I can't remember, I told my father about the Bibles. I failed to mention the danger, so all he knew was I intended to distribute them to the Chinese Christians I hoped to meet during my time in China. Therefore, he was very excited when he and Mom encountered a nice young man on their morning exploration of the ancient city of Canton. He turned out to be a Christian, and my father promptly told him about the Bibles and they came up with a plan for him to come get them at the hotel that night. Problem was my dad was so thrilled that he shouted the news to me across the large dining room where we were being served breakfast. I was utterly horrified. That night Mom and I waited in the hotel lobby for the young man. He did not come. We waited for four hours and finally went to bed. I was disappointed, to say the least.

The next morning I was still crushingly disappointed, and I told God so. He said, "When you know why, you'll be glad."

The next night I was walking around Souchow with a young Christian man from our tour group. He told me that a speaker had come to his church just before this trip. "Don't try to contact the underground church," he warned my friend. "If they're caught, they're tortured to try to get them to divulge the names of the others. It's very dangerous for them."

Instantly I knew why the young Chinese Christian had not come to the hotel. All the guides spoke English. There were the local guides who led the tour group around their city, and a national guide who traveled with each tour group the entire way. I'm sure they heard loud and clear what our plans were, thanks to my enthusiastic father. After that, the national guide watched me very carefully.

However God had other plans for those little blue New Testaments. China was newly opened to the West and the people were eager to learn more about the United States. Everywhere we went, I told our local guide, "You want to know more about the United States? Our Constitution and laws and government are based on this book. Would you like a copy?" They were delighted to accept that gift. By the time we left China, I had given away every one of those little Bibles. I had intended them for the underground church. Instead, they went to the government officials, one of whom kept asking me questions about God. It turned out he was also asking the other Christian couple the same questions. And two years later, a couple came to my church to talk about their trip to China. During their slide show, they mentioned this one local guide who kept asking them questions about God. They even had a picture of him. I looked at the slide. It was the same local guide who had questioned me. I still pray for him. I have a feeling I'll see him in heaven one of these days.

A Miracle On Belmont Avenue

My friend Darda Burkhart saw many miracles as the daughter of a missionary couple serving the "Graveyard of the Pacific," the treacherous west coast of Vancouver Island, Canada. At ninety-one, she still asserts God's will for all of us is to live a supernatural life. And she still does. Every day.

"It was the very last Christmas holiday we would have at the big old house on Belmont Avenue. For six years, this house had been a haven for servicemen and women. It was a place where they could find peace and be included in a family and its activities, rather than roaming around the city looking for something to do when off base.

"In one way it was sad, because we knew we probably would not see some of these wonderful servicemen and women again. Some of the guests were stationed at the military bases in Victoria, adding to our family. Some were friends, but I can't say for sure. After all, that's 70 years ago.

"We expected to have 25 people for the New Years Day feast. The menu included a large roast beef with mashed potatoes, good brown gravy, vegetables and dessert. The day before the holiday, Dad and Mother were in the kitchen preparing the vegetables and I was setting the tables when the doorbell rang. When Dad opened the door, a large paper sack was thrust into his hands. It contained a huge turkey, which someone had sent as a surprise. Dad took it into the kitchen and showed it to Mother. They wondered who had sent it and, more than that, what God was up to. Just then the phone rang, and Dad and Mother soon received their answer. Some China Inland Missionaries who had recently been released from a Japanese prison camp were on board an old tramp steamer that had anchored off shore. It was so derelict that it was a wonder it had made the journey across the Pacific Ocean and was still afloat. The crew had gone ashore for the holiday, but the missionaries were left alone on board. The caller wanted to know if Dad could do something for them.

"Dad said that he would. Immediately, he called the Immigration authorities, some of whom he knew personally, to see what could be done to bring the group to Victoria for the day. He discussed the matter with the authorities and was given permission to bring the group to his home, as long as he agreed to be responsible to guard them and return them to the ship. Dad readily agreed, hung up the phone, and then made some other necessary calls.

"One was to a friend who had a boat, and the two made arrangements to get the group from the steamer to the shore. The next call was for another driver to join Dad and pick up the people at the dock. The distance was not far, but gas was strictly rationed. With these critical arrangements made, Dad and Mother hurriedly began to prepare more vegetables, get the turkey ready for roasting, and I had to set more tables in the big dining room. Now the guests numbered 41, not 25.

"We didn't have many decorations because of the war, but it was still festive. A real Christmas tree stood in a corner of the living room. It exuded the memorable scent of cedar throughout the house. Icicles dripped from the branches reflecting the colored lights, and balls of gold, red, blue, and silver added to the feast for the eyes.

"When the missionary group walked into our home the next day, the atmosphere was electric. These were missionaries and their children who had paid a heavy price to serve the Lord in China. They had been captured and had spent four years in prison camp. Some of their group had died from the mistreatment, and the rest were malnourished and so thin that their clothes hung on their bodies. Every eye that welcomed them was wet with tears—tears of realization of the dangers and severe persecution they had suffered at the hands of their captors. Yet here they stood, freed at last and back on their own land. They looked downcast and nervous, as they came into this welcoming group of open arms.

"We brought the food in and placed it on the table. The bowls of mashed potatoes, gravy, carrots and green peas gave a vivid color scheme to the table. Then the people were invited to sit down. The children had never seen an orange, a beef roast or a turkey! The adults had not seen such an abundance of food for as long as they could remember. Aromas of beef and turkey filled the house and they reveled in the scents. They sat at the table wide-eyed with awe at the grace of God who had arranged for this time of fellowship with other godly people.

"After Dad asked the blessing on the food and the gathering, there was little conversation as the guests filled their plates with satisfying food that pleased both the eye and the palate. It did not take long for the dishes heaped with food to be emptied and filled again. (I remember Dad savoring his portion, the tail of the turkey, with his eyes closed and looking as if it was the best thing he had ever eaten.). When the time for dessert came, Dad, Mother, and I served each person a dish of sliced peaches with a large dollop of real whipped cream. A big plate of dark slices of Christmas cake full of currants, nuts, and candied orange peel with the coffee was a lovely taste treat to end this momentous meal.

"Slowly our guests began to talk quietly to some of those at the tables. When everyone was sated and the conversation began to flow, Dad asked the senior missionary to tell them of their experiences and of the trip across the ocean. The man rose and spoke haltingly of some of their deprivations and the loss of one of the fathers. His descriptions were painful to hear, but they taught us of the price some had paid to tell other nations about Jesus' love and salvation. The missionary recounted the instances of God's faithfulness to them in their dire circumstances and how He upheld them time and time again with His Word and comforting presence.

"He then remembered a little book he carried in his pocket, reached in and pulled it out. As he flipped through it, he told of being in Hong Kong the night before they left China. He went to a pagoda on the crest of a hill, where he could look out over the city. His heart was breaking for the people he had learned to love, and he prayed earnestly for the land he had to leave and its unknown future. He said that as he looked around the inside walls of the pagoda, he noticed some English names with Scripture references written underneath them. He read these names aloud.

"Suddenly, someone gasped. A stunned silence fell over the room, and all our eyes quickly turned to a couple of the sailors sitting at the table. The two men stood. They said they were the ones who had written their names and those Scripture verses on that very wall in Hong Kong!

"One of the other servicemen took Dad aside and asked if he could take up a collection for these missionaries. "Certainly, go ahead and do it," Dad said. It didn't take long to gather a nice amount of money, which was then handed to the amazed missionary. Word got out to others about this amazing event, and people began to bring gifts and other needed items to the house. One Christian man who owned a shoe store opened it up and fitted every one of them with new shoes.

"That amazing day had yet one more emotional moment, for the daughter of one of the missionaries was a nurse in Toronto. Despite the protestations of her parents, Dad decided to make a long-distance call to her. When he made the call, he learned that the daughter was a patient in the hospital where she worked. She had undergone serious brain surgery and was now in recovery. Someone brought a telephone to her room so she and her parents could talk. We could overhear their conversation and tearful sobs, and it affected each one of us deeply. Once more eyes were brimmed with unshed tears, but hearts were full of gratitude to God for having a part in such a wonderful day.

"At the end of the day, Dad and his friend transported the missionaries back to the dock, where the boat took them back to the rusty steamer. Each one wondered if they would ever meet again this side of heaven. That momentous day was a fitting climax to Dad and Mother's years of ministering to men and women from many walks of life whose lives had been interrupted by war.

"Looking back, I am awed how God arranged this healing time for the missionary group. He had the steamer dock at a certain port where there was a man who had the connections to allow them to visit this loving, caring family, who had the house big enough for the entire group to join those already there, and that God had also made sure there was more than enough food for all who were assembled.

"Somehow, I think that having at the table the two sailors who wrote their names on the pagoda wall, made some special connection with the missionary and the land he loved. God's tender care in giving them this special loving start to their new life on a New Year's Day was miraculous, and I got to be a part of it."

19

What God Alone Can Do

Chariots of Fire

When Eric Liddell left fame and fortune to serve as a missionary in China, he probably thought little about the life he'd left behind. Titles, medals, Super Bowl rings, trophies and the rest are all artifacts of past glory. If you asked most people who won the gold medal for the 400 meter race three Olympics ago, I doubt many could tell you. Eric's story would have been forgotten had it not been for a movie that came about under circumstances that seem suspiciously full of the fingerprints of God.

In 1978, David Putnam was staying in with a friend in Dunaway. He was sick and could not leave the house. Looking for something to read, he found a book, *History of the Olympic Games*. When he got to the 1924 Olympics, he saw a paragraph about Eric Liddell who refused to run in the 100-meter race because the heats were going to be run on a Sunday. Instead, he opted to run in the 400 meters and won. Putnam said that's where the movie came from.

Putnam became Producer/Director of "Chariots of Fire," his first major film. He'd made lots of short films, ads, etc., but never a full-length movie, especially one requiring costumes, locations, and props for a period piece. And it had to be completely created under his care. There were no books, no documentaries, nothing but that paragraph in the very old book of athletic events. Putnam hired a writer who began interviewing people. Putnam and the writer began researching Eric's life. They made inquiries, put ads in the paper asking for anything they could find on those particular games. A box of original scrapbooks from the 1924 Olympics showed up. A box of letters written by Aubry Montague arrived. He was one of the team members and had written home to his parents every day.

All through the process, pieces fell into place. Then they began to shoot the movie. It was a very strange production with odd things going on throughout the filming. All of them noticed—cast and crew. They couldn't do this shot and then something happened and they got a better one. This happened over and over. Putnam said, "The sequence on the sand, the opening to the movie at Saint Andrews, we shot it twice. We shot it first on a very quiet, calm day. A quite boring shot. The sea was boring. But thank God there was a piece of sand put in the lens and there was a scratch on the film, the whole sequence. So we had to go back, and the following day it was much more blustery, so you have the white horses on the sea and it's an incomparably more interesting, and better shot."

What touches me about these remarks by a decidedly unreligious man, is the way he was obviously guided to the book, then provided materials , and then the unusual circumstances that caused the film to be much better than it would have been without the intrusion from outside the project, the introduction of a different energy, a supernatural one. It led David Putnam to say, "I've absolutely always believed we were vehicles for a film that Eric Liddell, or Someone connected to Eric Liddell, decided to have made. I will go to my grave believing that."

I'm pretty sure God, not Eric, wanted that movie made and oversaw its production for maximum impact. He's really good at that. And, just to emphasize His blessing on the project, the film won Best Picture and a number of other Academy Awards. Putnam was truly astonished. It was his first full-length feature film and he wasn't sure anyone would like it. He said if he had known he was going to win, he would have gotten a haircut.

Most likely Eric would have been surprised to learn there is a movie of his life, and an Eric Liddell Centre in Scotland. It's not a museum with memorabilia from his Olympics and other competitions. Their website describes it as "a local care charity and community hub founded in 1980 in memory of the 1924 Olympic 400 meter gold medallist, Eric Liddell. We are working hard to change perceptions of living with dementia, disabilities and mental health issues - we aim to show living a full life can be achieved with the correct support. In doing so we support some of the most vulnerable people in Scotland's capital." I know Eric would prefer that to a museum full of old medals and trophies.

The director of the center said one day a young Japanese woman came by. She told him when she was a little girl, she saw the movie and was so inspired by Eric's life that she became a Christian.

I think it's significant that David Putnam was sick and housebound and just happened to select, out of all the volumes in his friend's library, the book on the Olympics and the one entry that caught his eye was the paragraph on Eric Liddell. Making that movie changed David Putnam. It touched him with the breath of God in the supernatural things that happened all through the filming, including the mysterious sequence-long scratch from a single grain of sand.

Shackleton

In the last desperate attempt to reach help, Shackleton took five men in a 22-foot boat to make their way from Elephant Island, which was off any shipping routes or where whalers and sealers might be hunting, to South Georgia, 800 miles away, where the whaling station was located. They took four weeks' of food and water and set out, a tiny speck of a boat in a vast violent sea. They left behind twenty-two starving, disheartened men, who knew this was their only chance for rescue. But there was no guarantee they would find it.

Worsley, who was navigating had a sextant but it required being able to see the horizon and the sun, neither of which was visible most of the time. He managed by dead reckoning, a seat-of-the-pants kind of groping his way with senses honed from many years in treacherous seas. Seventeen days later, drenched to the skin their limbs swelling and numb with frostbite, they reached the island and Worsley finessed the boat to shore without breaking it up on the rocks. Miraculously they had made it to South Georgia. There was only one problem. Stromness Bay Whaling Station was on the other side of the island. There was no way the boat or the men could endure another voyage, so Shackelton made the decision to cross the island on foot. Three of the men were too weak to go, so he took Worsley and Crean and the barest necessities, leaving the rest with the other men. For equipment they took only a length of rope and a carpenters adz. They were too weak to carry anything else.

At 3 a.m., taking advantage of the full moon, Shackleton, Worsley and Crean, their legs still numb from frostbite, set off on boots that had screws from their little boat in their soles for traction. The one map they had was of the coastline only. No one had knowledge of what lay ahead, or where the whaling station was in relation to where they were. To make matters worse, they were physically unprepared in any way. They were starving, their clothes ragged, and they were climbing the slippery ice on legs that had not walked much in four months. Shackleton reported, "We were now feeling the strain of unaccustomed walking and our muscles were out of tune." Caroline Alexander, who wrote the screenplay and two books on the expedition, described the ordeal this way, "Beneath the deceptive layer of snow lay ice fields pitted with crevasses. One misstep would be fatal. They struggled through a bewildering confusion of ridges and plateaus. Time after time they would ascend a summit only to find a precipice on the other side."

At 6:30 in the morning of the second day, the men stumbled to the door of Stromness Whaling Station. They had been climbing for thirty-six hours. That night a blizzard struck. Safely in the stationmaster's house, Shackleton knew if they had been caught in a blizzard while they were on the mountain, they would not have survived.

For his I-Max film, George Butler, Director/Producer of the documentary, "The Endurance," went back to South Georgia in April 2000. He brought with him three of the world's best mountain climbers, including one considered the greatest mountain climber in history, the first man to climb Mount Everest without oxygen. Butler had the goal of having them try to make the Shackleton Traverse. He said, "They had ice axes, crampons, proper boots, watertight Gortex clothing, tents, food, and compasses, but they couldn't match Shackleton. The extraordinary part of this story is what Shackleton, Worsley and Crean were able to do, which was nearly superhuman."

It took nearly four days for three of the best mountain climbers in the world to do what Shakleton and his two companions did in thirty-six hours. Butler added, "There have been some changes in the glaciers, which have receded, and Shackleton, Worsley, and Crean did have a good blanket of snow across the interior to cross, but the fact of the matter is they didn't know where they were going and they were doing it after sixteen months or so of deprivation, so their traverse is even more extraordinary."

Later in his memoir, *South, The Last Antarctic expedition of Shackleton and the Endurance*, Shackleton wrote, "When I look back at those days I have no doubt that Providence guided us, not only across those snowfields, but across the storm-white sea that separated Elephant Island from our landing-place on South Georgia. I know that during that long and wracking march of thirty-six hours over the unnamed mountains and glaciers of South Georgia it seemed to me often that we were four, not three. I said nothing to my companions on the point, but afterwards Worsley said to me, 'Boss, I had a curious feeling on the march that there was another person with us.' Crean confessed to the same idea. One feels 'the dearth of human words, the roughness of mortal speech' in trying to describe things intangible, but a record of our journeys would be incomplete without a reference to a subject very near to our hearts."

Tom Crean's daughter Mary Crean O'Brien, said, "The fourth man was, I suppose, the Man Above. They must have been deeply religious at the back of everything. They must!"

At the end of his memoir, Shackleton wrote, "We had seen God in His splendors, heard the text that Nature renders. We had reached the naked soul of man."

Shackleton had been a seeker of fame and glory driven to make a name for himself as an explorer, but when his ship was lost, he told his men, "Ship and stores have gone—so now we'll go home." From then on, he put all his will and energy into taking care of them, keeping up their morale, and expending all his energies and last strength in heroic efforts to rescue them and get them all home.

In his Director's commentary, George Butler gave details of Shackleton's strategies to keep up morale, something that had been lacking in previous expeditions by others under similar conditions. All had ended badly, with insanity and deaths resulting from the intense suffering. I recommend Butler's PBS video to you, for there is far too much to include here, but I want to add just one incident. On the 800-mile voyage from Elephant Island to South Georgia, two of the men lay near death from exposure and starvation. Butler said Shackleton kept his fingers on the pulses, literally, of both men, and when one would drop dangerously low, he would order hot drinks for everyone, and the men never knew it was on their account that this had been done.

As I watched the documentary, the story told through the diaries of the men, and sat looking at the faces and listening to the voices of their children and grandchildren telling what they knew firsthand from their adventurer ancestor, I couldn't help thinking that Shackleton had done much more than he realized. He made possible generations of people who would not be alive but for his single-minded determination, and the providence and divine guidance of God, to save their lives.

Shackleton's ship was named for his family motto, "By endurance we conquer." In all of history, no other expedition has ever made it home after so much time and adversity in the arctic. To me, it's a powerful "lifeboat" story, one that stands in history as a towering straight wall that inspires me to go on when I face terrifying climbs over uncharted mountains in the icy dark.

The Red Sea

Over the past year I've had the blessing of a lot of phone calls from my son John. He had gotten into the habit of calling me as he drove the hour and a quarter home from work. Where he lived, there was no cell service. No internet. Even his land line sounded like he was in a tin can and would suddenly drop the call. It was maddening. So we talked a lot on those long drives, especially as he tried to find his way through the intense trial he and Shelly were going through. Even that was difficult because there were spots on the stretch where the signal disappeared, usually during the most important parts of the conversation. And, of course, the closer he got to home, the less we could hear each other. We could talk for about twenty minutes, not counting the two blank spots. It was still better than nothing because, as I said, once he was home, it was almost impossible to hear one another.

Then he got the eviction notice. That led to more pressure, more anxiety, more worry.

I sent out the prayer call. Friends and family encircled John, sending emails of emotional support and words of encouragement. All of us felt God wanted him to be in a different place. Immediate benefits of being closer to work came to mind. He wouldn't have to spent $300 a month in gas plus wear and tear on his car or drive in the dark in the rain, which is scary when you don't see well at night and the road is rural, remote, and unlit. Nevertheless, in a pandemic, with housing availability at 1%, it felt to us a lot like what the Israelites faced at the Red Sea.

But God is good at Red Seas. When circumstances are most impossible, that's when we get to see He is mighty indeed. I knew that, and I also figured, since I'm writing a book on the supernatural normal Christian life, that God wanted to do something in present time, not remembered from thousands or hundreds or even fifty years ago. As I write this story, it's the last one that will be added to this book. Dan has already put everything else into layout and prepared the cover. But God told me not to fret that I wasn't able to complete the book sooner; He wanted to make a point, and, for that, I had to wait for the end of the story.

I'll give you the short version. During the ordeal, John kept telling God he just wanted to be wherever He chose. He didn't care where it was; he just needed a place he could have his piano and his dog. Mia is a silvery blue Weimaraner/pit bull mix. A lot of places get queasy around pit bulls, even as cute as Mia is. He wondered if he should try to find her another home, but we all felt God had a place that would welcome Mia.

The most spectacular thing that happened during John's search for a place to live was how consistently and emphatically all possible doors slammed shut. I already told you about the lenders who promised to call John back and never did. There were also those places that popped up on his real estate app and disappeared by the end of the day when he would have been free to make his interest known. There were places that had regulations, such as age or restrictions on dogs. When he talked to one, the man asked if Mia was a service dog. John told him no. The man said, "You could have lied," and John said that's not what he does. He wouldn't lie about his age, income level, or claim any disabilities either.

Doors continued to slam shut.

One day when Carol, Debra and I were gathered at my house to pray, John called. I asked if we could all pray for him. He said that would be good. So John got a 3-D prayer, each of us speaking what the Holy Spirit put on our hearts. Debra gets pictures and words, and sometimes words begin to tumble out of her mouth. When that happens she says she's being Balaam's donkey's lips. In other words, if God can speak through a donkey, He can speak through her. This is what she said:

"God has a place picked out for you, it is smaller, centrally located, more convenient, and the location itself is important. The new home equals ministry, opportunity, and an open door. It is not a house; it's a home. Reminder: it's not a new house, it's a new home. God was very clear it's not just a house, it's a home, and it will feel like home. You'll know when you walk in. It has a fenced yard."

Some weeks later, a place became available. John went to see it. It was a 4,000 square foot house that had been divided into four apartments. It had a fenced yard that all the tenants shared, and no place for washer and dryer. John wasn't thrilled, but he put in his application. He had told God he would be glad to be wherever God chose, and he wasn't going back on that. He figured if this was God's choice, he would make it work.

Email from John:

"Hi, mom,

The owners for the apartment messaged me today to say that they rented it out to someone else. She also said her property manager had a property she'd like to offer to me. It's only about 700 square feet but it has a yard and it's a house rather than an apartment. I'm going to see it tonight after work. Please pray. I just want what God wants. I've seen pictures. It looks nice. I'm hopeful. It's 9 minutes from work."

That evening I got a phone call from my son. "I'm just leaving the driveway of my new home," he said. He had gone to see the property manager, and the owner was there. The owner said he stopped listing the place because immediately he got fifty phone calls. It was overwhelming. So he took it off the market and still got ten inquiries. John talked to him a bit. The man wanted to see a picture of Mia. Then he told the property manager, "He looks like an honest man. Give him the keys."

Cautiously I asked John, "How did you feel when you walked in?"

He said it was like when you meet someone new and you think, *I think I'm going to like this person.*

I asked, "Does it have a fenced yard?" It did indeed. It's the length of a car all the way around the house with room for his barbecue and outdoor furniture. The kitchen is all new stainless steel appliances and it has hookups for washer and dryer. And it's only nine minutes from work.

But it is definitely smaller. John went from a four-bedroom house to 700 square feet. The first night, he called me in distress. In the front room boxes were stacked in every direction all the way to the ceiling. He couldn't even get to his piano. It seemed too cramped to really be the home Debra said he would find it to be. As John spoke, I got the words, "It's expandable."

I told Debra and Carol. Carol immediately sent John a story about the home where she, Randy, and their two little girls lived when they were in Willits. It was about the size of John's new house, but all four of them fit in nicely and had a wonderful time together. In fact, Carol looks back on it with great fondness. Debra responded with more words from Balaam's donkey's lips. She got the word, "contentment." She said that contentment would be growing stronger, "and out of that contentment comes peace and the recognition on his part that he was dealing with a lot of distractions at the home where he was before." He would be feeling peace and recognizing a release of pressure. "God will tell him more as he settles in."

John is getting used to new hours. He no longer has to get up at 5:15 a.m. In order to get to work on time. He no longer gets home after 6:00 p.m., and Mia no longer does the "pee-pee dance" after twelve hours in the house. John keeps unpacking and more and more of the place becomes space instead of a wall of cardboard boxes. He has unearthed his piano, and playing it always gives him comfort. The cell phone and internet work just fine. He still calls me on his way home, though the drive is short. We just keep talking while he makes his dinner.

If the Israelites could have gotten away from Pharaoh's army just by going fast, no big deal. "We got away." But God hemmed them in so there was no chance of escape unless He parted the Red Sea. Then it was a miracle, something they could remember forever. When John was hemmed in on all sides, he needed a miracle, and he got one. He will remember it forever. If he could have done it on his own, he wouldn't have needed God's intervention. It would have shown how wonderfully diligent and resourceful he is. Or serendipity. "How nice that these doors just happened to open!" Instead, all the doors slammed shut in his face. There was no way he was going to get what he needed. Except for God: "He looks like an honest guy. Give him the keys." It wasn't listed! And there it is, saved for you. Because when God has something for you, He doesn't let it be first-come-first-served, someone gives him a better offer. He saves it for you. He's the Papa who knows how to give you a home and a yard for your dog, and a memorable experience showing you what He can do for you. He knows what you want. He knows what you love. John loves to cook. Papa gave him a wonderful kitchen. There's room for his piano. It isn't an apartment whose tenants might not appreciate Chopin and Satie. It has a big back yard with lots of room for his outdoor furniture so Shelly and he can look at the stars.

On the weekend, John found a little laundromat only four minutes away, and directly across the street is a fish market, a rather famous fish market, with an impressive array of smoked fish. John bought a smoked steelhead that he pronounced "ambrosial," not too salty and not like licking an ashtray, which is how he says a lot of smoked fish tastes. Best of all, he's feeling the release of pressures he didn't even know he was under.

I was just finishing up this story, preparing to email it to John to check one more time when he called. He was on his way to see a patient and wanted to give me an update. He said he's in his second week at the new home and he still has half a tank of gas. At the previous location, he would have to fill up every couple of days. Previously he didn't get reimbursed for mileage or time. Now that he lives near work, this hour drive to a patient's house will earn him both.

John now has a storage shed and a locking mailbox that weren't there when he moved in. His landlord provided them after John inquired about such things. He didn't have to beg or follow up on them. Expandable. That's what God said. He also told me a couple of stories about his adventures at the laundromat. I'll just say he's doing that kindness-thing I wrote about in the story of

Ebed-Melech, the kindness that makes others feel encouraged and uplifted and better about life in these days. The stories reminded me of what Debra said about the location of the new place being important because it equalled ministry. When John drives through town, he sees people wandering, vacant, lost. One woman stepped out in front of his car without even looking. A man was shouting on the street at things that weren't there. John has been love bombing them. He has a lot of weapons that are not physical, but mighty through God, and he knows how to use them. He has Jesus-authority to open prison doors and set the captives free. I'm thinking, with his medical background, he can pray sharpshooter prayers for the man whose brain is shorted out through drugs. I have such a strong sense that John will get extra help when he opens his mouth on their behalf, "for it is not you who are speaking, but the Spirit of your Father speaking through you." (Matt 10: 20) Who knows what God will do for these people? He moved John there to change what would be without him. John has been there only a short time, and it's been happening in abundance already. He said he can tell. Me too. He's doing what Jesus said. He's being a light in the world.

To me, the major supernatural of this story is not the timing and the way the provision of the house came about, miraculous as it is. It's the transformation I'm watching happen in my dear son's life. It's hearing about his conversations with God, his total surrender, his desire for the will of God, his trust in Him during these worst of days for Shelly and him. The way the house came about is spectacular, but God never does just one thing. Preceding the crossing of the Red Sea were ten plagues during which Moses was changed from a man who argued he couldn't do what God asked to the one who trusted God in everything. I've been watching that happen to my son, who meets with Yahweh every day and talks with Him face to face as friend to friend. There's a shine on his face people can see, the image and character of God. And I'm hearing God sayin' in my heart, "You ain't seen nothin' yet."

20

The Bible

After all these stories with evidences large and small of the supernatural ways God intervenes in human life, why would I turn now to the Bible? Isn't it kind of inert—an ancient book that has been examined and discussed and preached from for thousands of years? Why would the Holy Spirit direct me to this subject at the very end of this book on the supernatural normal Christian life? Because that life is rooted and grounded and founded on the Bible, and everything about the Bible is supernatural, from its structure and coherence to the history marked by Divine intervention, all the way to the prophetic—both what has already been fulfilled and what is yet to come. The Christians of the First century were able to survive vicious, persistent persecution because they believed in the finished work of Christ and that God had spoken through people who had written the Tanakh and what was currently being written by those who knew Jesus personally. They were able to avoid being pressured into the mold of the dominant culture with its multitudes of idols, and the crazy hostility directed at them through that whacko Emperor Nero. And God spoke to them individually as well. One notable example is what Eucibius reported regarding the Christians and the siege of Jerusalem. You'll be reading about that when we come to the Olivet Discourse.

"For whatever things were written before were written for our learning, that we through the patience and comfort of the Scriptures might have hope." (Romans 15:4 NKJV)

Paul tells us what's been written in the Bible is for us, that we might receive patience and comfort that results in hope.

Reading the accounts of God's workings with humans all through time helps build our patience. The word in Greek is *hupomono*. Remember, it's not passive. It means endurance. We will have power to last. We can bear up under pressure. It also gives us comfort, but the word in Greek is not "consolation." This comfort from the Scriptures is not so we can feel better, like a small child in its father's arms. In Greek, "comfort" includes a sense of coming alongside and giving strength. It's like steel girders installed to help hold up a vulnerable structure. Together the words of Scripture give us the ability to endure, to last, to persist, and they come alongside to give us inner strength. That results in hope that does not disappoint—not wishful thinking, but solid confidence in the faithfulness of God. He will never leave you, fail you or forsake you. He is mighty to save. He keeps His promises. He loves you. His thoughts toward you are more than the sand. *More.*

The Bible can be trusted to provide the information you need to get safely where you have to go. It's like a globe of Earth that shows the placement of continents, oceans, and countries as they relate to one another. It's a map that shows us the routes that can get us to our destination. It's turn-by-turn guidance with accurate, up-to-date inclusions of all the most recent construction zones to be factored in. It helps you keep on track, know which off-ramp to take, and can guide you safely home.

Some people think the Bible is a book of rules. Don't do this. Don't do that. Some people think it's moral stories and fairy tales. I've also heard it called a love letter from God. This makes me think of various times God spoke as recorded in biblical accounts. Some people heard thunder. Some people heard words. The Bible is a supernatural book divinely authored outside of time. It is not obligated to reveal its secrets to anyone who is unprepared. At Mount Sinai, in the tabernacle, in the Holy of Holies, God made very strict rules concerning certain sacred places and items. Why? To keep people safe. We have no idea what holiness really is, or the power of God, or what His presence can do. Or His Word. I know Christians who read a favorite Psalm to cheer themselves up or quote a single verse almost like a protective incantation, but never look at any of the rest of the Bible. Because that's all they want from it, that's all they get. And people who expect fairy tales will get nonsense and gibberish, not realizing the Book Itself is keeping them from perceiving anything more. But for those of us who seek God in His Word, the Bible reveals all the ways we can know Him, understand His heart, His purposes for us individually, and become like Him bringing Him glory according to God's surprising design. His Ways aren't intuitive. "Love your enemies" is not intuitive in the least. But that's how Jesus says life works best. We were each His enemies and He loved us. Redemption isn't possible any other way. But when we take Him at His Word and act upon it, wow! Supernatural things happen. We get to see how very un-normal the Christian life is capable of being. It's exciting and mind-boggling and fun. And it's all available to you if you're really interested.

In the next chapters, I'm presenting things that most often confuse people. There will be a globe-type overview of the Bible as a whole, a map to show how to navigate some of the most confusing interchanges so you don't take the wrong off-ramps, and turn-by-turn guidance through some of the "contradictions" that contain surprising information in plain sight if you know how to look for it.

The Globe Overview

I always thought of the Bible as history and prophecy, eyewitnesses and letters. Yes it is, but there's more. It's an integrated message made of sixty-six books with more than forty authors writing over a period of more than 1500 years.

Because of Chuck Missler's meticulous scholarship and extensive background in a wide range of disciplines, from his specialty in technology and the information sciences, to quantum physics, world history and international finances, to high level military information, cryptography, and extra-biblical sources, I now understand what the message is about. When you know the Plan, you will not be caught unprepared for baffling current events or the strange happenings in the future. When you know its coming, you can say, "Oh, He said that would happen." And if you're not surprised, alarmed, or incapacitated by it, neither will your children be afraid. You may be the only ones on the block walking in peace, but isn't that like being shining lights in the darkness? All of you, your children included, were born for making a difference in this special time. And that means God has equipped you to be good at it.

Here's my overview of the Bible to give you placement and movement through history from beginning to end—the loss of relationship with God all the way to His restoration of all that was lost. There are lots of ways to get an overview of the Bible, but the one I'm offering here is my interpretation of how it goes together in an integrated message of repeating patterns throughout time, with the issues always the same.

First there was nothing but God. Since the Bible is God telling us our story, that's all we need to know. He was always God, and He chose to create our universe, speaking it into existence with all of its parameters fine-tuned to be perfect for life to thrive on Earth. Then He planted a garden and created Adam in His own Image, gave him dominion over Earth and its creatures and features, and established moral law through a single command: Don't eat of that tree. The consequence was also made clear: death. Then He created Eve, and they would visit together, Creator God and Adam and Eve, in the garden. That was perfection. No strife, no pain, no misunderstandings between humans or humans and God. Perfect communication in harmony with creation in which everything was wholesome, lovely, nourishing, and good. *Kalos*. When God pronounced His creations "good," that's the word used in the Septuagint (the Greek translation of the Tanakh). In Hebrew, the word "good" has the same overtones. God made it beautiful good.

You know what comes next. Satan tricks Eve into doubting God's goodness—Big Mistake #1—and she takes matters into her own hands—Big Mistake #2. She offers the fruit to Adam who eats it without any nudging from Satan. He made a totally free-will choice to take what God told him would kill him.

One concept we modern human beings don't understand well is how very orderly the universe is. We've got the John Wayne-thing going on—the lawless, rugged individual who answers to no one. He comes and goes as he pleases and is a law unto himself. We on the West Coast are especially prone to that cherished image of ourselves as children of the wild wild west. When God created the laws of physics, the moral and natural laws, they were irrevocable. All of the spiritual realm works by authority. When Adam forfeited his right to fulfill his charge as son of God overseeing the expansion of the Garden into all the Earth, populated by wonderful children all taught in the ways of God and enjoying what He had given them, he opened the door to entropy, a deterioration of all that was meant to flourish forever in fruitful fulfillment.

At the moment Adam lost the title deed to Earth to Satan, our own spiritual warfare began. Because righteousness is the very nature of God and built into the foundations of everything, God couldn't just say, "Well, boys will be boys." The crime had been committed. The price must be paid. The price was innocent blood, and now there would be no sinless blood flowing through any of the children of Adam. The only way to get Earth back was for another human man, one without sin, to die for the sins of every human being that ever was or would be. Nothing else would fulfill the requirements. God already had Redemption planned for us, but now there would have to be worked out through history a very detailed and complicated preparation that would not only redeem human beings, but creation itself. Thus began the nature of life on Earth that continues through this day: "The message is true, the struggle is hard, the conflict is long, and the war is great." (Daniel 10:1)

Here are the foundational issues: the questioning of God's goodness; the choice to decide for yourself what's good for you; and the resulting shock, shame, blame, and hiding. What is God's response? Notice that God does not yell at them. He knows full well where they are, yet He gives them an invitation to confess and reconnect with Him. He calls, "Where are you?" God's desire is to reestablish connection. We don't know what would have happened if they had chosen a different way to relate to Him after their transgression, but they did what they did and it started the pattern that will repeat in increasingly destructive spirals of disconnection from God, with shame and blame separating humans farther and farther from one another and, worst of all, from God Himself and the sound of His voice.

Fig leaves (which are large, but scratchy and itchy) are their attempt to cover up. God replaces the leaves with tunics of skins—covering their nakedness with innocent life slain for their sakes. It's the first "type" —a symbolic representation of what would be fulfilled in the Lamb of God Who takes away the sins of every human being ever born. Every one. Whether they appreciate it, acknowledge it, or accept it on their behalf. Before the beginning of time, Scripture says, the Lamb was slain. God already knew the potential of free will to choose what would be most damaging for themselves, and had already determined He, Himself, would pay the price to make it possible for them to be restored to Him forever.

It's also important to realize that God didn't kick them out of the Garden and never speak to them again. God would have explained sacrifice to Adam, what was clean and what was not suitable for offering to cover their sins. Every detail of the sacrifice was a sign post pointing to the Lamb of God Who, with His sinless blood, would qualify to buy back every human and Earth itself. God still wanted to be involved in the lives of His children and wanted them to know what was required to stay connected to Him.

Genesis says Adam lived more than nine hundred years after leaving the Garden and had many sons and daughters. Considering human gestation time was probably the same back then as it is now, and seeing as my grandparents had a child every two years, how many children could they have had in nearly a thousand years? A bunch! Also, since chromosomes were not corrupted at the beginning, siblings and cousins could marry each other and have children without any strange deformities or mental aberrations. Abram, you remember, married his half-sister Sarai. Same father, different mother.

The Bible doesn't say Cain and Abel were the only two kids on Earth at the time we hear their story. I throw that in for free just in case you wonder where Cain got his wife. They weren't little boys either. Abel had flocks and Cain tilled the ground. They had their own choice of occupation and they'd been at it for a while. At a specified time, they brought God their offerings. Abel's was accepted; Cain's was not. Why do you think that was? Did Cain bring lousy cabbage and bitter Brussel sprouts? Nope. Remember the type (the imprint representing the real thing)? The covering (atonement) for sin was the shedding of innocent blood. Cain brought the fruit of his labors, the work of his own hands. God corrected him, but Cain refused to change. He wanted God to accept what he chose to give, not what God had instructed them to offer. Cain was trying to force God to accept his offering, and when God warned him again, Cain was so angry he killed his brother.

So now you have Big Mistake #3—normalize your will in preference to God's, and Big Mistake #4—kill off your competition. Notice the theme of insisting on your own way and offering the works of your hands, insulted when God doesn't graciously and gratefully receive what you deem to be most appropriately pleasing to Him. See? Cain totally missed the point. It wasn't about giving to God something that was costly to you, it was about not being able to produce by your own efforts anything that would deal with the core problem. The payment for sin is death. In order to pay for your sin, somebody has to die, somebody innocent of wrongdoing, somebody with blood. Turnips don't qualify. Starting with the tunics of skins back in the Garden, death was the price, and an animal's blood was the covering that temporarily atoned for their sin and provided the picture of what would be the real sacrifice by the Lamb of God, Jesus of Nazareth.

My guess is that Adam had instructed all of his children in the right and acceptable way to worship God, how to build an altar, what to offer on it, what animals were clean and which were not suitable, and the specified element of fat. I have no idea what fat represents, though I'm sure there are commentaries about it. The thing it most signals to me is the detail, repeated in Leviticus and other scriptures, that says it was a codified offering, not just a dead animal thrown up on a pile of sticks and burned like bad barbecue. Cain was without excuse, yet when God told him the consequences of the murder, Cain wailed, "My punishment is more than I can bear!" The word "punishment" is actually "iniquity," and it means "warping" or "twisting." The word in Hebrew contains both the wrong doing and the punishment. I wonder if it's because iniquity is so horrific that its consequences carry their own curses and punishments.

Arar is the word in Hebrew for "curse." According to Zodhiates, *arar* means "to bind as with a spell," "to hem in with obstacles," "to render helpless." God pronounced these curses on Cain: The ground would no longer yield its strength to him, he would be a vagabond never finding a place he belonged, and worst, he was alienated from God.

Here's a bit of explanation to help clarify the differences in sin, rebellion, and iniquity. Sin is missing the mark. A woman chooses to have an abortion, believing society that says it's a good alternative to unwanted pregnancy. Rebellion is when a woman knows it's wrong, but chooses to do it anyway. Iniquity is when the woman says, "It's not a baby. Go ahead and kill it." This is particularly evidenced in late-term abortion. Hard to convince yourself it's not a human being when it sure looks like a baby. If you can talk yourself out of believing that's a life, something is wrong within your heart, and there will be consequences manifesting in your life in a multitude of ways that will bring more anguish than you can imagine.

Cain was making his own standard righteous and he pronounced God's ways unfair. Do we hear accusations that God's ways are unjust? Is there murderous anger because God refuses to accept our standard of righteousness instead of His own? It's iniquity—a twisting, a warping, a normalizing of our own standard and it twists people away from God, land, community, and even themselves.

Some people have treated The Mark of Cain as a permanent curse on his family line. Is it? According to Scripture, it's God's gift of protection. God doesn't hate anyone—-no individual, no people group. There are no hated races. Jesus always intended to pay for everyone's sins, rebellions, and iniquities, with the last category of disconnection with God being the worst. It's the normalizing of your way, saying this is right and God's laws in this area are inconsequential. It's the most serious of the types of transgressions. Yet, there's this amazing line in Psalm 103, composed by David long before the Lamb of God went silently to the slaughter: "Bless (affectionately, gratefully praise) the Lord, O my soul, and forget not [one of] all His benefits—Who forgives [every one of] all your iniquities, Who heals [each one of] all your diseases, Who redeems your life from the pit and corruption, Who beautifies, dignifies, and crowns you with loving-kindness and tender mercy; Who satisfies your mouth [your necessity and desire at your personal age and situation] with good so that your youth, renewed, is like the eagle's [strong, overcoming, soaring]!" (Ps 103:1 AMPC)

Skip ahead now to Genesis 4, where things are getting worse and worse. We're two chapters from the destruction of all living through the Flood. It says, "In those days men began to call on the name of the LORD." If the inhabitants of Earth were deteriorating fast, wouldn't it be a good thing that they started calling on the name of the LORD?

Turns out there are two ways "call on the name of the LORD" can be translated. One is they started calling Him by His proper name. The other is they started calling Him by other names, or the right name, but in a wrong manner. So you could translate this, "In those days men began to blaspheme (or defile, or disable or misappropriate) the name of the LORD."

God had given them His name and human beings were disregarding God's value, character, power, essence. Sound familiar? It's not a new thing. It's a repeating pattern. Interesting that Jesus says of the End Times, "As it was in the days of

Noah, so it will be at the coming of the Son of Man (Matt 24:37)

Yet, God is still found pursuing relationship with His children. How do I know that? Genesis is full of conversations between people and God. Even during some of the most wicked and depraved times when people were sinking into their own depravity in increasingly heinous ways, Enoch walked with God for three hundred sixty years. Do you think Enoch was off living under a tree somewhere communing with God? Scripture says He was talking to people about God and their need to turn from their wicked ways back to Him. That was also near to the time Noah was going to be told to build the ark. God instructed Noah, so obviously He was still talking to human beings. He told him how many years it would be till the flood. He told him it would be seven days before the waters began. He told him how to prepare, what dimensions, what kind of wood, the exact plan for a most sea-worthy vessel, and which humans to take. Noah obeyed in spite of ridicule for one hundred twenty years from those to whom he preached to no avail. God was still giving people a chance to change their minds.

Through the centuries, the knowledge of God's requirements for worship were passed to subsequent generations. God told Noah to take pairs of animals—two by two—but also seven (pairs) of every clean animal. How would Noah know what was clean and what was unclean? and what did he do when the ark came to rest and they went out on dry ground? He offered a sacrifice to God. Noah didn't make up a ritual hoping God would be appeased. He knew what God wanted, and he gratefully offered it in the day of new beginnings. After Noah offered the sacrifice to God on the strange new face of Earth, God gave a rainbow as a sign of His promise never to destroy Earth by water again. Notice He didn't promise not to destroy it again, just that it won't be by water.

By the way, just to address the cave man idea that we get in school, the original humans were made in the image of God. No Neanderthals with smaller pre-frontal cortexes. Adam was made in the image of God. He was given the honor of naming all the animals. He was entrusted with dominion over the whole earth. He had an unsullied mind. Creativity, insight, ingenuity, and brilliant thinking were normal for him, and Eve was no slouch either. They must have had really smart kids. Genesis goes on to enumerate various offspring populating Earth and what they did. One group was known for their musical instruments and another for their artistry in precious metals.

Why does this matter? I'm realizing how much I've accepted all my life concepts that aren't accurate if I really consider what the Bible says. That includes various versions of the story of Adam and Eve and their expulsion from the garden. People think God had a fit and threw them out in a rage, like a father disgusted with his children for sneaking out at night. Really? Then why did He cover them with tunics first thing? He covered their nakedness, their exposure, their shame. He promised (in the symbolism) redemption and a way to stay in contact even all the eons before Jesus did the actual deed. Some people think He was so mad at His children that He quit communicating. Some people still think He's mad at them. It's not true. That's never been His heart. We're not even half-way through the first book of the Bible, yet this repeating theme shows us God did not abandon us—then or now.

From Noah's three sons, all the people of the post-Flood world came. For this mapping of history, I'll just follow Ham's line. I want you to see the patterns again. Ham had a number of rotten offspring, one being Canaan (from whom the Canaanites came) and one named Nimrod, whom Genesis identifies as a mighty hunter before God. A better translation is "Nimrod put himself before God." In other words, he set himself in competition with God. This is expressed more fully in Nimrod's legacy. He founded Nineveh, a wicked city, Babylon, a very wicked city that has a big role in the final drama of Revelation, and Babel, in which a gang of intellectual types decided to build a tower that would make a name for themselves. Many think it was to be used to observe the movements of stars and heavenly bodies in an attempt to know the future. It was forbidden knowledge they were after, and God scrambled their languages and scattered them to put a stop to their grasping for power. Sound familiar?

It is likely that all occult knowledge originated in Babylon, and the original Plan of Redemption that was set in the stars was corrupted into our present Babylonian astrology with its openings into further occult practices.

While all this was going on, God was still going forward in His Plan of Redemption. He called one man, Abram, told him to leave everything he knew and go to a land He would show him, and Abram did that. The plan was to create a people who were unique among all others on Earth, a people who would receive revelation from God and become the means through which His redemption would be made available to all human beings. They would demonstrate the wisdom of His ways, living by His Laws and sustained and protected by His supernatural interventions. Through them others would see His mighty power and know that there is only one true God—Yahweh, the God of the children of Israel.

Interestingly, when the Hebrews were about to invade the Promised Land, Scripture says the inhabitants therein were remembering about the Red Sea and still so shaken that their hearts were melted, even though it happened years before. Yahweh had certainly shown Himself mighty on behalf of His people. It impressed Rahab enough that she risked her life to hide the two spies. Through her and the scarlet cord in her window, her whole family was saved, and she became a follower of Yahweh and the mother of Boaz, who married Ruth, from another wicked race, the Moabites. They had Obed, Obed had Jesse, and Jesse had David, who became King of Israel. To me, Yahweh wasn't showing off to scare all the people in corrupt cultures to death, He was giving them a chance, as He did in Egypt, to choose Him over the useless idols they worshiped. Some did, as we see all through Scripture, and these two ladies became honored mothers in Messiah's bloodline. But back to Abram.

This commitment of God to His people was so crucial that God "cut a covenant" with Abram. It was an ancient ritual—splitting animals in two and then both parties passing between the pieces, their feet and robes stained with fresh blood. It was a very serious kind of covenant, not to be taken lightly. But this covenant would be so important that God Himself passed between the pieces while Abram slept in a heavy, supernatural sleep. In the dark a smoking furnace and a burning torch passed through the pieces. The Bible is an integrated message, and even though there are sixty-six books and hundreds of years between them, the types, images, and figures of speech are consistent. When you see torch and furnace, ask yourself where you've seen those before. Maybe atop Mount Sinai? God descending like a smoking furnace melting granite to black metamorphic rock. And the torch? Jesus is the Life and the Life is the Light of men. (John 11) Thus, the covenant was confirmed by God Himself, an unconditional agreement that cannot fail. This is before circumcision, a covenant cut in the flesh. It's before Abram's name change. At this point, Abram has done nothing to deserve any of the promises God is making to him except he left everything to follow God, and it turns out that quite a few times he didn't do that very well. But it doesn't depend on Abram—or us. When God cut that covenant it was all on Him to fulfill. I can't emphasize that enough. If you don't understand this unconditional covenant and the seriousness of God's commitment to His Word, you won't understand the rest of the Bible—or the rest of Time.

Though Sarai was getting up there in years, God intended her to be the mother of the child He promised would be Abram's heir. You probably know about the side route the couple took in order to help God fulfill His promise. I think it's significant that God didn't throw Hagar or Ishmael away. He intervened supernaturally to preserve their lives, and Hagar had a personal encounter with Him, and has the honor recorded in the Bible of giving Him a name in gratitude for His kindness. God doesn't throw anyone away.

Of course, the Type that stands out to us most is the one that happens on the top of a hill where Abraham is told to sacrifice Isaac. Again, children's Bible stories not withstanding, Isaac was not a little boy. He was around thirty, and could easily have overpowered his aged father. But he agreed. He lay himself on the altar. Human sacrifice was a common practice in those ancient days, and child sacrifice was considered especially pleasing to the gods. So it wasn't as shocking to Abraham as it would be to you or me, but it would be painful to Abraham nonetheless, even though he believed God would resurrect Isaac or do something else miraculous in order to fulfill through him the promise He spoke to Abraham. It was a type. God Himself provided the innocent—a ram caught in a thicket by its horns. There on Mount Moriah, Abraham spoke the first compound name of God recorded in the Bible—YHWH-Yireh (or with vowels added for pronunciation "Yahweh-Yireh" or "Jehovah-Jireh"). On the mountain of God it will be provided. As promised, it was.

Isaac had two sons, Jacob and Esau. God Himself told their mother Rebekah that the younger would prevail over his brother, but she still took matters into her own hands to help God out. Jacob had doubts and fears, but his mom said she'd take the responsibility on herself and so Isaac, his eyes dim with age, gave the entire spiritual blessing to his younger son, who smelled and felt like his older, hunter son, since Jacob, at Rebekah's urging, was wearing Esau's clothes and had covered his arms and neck with hairy goat skins. Esau came in right after Jacob left, only to find his father had nothing left with which to bless him. Esau was understandably furious, but he seemed to have forgotten the birthright was no longer his. He had sold it to Jacob for a bowl of red lentil stew. Genesis says, "he despised his birthright." In this story, you can see that nobody did the right thing. Everybody took matters into their own hands to make things come out the way they wanted, and it got worse after that.

During his flight, Jacob wrestled with an angel all night, saying he wouldn't let go without a blessing. The angel shortened the sinew in Jacob's hip to give him a permanent reminder of the night, and also changed his name from "Heel-grabber" or "supplanter" to Israel—"Prince with God." After that, Jacob went off to find a bride, fell in love with Rachel, but her father switched sisters on him on their wedding night and he ended up with Leah, her older sister. Thus began the offspring wars with both wives supplying themselves and their maid servants to try to get more kids to establish their position of favor with their husband. It's really quite ugly. The Chinese word for "trouble" is "two women under one roof." Here you have four women, and twelve sons and a daughter all under one roof. And the favoritism that started with Isaac over Ishmael, was exacerbated with Rebekah favoring Jacob while Isaac favored Esau. It was even worse after that, Jacob lavishing gifts on Joseph, the son of the wife he loved most, which led to the jealous brothers throwing Joseph down a well, then selling him to a caravan of Ishmaelites (yes, nomads descended from Hagar's son), that led to Joseph's getting thrown into prison and then taken out to interpret Pharaoh's dream. So now Joseph was second in command in the most powerful kingdom of the known world. Seven years of plenty passed as God had shown Pharaoh they would. Joseph oversaw the storage of grain. Then seven years of famine as per Pharaoh's dream. Back home, Jacob and his sons were starving, so they sent all the brothers except the youngest to Egypt to buy grain. In the short version for this overview, I'll just say Joseph was reconciled to his brothers and Pharaoh invited the brothers, their families, and their dad to come live in Goshen the best land in Egypt. That's how the children of Israel came to be in Egypt. There were seventy people when they arrived, and they quickly multiplied and prospered for the next thirty years till Joseph died and Pharaoh died and a replacement Pharaoh who did not know Joseph and who was nervous about all the Israelites came along and somehow got the Israelites to change their understanding of themselves from honored guests to worthless slaves.

God called Moses through a burning bush and gave him the charge of going to Pharaoh and getting the Israelites set free. When Moses asked His name, God told him, "YHWH, I AM." Hebrew mostly doesn't use vowels, so scholars put some in to enable us to pronounce the words. Thus you get "Jehovah" or "Yahweh" for the I AM name of God. YHWH is a verb, not a noun. God is always working whether we see it or not.

A Brief Word from Our Sponsor

Let's pause a moment here at Exodus. There's such amazing stuff in it. We all know about the plagues, "Let My people go!" We know about the Red Sea and cheer when God takes off the chariot wheels of the pursuing army. In other words, we all know the plot. And that has merit. It's important that we see God's deliverance when we feel hemmed in with impassable mountains on one side, the Red Sea before us, and Pharaoh's army bearing down with charging horses and flashing chariots. But there's something about reading the words. It's then that God can speak to us directly, pointing out things we hadn't noticed before. I always feel as if Someone has been typing in my Bible because there are so many things I don't remember seeing.

Here are a couple of things I noticed in my recent readings.

1. Aaron came to meet Moses. Yes, okay. We know that. But here's the part I didn't remember. God told Aaron to meet Moses in the mountain of God. What mountain? Aaron hadn't seen Moses in forty years. He had no idea where his brother was. Maybe he guessed Moses had fled to the land of Midian, since he was trying to get out of Egypt, but it's a big place and Moses was one small person whose intent was to hide.

Exodus 4:27 says, "The Lord said to Aaron, Go into the wilderness to meet Moses. And he went, and met him in the mountain of God [Horeb, or Sinai] and kissed him." (AMPC)

So there's Aaron, a slave, the son of slaves, 400 years' worth of generations who have not known anything else. But God spoke to him and he didn't freak out or think it was a ghost or a demon or anything hostile or creepy. He knew it was God and obeyed. How did he know where to go? It was three day's journey with no GPS and yet he found the mountain of God and Moses upon it. By the way, Mount Sinai is not a small mountain. Those who have been on it have said it's the tallest peak in the mountain range. But back then, before God descended on its top and melted it black, it looked like all the others, just a little taller.

Anyway, Aaron found Moses and God talked to both of them. It's interesting to me that Scripture does not record whether Aaron found this alarming. Also, when they got back to Egypt, the people had apparently not forgotten about their ancestors or the promises God made to them because they were not surprised when they heard what the God of Abraham, Isaac, and Jacob had sent them to say. They didn't look blankly and say, "Who?"

Another thing. I had always heard God was silent for 400 years while His people were suffering under cruel taskmasters. Really? It never says God turned His back on them. Somehow the Hebrews managed to maintain crucial aspects of their identity even before they became the nation with God's laws and tabernacle and the rest. How do I know? When they left Egypt, they went out by tribe. Two million people leaving in an orderly fashion, no confusion among them as to where each one belonged. That was possible because they kept meticulous genealogies. You can see that many times through the Tanach, and again in the genealogies of Jesus. They remembered their ancestry all the way back to Adam and Eve. And they knew, through Abraham, they had a covenant with God. They were also circumcised in Egypt. Moses was.

Another thing, while we're at it. I heard they were beaten down with no identity except that of worthless slaves. I actually bought that, until God told me this morning to rethink it in the light of the Scriptures. When they left, they went out boldly. If you've been beaten (and all your ancestors too), no sense of identity or destiny for centuries, you probably wouldn't be able to manage "boldly" with any authenticity. But they did. And they carried with them Joseph's bones. He'd requested in faith that the promises God gave them would be fulfilled. Somehow they knew where he was and took him with them.

Also they weren't sickly and skinny—weak from starvation. Pharaoh had given them the best land in Egypt and they knew how to grow crops and nurture flocks and herds. You may remember they complained to Moses in the wilderness that they would have been better off staying in Egypt eating leeks and onions and sitting by the "fleshpots." When they were given instructions for Passover, nobody asked how to slay a lamb and roast it. They knew how to make bread. One of the dishes for the Passover meal was a combination of apples and raisins. They had herbs. They had hyssop. They were in good health because God made sure they'd be fit for the journey. They also knew how to dance and sing and they had musical instruments and it says Miriam was a prophetess, so they did have prophets; we just don't have record of anything they might have said to the people. I guess God thought we didn't need to know.

Anyway, after they crossed the Red Sea, Moses sang (and all the people with him) and then Miriam sang and played the timbrel. Scripture says the other women played timbrels too. So much for the portrayal of the Hebrews as a nation of bedraggled, hangdog, groveling skinny slaves. God kept them distinct even in slavery, and they knew who they were.

Then there was the time at Mount Sinai—nearly two years—and the wandering in the wilderness, all with the presence of God in a pillar of cloud by day and a pillar of fire by night. They saw God descend on the mountain like a furnace, and appear at the door of the Tent of Meeting to talk directly to Moses. They didn't choose to talk to Him directly, but they were quite accustomed to His visible and audible presence. And there were a lot of words too. Communication with God was normal, usual, expected. It was woven into their history and their very beings. Even when they later became terrible idolators in direct rebellion in spite of multitudinous quite clear warnings and wooings from God through a whole bunch of prophets through many decades, He didn't stop trying to communicate with them.

The other thing that struck me this time I read Exodus is what God said as the plagues were getting more intense. The reason this stood out to me is because God is going to do a lot of very intense things in the days that lead to the end of all things. Hebrew prophecies are in patterns. God is always communicating. In the past, I've read the plagues as a way God showed everyone that He is bigger and mightier than the Egyptian gods (each plague demonstrating His superiority over one of their gods). That's the obvious purpose. But now that I understand His heart, that He is not willing that any should perish, I read these words differently: The "they shall know that I AM" is about revealing to them the insufficiency of what they've trusted in, and who is really the One they can rely on. Proof of this is Plague Number Seven, the devastating storm of fire and ice. The Egyptians heard the warning, "Get your servants and herds to safety." The storm did not affect the land of Goshen; it pounded only the fields of Egypt. Those who had learned from the previous six plagues took heed and got people and animals to safety. Those who didn't left them out in the open, and all of them died. See? It wasn't the Israelites who were warned; it was the Egyptians. And some scholars said when Moses and the Israelites left Egypt, some Egyptians went with them. They were convinced Yahweh was the true and only God, and wanted to belong to Him. It's the heart of God. He's not a bully pulling Alpha moves on powerful kings; He's the Alpha (and Omega) Who sent His Son to pay for their sins and give them a chance to be accepted into His Family.

A quick word about heart-hardening. Some people get upset because God says He will harden Pharaoh's heart, as if He's setting him up to knock him down, a celestial bully. In the first plagues, Scripture says Pharaoh hardened his own heart. If you put a cube of butter and a lump of wet clay in the sun, one will soften and one will harden. The hotter the sun, the faster and more obvious the nature of the substance. In the later plagues, God turned up the heat, and the obdurate heart of Pharaoh became harder than even he knew it could be.

In Exodus 9:16, Yahweh says to Pharaoh, "But indeed for this purpose I have raised you up, that I may show My power in you, and that My name may be declared in all the earth." His name. His character. He wasn't trying to kill everyone; He was trying to wake them up. It will be the same in the Day of the Lord. He wants to show them what they trust in will not hold up. It can be devoured, bring sickness, be destroyed in hours. This exposing of insufficiency is intended to lead to a change of heart. "God is not slack concerning His promise, but that all would come to repentance"—turn around and follow Him, in Whom there is Life in all its fullness, goodness and fulfillment.

For a brief moment, Pharaoh saw the light. "Then Pharaoh called for Moses and Aaron in haste, and said, 'I have sinned against the LORD your God and against you. Now therefore, please forgive my sin only this once, and entreat the LORD your God, that He may take away from me this death only.' So he went out from Pharaoh and entreated the LORD. And the LORD turned a very strong west wind, which took the locusts away and blew them into the Red Sea. There remained not one locust in all the territory of Egypt." (Exodus 10:16)

I think it's significant that, each time God got rid of something, there wasn't one left—from lice and flies to frogs and locusts, not one remained. This is supernatural. As is a darkness for three days so thick it can be felt. But in Goshen, there was natural light in the houses. It wasn't lamps they were lighting. God was making a distinction, lights that could be seen like a city on a hill. It's one of those repeating images of God making a distinction between His people and all others, not to show their superiority, but to beckon them to come in. That was the original Plan for the children of Israel. Through them, Messiah would come. Through Him, the whole world could be saved—if they chose to be.

At Mount Sinai, God gave His people additional promises, some conditional, some not, and something no other peoples had: His Law—His ways, His instructions on how to live best, and His presence. They wandered, their slave-mentalities being replaced in the wilderness by dependence and trust in God. As we know, they didn't do it perfectly. Like us, they floundered, forgot, complained. Nonetheless, God guided them and remained with them, as He does with us. As He revealed to Moses, long-suffering is one of His attributes.

However, there was one incident that could not be tolerated. It was more shocking than the one with the golden calf. It was in the wilderness of Zin. Once again, after so many miracles of provision, the children of israel once more raised their complaints asking again why Moses brought them out there to die of hunger and thirst. When Moses asked God what to do, for indeed there was no water anywhere, God told him to take his rod and speak to the rock. But Moses, frustrated and furious with the people, struck the rock twice. After all his faithfulness under incredibly difficult circumstances, that one act caused him to be kept out of the promised land.

This has troubled me for years. What if I live faithful and obedient all my life, experiencing God repeatedly in supernatural ways, only to have a lapse of temper under extreme circumstances? Would I lose the final fulfillment of my destiny on Earth? I don't mean I fear losing my salvation, because it's not dependent on me, but it made me nervous. I read commentaries that said Moses made the people think God was mad at them. I read that he was acting in the flesh, not obeying or honoring God's holiness. But they all agree it spoiled the typology of Jesus, the Rock of our Salvation, who was struck just once.

Okay. I get that, but I felt unsatisfied. There was more to it than that I could feel it. And now I can ask Papa like a little child, no longer in the demeanor of a soldier in the army who does not question orders or the decisions of the Superior. So today I asked. The answer surprised me. I'll give you the short version.

When Moses struck the rock near Mount Sinai, it split from its 40-foot high crown to the bottom. It had to be struck to be the symbol of what Christ would go through for us. But when the people thirsted again, God said to speak to the rock. What He showed me today is we now need only ask, and living water will pour out in our times of thirst and need. The extreme price was paid. We have gentle access through Him, our Rock, for whatever we require for life.

But wait. There's more. I asked God if Jesus had already risen, all sins forgiven, when this happened, and Moses asked for forgiveness, would he have been allowed into the promised land? It's a theoretical question, of course, because time would have been twisted along with our brains to even ask the question, but it applies, you see, to me in this present day. If I, who love and serve my God with all my heart, do something that so egregiously violates the representation of Christ to the people, can I be forgiven? Can you guess the answer? It's yes. Which is a good thing, considering that I violate the image of Jesus, my Savior, all the time, misrepresenting Him, making people think God is mad at them by my tone and frustration, misusing the authority He has given me by dropping into the flesh instead of walking by the Spirit. Oh, how I love Jesus! What a relief to know His resurrection proves that every sin for every human being ever created has been paid for, and the payment in full has been accepted completely. It is finished. It is over. None of my lapses cannot be forgiven. I need only ask.

Now back to our overview. After the death of Moses, the Israelites, led by Joshua, went into the promised land and settled there. They still had many struggles with the attractions of the world and the idols and enticements it offered. Kingdoms rose and fell and the chosen people, under judges and kings and warned by prophets, obeyed and disobeyed, and gave themselves over to blatant idolatry which led to the splitting of the Jews into the Northern Kingdom (Israel) and the Southern Kingdom (Judah). The Northern Kingdom was so idolatrous that all the Jews who wanted to keep worshiping the right God the right way left for Judah. Thus, all the tribes were preserved in the Southern Kingdom. There are no lost tribes. Why is this important? Because Revelation says there will be 144,000 amazing Jewish men evangelizing with power during the Great Tribulation—12,000 from each tribe. All tribes are represented.

The Northern Kingdom became so blatantly idolatrous that God used the Assyrians to bring judgment, conquering and scattering them. Meanwhile, the Southern Kingdom made it another two hundred years before their idolatry finally required divine judgment through conquest by the Babylonians and captivity for seventy years. Then, right on schedule, the Jews were allowed to return to their land, but they never returned to their idolatry, though they had other problems, including Rome.

After Alexander the Great conquered the entire known world and made Greek the universal language and then Rome built vast networks of good roads and a new Temple in Jerusalem, when everything was in place for God's miraculous intervention in the history of all things, in the fullness of time, the Word became flesh and walked among them, not only to show us the Father and give a course-correction for what had been adapted and corrupted since Mount Sinai, but to live without ever missing the mark of God's best for a human being though He was harassed by Satan himself and even His own family all His life. Then Jesus paid the ultimate price—in full—rose from the dead, ascended with a promise to return, and sat down at the right hand of the Throne of God. After that, eyewitness accounts were written (the Gospels) letters (also called "Epistles") provided instruction on the Christian life, and prophecies of the future established the foundations of the group that would be called the Church, the Body of Christ, and, most astonishing of all, His Bride.

Then comes the Book of Revelation. To me it had been a horror—unimaginable suffering and anguish from the outpouring of God's wrath upon those who refuse to love Him. But Chuck Missler's careful turn-by-turn guidance through that book convinced me the Book of Revelation is not about punishment and spectacular devastations like the finale of a movie where all the bad guys get theirs in fireballs, 50-pound hailstones, bizarre and deadly poisonous creatures, etc. In his extensive examination of the text, referencing the whole of the Bible with insights and correlations with ancient cultures, the decoding of symbols, the understanding of interweaving prophecies and covenants with the Jews, and the ways all evil will be eradicated once and for all, I now understand the wisdom of God's Plan of Redemption—not only for human beings, but for everything He created In the Beginning.

If you've been nervous about Revelation, it might make you feel better to learn what Chuck Missler says about those scary pages. He says the only connection that book has with Christians is the first three chapters. After that, all references to Jesus are in Hebrew terms. He is called by Hebrew titles, such as Lamb of God and Root of David. The rest of the book shows what is going to take place and why. And all of it has to do with the redemption and transformation of the chosen people and God keeping His promises to them. Someone said more people will be saved during the Great Tribulation than all the time before. I guess so—144,000 Jews finally connected to their long-awaited Messiah. They'd be pretty excited. It made me feel better about all the hard things that are going to be coming down. Sometimes it takes a lot of shaking to show the realities of the spiritual realm, what we're actually dealing with, and Who is God and who is not. Ezekiel talks about this a lot in the last chapters of his prophecies. In Ez 30, God is executing judgment on all the kingdoms that have tortured His people and each part ends with God saying, "Thus will

I execute judgments in (insert name of kingdom), and they shall know that I am the LORD." It gives even the most hard-hearted a clear choice. Who will they have on their throne?

After the Lamb that was Slain takes the title deed from the hand of the One seated on the Throne in heaven, He begins to open the seals. That starts the horrors—seals, bowls, trumpets—until autonomy and self-sufficiency are exposed as totally inadequate to provide security or satisfaction. All who are alive on Earth have a clear choice. Supernatural things are happening in alarming manifestations of both evil and good. The true nature of the battle is revealed. Some of God's people realize their idolatry, their adultery with the world and its values, and recognize, with a shock, the One they pierced. They cry out to Messiah, He comes back, rescues them and sets up His rule on earth for a thousand years. At the end, Satan is released from where he's been chained, and all who still want to be their own god join with him for one last battle against God, which doesn't last long. New heaven and Earth, all has been completely redeemed, all promises fulfilled, all evil destroyed. The End. The *telos*—the intended End. It's kind of a sandwich with the Jews on both ends and the church in the middle. The Church did not replace the Jews. If you've been taught Replacement Theology, you might want to take up the matter before God and His Word. Quite a lot of the Bible won't make sense if you have to work things to match that theology. But don't take my word for it. Here are just a few statements God has made:

"For thus says the LORD: David shall never fail [to have] a man [descendant] to sit on the throne of the house of Israel, ...And the word of the Lord came to Jeremiah, saying,Thus says the Lord: If you can break My covenant with the day, and My covenant with the night, so that there should not be day and night in their season,Then can also My covenant be broken with David My servant, so that he shall not have a son to reign upon his throne..." (Jeremiah 33:17-21)

And here is more: "For thus says the Lord—Who created the heavens, God Himself, Who formed the earth and made it, Who established it and did not create it to be a worthless waste; He formed it to be inhabited—I am the Lord, and there is no one else. I have not spoken in secret, in a corner of the land of darkness; I did not call the descendants of Jacob [to a fruitless service], saying, Seek Me for nothing [but I promised them a just reward]. I, the Lord, speak righteousness (the truth—trustworthy, straightforward correspondence between deeds and words); I declare things that are right." (Isaiah 45:18, 19 AMP)

And let's not forget the many times in the New Testament there are references to Jesus' second coming and his ruling during the thousand years. One of the first and most memorable of these promises is made to Mary (Luke 1:32) when Gabriel tells her "He shall be great, and shall be called the Son of the Highest: and the Lord God shall give unto him the throne of his father David: And he shall reign over the house of Jacob for ever; and of his kingdom there shall be no end."

God keeps His promises, especially when they're unconditional. He does not change His mind when He's already given His Word in an oath. Why does this matter? Let me tell you a story.

I know a man who had a daughter. In his eyes, she was a bright and beautiful star. All his attention went to her. Years passed, his daughter always favored, treasured, nurtured—the center of all his hopes. Through her he would establish his rich, enduring legacy. To guarantee this future, he made promises of provision and abundance always. But his daughter began to go her own way, and at last she disappointed him so many times that he became angry with her—angry enough to find another, one who would obey him and faithfully do his will thoroughly, completely, and without question. She pleased the man so much that he adopted her, totally abandoning the former favored one. He lavished his new daughter with attention, devotion, and honor. He granted her great privilege and approval, with promises of provision and abundance always. As he neared death, because of his close relationship with his adopted daughter, he made her officially his heir—the only one—and left nothing to his original daughter. All promises formerly made to her were nullified. He felt justified in this because she hadn't measured up to his requirements and desires. Furthermore, the gifting of all of his estate to his adopted daughter would leave a lasting message of rebuke and reproach that the rejected one would never forget.

How do you feel about that man? It's a true story. Do you think Yahweh is like that? God keeps His promises. He delights in it. He is faithful. He is loyal. When He says something, He means it. He is not arbitrary, unreliable, or capricious. And because He is faithful to keep His promises to Israel—all the way to their glorious destiny with Messiah Jesus—we can be sure He will be as faithful to us, though we, too, often fail, stumble, take matters into our own hands, get distracted, distrust, complain, and wander around.

21

Contradictions, Confusions

Maps

I remember the old accordion-fold maps, spreading one out across my lap and trying to get myself oriented. Where are we now, and where do we want to go from here? My dad was driving us in his converted van, Beluga, across the country from Los Angeles to Cape Cod. My father had given me a map, the blind person trying to read the tiny names and numbers on the vast expanse of paper, then shouting directions to the deaf man. I think I had nightmares for months afterwards.

We were following directions to visit relatives and friends in New York and New Jersey. The overhead signs were maddeningly inconclusive and traffic was fast in those skinny little lanes. We would have been hopelessly lost were it not for directions over the phone from my cousins, who knew exactly which roads to take. It really helps to have some idea of how to go, described by someone who knows the way.

After more than four decades of reading the Bible, I think I have a fair idea of how to find my way around it. I'm hoping this chapter will help you do the same. Below are some examples of how to find treasures on your way through the Bible in areas that might not be familiar to you. You may find some parts daunting or dry or mystifying. Specifically, Leviticus. Some people skip that part because they think it doesn't apply to us modern folks. Why do we need to know the significance of the color of the hair in a particular kind of bump on the body? There are all manner of treasures in Leviticus, and 2 Timothy says every bit of this God-breathed book is for our instruction, so let me give you some thoughts on this strange, detailed, ancient book.

I look at Leviticus as an astonishing revelation of insights into things the Israelites couldn't know. They were in Egypt 430 years, thirty as honored peoples, the rest as slaves. As Pharaoh's workforce they knew how to construct large building projects (handy when it came time for them to build an altar for God at the foot of Mount Sinai—not so good when they made the one for the golden calf. But that, and suffering, and having a slave mentality meant they needed a major reset. Leviticus does that. One example is the ox in the ditch. There are other animals named, but I mention the ox because it's a big animal so pulling it out would be inconvenient, to say the least. One of the Ten Commandments tells us to honor the Sabbath and do no work on it, but in Leviticus, God says if you see you're neighbor's ox in the ditch, pull it out. Even if it's on the Sabbath. Even if it's your enemy's. Don't just leave it there. To me, this separates the Judeo/Christian faiths from all other religions. I don't know much about Islam, so I'll talk about what I do know. Hinduism and Buddhism tell you to leave things alone. If your neighbor's ox dies because of neglect or whatever, his loss causes him to suffer, which helps with working off his bad karma. If it's your enemy's ox, so much the better. He deserves it and then some! But Yahweh says to pull it out. It's a compassionate way of moving through life, and it isn't something that comes naturally, especially to slaves.

What about those lumps and bumps on the skin and what color they are? Who cares if the hair sticking out of them is yellow or white? If you were a leper, I bet you'd care! And how long do you think it would take for a normal human being to figure out what that color and configuration means? And what should be done about it? And when it would be no longer contagious so it would be safe to rejoin the community?

God gave them a plethora of detailed medical information (see Leviticus 13 for a crash course in diagnosing leprosy) and designated a group of people to be trained in such things. God turned former slaves into priests who have, as part of their calling, understanding in healing. Overtones of us as priests of the Most High, called to bring healing to the wounds of our fellow human beings and help them back into fellowship with the community from which they were estranged.

From the Book of Joshua

Understanding the intent, the message, and the structure of this miraculous Bible gives me confidence that God will speak to me through everything I read. I want you to have that confidence too. This next kind of approach to Bible reading may be easier for you to apply to your daily life. I'm breaking it down into things that struck me. I hope it inspires you in your own discerning of what God wants to say to you as your read His Word. These first examples are from the first chapters of the book of Joshua.

1. The Israelites are heading off towards the Jordan River. Joshua tells them the ark of the covenant will go first and they are to keep it in sight because "you have not passed this way before." Boy! Does that sound like good advice for today? Keep the presence of God in sight because we have not passed this way before.

2. The Israelites have just crossed the Jordon River in flood stage—on dry ground. The Canaanites have heard of it (and the Red Sea and the defeats of two scary, gigantic enemies). They are in abject terror of the Israelites and their hearts are melted within them. Sounds like a great time to attack, doesn't it? Get them while they're weakened by fear. But that's not what God does. Nope. Now that you're over the river barrier and on their land, let's have all the males get circumcised! Let's incapacitate all the fighting men for several days. Why? Because none of the boys were circumcised dur-

ing the wandering in the wilderness. Hey, wait! What happened to the momentum?

Of all the stories in the Bible, this one just grabs me. The world says strike while the iron is hot. Maximize your advantage. Get the job done. But God says renew the covenant. Remember your roots. Consecrate yourself. Remember what all this is about. Keep the Main Thing the main thing.

To me it's about the absolute necessity of being aligned with God before you go into battle. It's all about relationship. It's not about how mighty and scary and superb we are; it's always about being connected to the One to Whom the battle ultimately belongs. "It's not by might nor by power, but by My Spirit says the LORD." When we think it's our might and power we stop being connected to God, dependent, trusting, submitted, inspired, and sustained by Him. We no longer abide in Him, and that leads to all sorts of bad things you can read for yourself in the Book of Judges. This startling series of events before starting the conquest of the Promised Land shows me what matters most to God—and what we need to do first—consecrate yourself. Circumcise your heart. Remember you are in Covenant with the Lord of the universe. It's a great starting place. If God be for you, who can be against you? No weapon formed against you will prosper. In Him, we are more than conquerors.

3. And this is the foundation of all our successes in all circumstances: Joshua 1: 2-9. It's keeping the word of God in your mouth—repeating it to yourself, mulling it over, meditating on it day and night so that it might become part of the fabric of your understanding, the worldview from which you perceive, think, process, and act, that you may know which way to go and what to do and not turn aside or waver or be distracted or deceived. And then your way will be fruitful and then you will have good success in the things that matter most. God commands Joshua, "Be strong and very coura-

geous. Do not be afraid or dismayed," Why? "for the LORD, your God, is with you wherever you go." (Joshua 1:9)

Some Things Are Literal

The Bible has more than 200 kinds of figures of speech in its text, including metaphors (Jesus is a rock), similes (the Kingdom of God is like a mustard seed), types, symbols, synecdoches (where the part stands for the whole and vice versa, such as He sets a table for me in the presence of my enemies) ... People who really want to understand what God is saying will recognize those devices as ways to increase understanding if they're willing to put in the effort to explore them. How is God's Kingdom like a mustard seed? How is Jesus a rock? What does it mean for God to spread a table for us in the midst of our enemies?

What I've found is there's a lot that scholars deem allegory that turn out to be more literal than I would guess from living a normal human life. One is what I saw one day as I paused at a stop sign before turning onto the street that ran past the legalistic church I no longer attended. In that church we were taught to pray that those who left would come to recognize they were deceived by the world, the flesh, or the devil. We'd ask God to send a messenger from Satan against them to torment them and show them their peril and, if that didn't work, that God would take their lives before they lost their salvation. We were basically cursing them. As I paused at the intersection, and knew it was the time of day they would be praying those prayers for me. Right then, I heard "Bless those who curse you." So I did. Immediately I saw my words, like sabers of shining steel, flying out to meet sabers that were coming from the upper story of the church. I blessed, they cursed, and our words met above the middle of the street, clashed, then returned to the ones who had spoken them. I got back blessings. They got back cursings. It was a startling vision of the realities of the invisible realm. The Bible says words are like swords, knives, arrows. Proverbs has a whole bunch of references to body parts—bones, mouths, ears, eyes—and in our practice, Dennis and I found strong and startling connections between violations of God's wisdom and certain crippling conditions in the physical body. It's wise not to assume most of what the Bible says is figurative.

Many things that have been considered symbolic or interpreted according to human reason will be more trouble than they're worth. Sometimes you just need to look at them literally. If that requires less twisting and adjusting, it's probably more accurate. For example, Adam and Eve. I've heard "scholars" say Adam and Eve were symbolic of tribes. They weren't specific individuals. Here's some evidence that Adam was a real person—and this may surprise you. The Chinese word for "happiness" or "blessing" is comprised of four other words: "God;" "one" or "first;" "mouth" or "person;" and "garden." God plus the first person in the garden is a blessing. The garden even has four rivers crossing in its center. Ecclesiastes says God has put eternity in their hearts. It moves me deeply that God made sure my ancestors knew there was One Creator God, Shang Ti, and that the original blessing is to be with Him in the Garden.

Here's another: Luke 3:38, Luke's genealogy of Jesus. It works backwards through all those names, and ends with "Seth was the son of Adam and Adam was the son of God." Whew! Gives me goosebumps! By the way "son of God" is a term that is used only for direct creation. When God made the angels, they were direct creations, so they are called sons of God. When Adam was formed, He was a direct creation. That's why the genealogy in Luke ends with Adam, the son of God. After Adam, the rest of us are called sons of Adam. What's really amazing is what we find in Matt 10:30, "But as many as received him, to them gave he power to become the sons of God, even to them that believe on his name." Really?

God gave us the power to become the sons of God? We can, by believing, trusting, cleaving to, and relying on Him, become direct divine creations—truly new creations in Christ.

Another story in the Bible that has been disputed as myth is the Flood of Noah's day. Naturalists such as Hutton and Lylle believed all of Earth's formations were the result of slow processes of erosion and sedimentation over long periods of time. No catastrophes, please. Hutton and Lylle were only confirming what the prevailing worldview was saying—that Earth was made by natural means, not created by God. Science was making a supreme being unnecessary since we no longer need deity to explain things we don't understand, such as thunder and lightning.

Your children will be exposed to all kinds of statements of "fact" regarding evolution and the assertions of scientific materialism. Here's a quote from a Readers Digest documentary on the Grand Canyon I watched recently. "Although the canyon might appear as though it had been produced by some sudden and cataclysmic occurrence, in *fact*, the events that produced it were simply part of a slow, orderly process of erosion." It's helpful for your children to be aware of this kind of assertion and not become so used to hearing it that it sounds more like truth to them than the evidence to the contrary. The Bible is not myth, fairy tales, or legends. There is verification and scientific evidence for the Flood. If you want to go for a really wild ride, listen to the lectures of astrophysicist Dr. Jason Lisle. His talks on dinosaurs are brain-bending. His biblical verification is exciting. His information on the Flood with the latest scientific research changed the way I saw that event and spurred me to revise one of my books.

Here's a little extra surprise, just for fun. The Chinese word for "boat" is comprised of three other words: "boat" or "ship;" the number eight: and the word "mouth" or "person." Scholars agree that the Chinese language is at least 4000 years old. Noah had three sons. One was Ham. It's from Ham that the Chinese descended. Do you think Ham might have told stories about his time on the ark to his children?

Why does any of this matter? The Bible is a supernatural gift from God. It has what we need to know, especially as things get more and more strange. But some of what we take for granted, criticisms and questions about various parts of the Bible, can undermine our confidence in its veracity and lead to weakness in our faith. The Bible is intended to provide information that will keep you strong because it's rooted in the truth of God. In these days of human reason and the belief in the reality of the material world alone, it helps to have something a bit startling and miraculous to keep us aware this is not all there is. We have a divinely authored book, given from outside time.

Proof of Divine Authorship

In "Beyond Coincidence," Chuck Missler offers two hours of teaching on the science and structure of the Bible that could not be the result of mere recollections written by men. Here's just one of them.

Missler said there are two constants that are dimensionless. One of them is Pi. It's the relationship between the diameter and the circumference of a circle. The other is "e," the base of what we call natural logarithms.

Hebrew has the peculiar characteristic that every letter has a numerical value. So every word has a numerical value. Here is the first sentence in the Old Testament, "In the beginning God created the heaven and the earth." If you take the number of letters in Genesis 1:1, multiply it by the product of the letters, and you do the same thing with the number of the words, divided by the product of the words, you come up with 3.1416, which happens to be the value of Pi, more accurately than you probably used in school.

John Napier discovered logarithms. He also is the guy who promoted the use of decimal points in fractions. He happened to be an activist in the Protestant reformation in Scotland. It's interesting that whether it was Sir Isaac Newton or other great scientists, these brilliant thinkers took the Bible seriously.

"e" is very widely used in mathematics. In Napirion logarithms e appears in exponential functions. It's the only function having a rate of growth equal to its own size.

It's the fundamental function for equations describing growth or many other processes of change. For that reason, you find it in wave mechanics, electrical theory, advanced math, and distribution of prime numbers. It's usually approximated 2.71828

If you take the first line in John 1:1, "In the beginning was the Word and the Word was with God and the Word was God," and take the number of letters times the product of the letters, divided by the number of words times the product of the words, you get e to 4 decimal places.

Missler says, "This is a kind of sign post there is a marriage between the real creation and the message from our Designer."

How does this affect you? I'll tell you what it does for me. It reminds me that everything in the Christian life is supernatural, and the Author of the universe is the Author of the Book is the Author of our salvation. He is Mighty. His weapons are mighty. And one of those weapons is the Word of God—not only the Bible itself, but energized by the One Who was in the beginning before anything, the One who spoke and it was so. He gave us prayer—words we could speak to Him and words we could speak on behalf of others. And through our partnership with Him, there are mighty, supernatural, divine, and eternal possibilities that He wants to bring about through us for such a time as this.

Contradictions and Confusions

The Bible is our supernatural active guidance system. We need it now more than ever. But some are insecure about trusting it to give good insight because they've been told there are too many contradictions. Are there really? Often scholars cite discrepancies in the Gospels. One book says there was one blind man healed. Another says there were two. There are discrepancies among the four accounts, three who claim to be eyewitnesses, and Luke, who says he researched from the largest events to the minutest details. This kind of confusion about accounts can dismantle your confidence in the Gospels. So I'm presenting some thoughts I've assembled from Bible teachers and some I've figured out on my own. I want you to have security when you read the Gospels because it will make a difference when you read your Bible. You can trust what it says about Jesus, His words, His ministry, and what others heard and saw. It's all important. Every detail. It all means something. All of it.

Controversy, Confusion, and Clarification

One of the biggest subjects of controversy is Jesus Himself. Who is He really? How can He be God and Man? Is He half and half like a pie cut down the center that can be separated into two pieces, operating out of one sometimes, and sometimes out of the other? Is He inferior to the Father? Jesus clearly says, "My Father is greater than I." (John 14:28) and yet He also says, "I and the Father are one." (John 10:30).

Let's take care of the "one" issue first. The word in Greek does not mean one person, but one in essence, power, and quality. When Jesus prays in John 17, He asks that His disciples would be one in the same sense that He and the father are one. No one thought He meant the disciples should become one person. Jesus and His Father are One—in essence, power, quality, design, action, agreement. They are not one person but two persons, and yet both of them are God.

The truth that Jesus is God before all time is expressed in numerous Scriptures. My favorite is John 1:1 (In the beginning was the Word and the Word was with God and the Word was God), but you also have Him with flaming eyes in Revelation 1 and throughout that Book where His glory has been restored and John (and we) get to see Him as He really is—-as God in the fullness of His original glory.

But before that, when He was incarnated for our sakes, He had other work to do. The Greek says He continued to be God when He became human and continued to be a man. But He voluntarily emptied Himself of His glory and took on the humanity of a human being so He could be the sacrifice for our sins. As the Athanasian Creed states, Jesus was equal to the Father as touching His Godhead, and inferior to the Father as touching His manhood.

Why is this important? Because our salvation depends on all the elements that had to be in place for the sinless sacrifice to be possible and to be accomplished. If one detail was not fulfilled, we'd all be doomed—forever. It has to do with His being our Kinsman-Redeemer, but more about that later. Technicalities aside, without Jesus on the cross, we would not know that God Himself entered into our suffering because of His overwhelming love for us.

Now back to the identity of Jesus. You'll hear all kinds of things said that demote Him, especially from those who cite His own words where He says His Father is greater than Himself. Plus, He calls Himself the Son of Man. Many claim Jesus never said He was God, that His disciples deified Him. You get the "He was a good man," or "He was a great teacher," remarks, and a lumping Him together with a list of other great teachers including Confucius and Lao Tsu.

A Jewish friend of mine said Jesus' father was a Roman soldier. He said, "You can tell because in all the pictures he has blonde hair and blue eyes." Really? There are photographs of

Jesus? I ignored my friend, because before I was a believer, I, too, didn't care about Jesus anyway, but it's actually something a lot of people still believe—and say.

Just a word about that. If you were Mary and had a fling with a cute Roman soldier, you might be tempted to fabricate a story to explain your pregnancy before marriage (though that would be a pretty wild one to make up), but now your kid is thirty-three years old and they're flogging Him mercilessly in preparation for the worse torture you know will be coming next. Would you stand by and let your beloved son be brutally murdered to cover up your guilt? Same for the disciples. People say they stole the body and made up the story of His resurrection. If you were one of them, would you have spent the rest of your life spreading the lie? For what? It didn't make them rich or famous. It got them beaten, scourged, thrown into prison, stoned, crucified upside-down, beheaded… Why would they go through such trouble and torture to cover up their lies? Why would they died for Him if He wasn't really Messiah? For that matter, why would anyone die for Him? For more than 2,000 years, that's been happening, and it's happening now. This morning Stephanie sent me an email asking for prayer for Christians in Afghanistan who are being beheaded for their faith. It points out how foolish people can be when they want to discredit Jesus, declaring Him just a man. As the Apostle Paul said, if Jesus isn't Who He said He is, we of all men, are most miserable.

Of course, the Good News is Jesus is really Who He says He is—fully God and fully man and it will take all of Eternity for us to understand the fullness of what God did to redeem us back into fellowship with Himself. It seems I can hear God saying to me now, "You have no idea! And you have no idea how much I love you, every one of you.

One more thing I want to clarify. I've thought about this a lot. There are some who believe Jesus always accessed His God-powers while He was on Earth. He could walk on water, calm seas, multiply food, transform water into really good wine, heal the sick, raise the dead, cast out demons, know what people were thinking, and disappear in a crowd. Scripture says He divested Himself of His God-capabilities and entered Earth's arena as a baby who could have been murdered, helpless to care for Himself, dependent on His parents just as we, as human beings, were.

Why does this matter? Because Jesus said we are to do what He did and more. How did He do it? In total dependence upon God, the way we can do it too. You want biblical proof? Here are two.

"But when they deliver you up, do not be anxious about how or what you are to speak; for what you are to say will be given you in that very hour and moment, for it is not you who are speaking, but the Spirit of your Father speaking through you." (Matt 10:19, 20 AMPC)

"But if it is by the Spirit of God that I drive out the demons, then the kingdom of God has come upon you." (Matt 12:28)

In one case, Father God provides the words. In the other, the Holy Spirit is doing the driving out. Jesus had help, enablement, insight, authority, miraculous manifestations by the power of Father God and Holy Spirit God. That's how we do it. Want to try going up against a demon in your own strength? I remember reading about seven hot-shot big brothers going after a demon in the name of Jesus whom Paul preaches. The demon-possessed man said, "I know Paul and I know Jesus, but who are you?" They left beaten and bloody. But James 4:7 says, "Submit yourself to God. Resist the devil and he will flee from you." And Jesus said, "In My name, cast out demons, heal the sick, raise the dead…" See? Jesus didn't use any of His divine power on Earth so He could show us what's possible for human beings to do, including resisting the wiles of the devil and losing our tempers when we're insulted and unfairly accused.

I can't resist telling you a couple of other short things. A few winters ago, the lake was so full it was going over its banks. One day wind was whipping it up so hard it was smashing the docks that jutted out into the lake. Carol's back yard is a few yards from the lake. She could tell the water was getting higher and more destructive so she went out and yelled at the wind and the waves. Just like Jesus. You know what? They stopped! Of course, she told me. A couple of years later when Lake County was surrounded by fires, a powerful wind was driving the flames from a wildland fire down towards where Darda's son Dale lives. I remembered what Carol did and went out and commanded the winds to stop. My friend Elizabeth was reporting on the fire for her newspaper and she told me firefighters had said the fire was right at the pass above Nice. As the flames began to climb up towards the opening, something seemed to drive them back. This happened several times. It should have been easy for fire to rush up the sides of the mountain and into the homes beyond, but it kept being driven back. The firefighters found this so remarkable they told Elizabeth about it. Dale called and said where he lived not a leaf was moving.

Discrepancies in the Gospels

What about the discrepancies in stories? I'll explain it to you from my experience as a writer. In this book I have recounted events from my life to illustrate various points. For example, whenever I went to visit Bea Cull, Stephanie drove me there. She had gone to the Christian school at the legalistic church and was trying to figure out the Truth. We went a lot of places together, and other people drove me too. Drivers to WWW conferences included Nathan, Nancy, Gail, Darda,

Dan, and my dad, but when I wrote about it, it sounds as if I'm there alone. The truth is I rarely went anywhere by myself because, by 1985, I was already 80% blind. But I have chosen not to mention friends, drivers, or other human beings who might have been there with me. Including them wouldn't make it more true; it's unnecessary detail and it would complicate and slow the story down.

Now let's take a look at a couple of the most confusing of these incidents: the Second Coming, and the anointing of Jesus by a woman with spikenard (nard). Let's take the woman first—because it's the one that bugs me most.

In an attempt maybe to help God out, scholars and preachers and teachers and commentators have tried to harmonize the Gospels, assembling together accounts they see as having discrepancies by incorporating the details in a whole. It's like piecing together three testimonies to get the entire picture. Only one problem. They're ignoring the glaring and obvious differences.

Recently I heard a talk by a popular and highly respected preacher. He gave a very convincing presentation of the anointing of Jesus saying it happened in the house of Simon the Leper and Martha, Lazarus and Mary were there. He said Martha was busy in the kitchen and Mary anointed Jesus's head with the precious oil. Really? John says very clearly that Mary anointed His feet and wiped them with her hair. And what was Martha doing in Simon's kitchen? Also, some people try to say Mary was the notorious sinner, blending two other accounts. Really? That would make Jesus' friend Mary a notorious sinner. I think they see the name and immediately equate her with Mary Magdalene. By the way, nowhere in the Bible does it say Mary Magdalene was a prostitute. That's a tradition from the Middle Ages. Scripture says Jesus cast out seven demons from her. It's not a sin to have demons. It's a miserable condition, but it's not a sin. And where does all this romantic insinuation come from? There were several women who traveled with Jesus and the disciples and supported them with their own means. If there were hanky-panky going on, do you think the Pharisees wouldn't have pounced upon that as a leopard on a gazelle? But they never did. Why not? Everyone knew it wasn't true.

So what's the deal with those women and their expensive, fragrant spikenard? Easy. Three women, three different anointings. One was in the house of a pharisee (the notorious sinner was the woman in that account). One was at the house of Simon the leper. She poured the oil on His head. One was at the haven in Bethany, Mary's act of pure devotion. Also, they were different times. In John it says it was six days before the Passover. In Mark, it specifies it was two days before the Passover. Did the writers forget what day it was? No. It was a different day. See? Easy. It's all there in detail. We just have to read it and let it tell its own story.

Okay. Now we have the plots straight. There are two houses in Bethany, one owned by Simon the leper, one by Lazarus, Jesus' friend. There are two Simons. One was the Pharisee and one was the leper. Two of the women poured the spikenard on Jesus' feet and wiped them with their hair. One was a notorious sinner. One was Mary. The other woman, the one in Simon the leper's house, poured it on His head. It was considered a greater honor for the oil to be poured on the feet. You have the notorious sinner, so grateful that she couldn't stop weeping and caressing His feet, and Mary, who had sat at Jesus' feet and understood Him. Of her, Jesus said she had chosen the better part—better than serving—working working—and with a grumpy attitude, too. Two women from the opposite ends of the spectrum of relationship with Jesus, and both of them pouring out their dowry, their entire future, because all they wanted to do was somehow give Him something back for all He had given to them.

Interestingly, those who poured the oil and wiped it with their hair got it all over themselves as well. I think that always happens when we truly worship in overflowing gratitude and love. It also reminds me of the sacred anointing oil for the tabernacle. God gave Moses the formula which was strictly forbidden for personal use. But since it was poured on all the utensils, guess what happened to anyone who picked one up in the course of serving the Lord? Exactly! It's a by-product of service and devotion, fragrant and pure and rare.

Principles

In Bible study, there's the Law of First Mention. That's always a clue to pay attention. It kind of sets the pattern, the tone, the direction of the thing which will be developed throughout the Book. There's also a principle of repetitions. If God says it more than once, it's emphasized. My favorite of these is, "I will never leave you or forsake you." You find it in Joshua 1:9 and Hebrews 13:5. It shows up other places as well. I always find it wonderful when it's in both Testaments. Same God. Same Word. Same message throughout.

This story of the anointing is there four times—one per Gospel. Matthew and Mark are almost the same, but there are always different details, and they reveal different things about the narrator and his purpose for the telling. The sinful woman's story especially touches me because Jesus says she who has been forgiven much loves much. When I attended a legalistic church, I thought I was keeping all the rules (Oswald Chambers calls it being "obsessed with our own whiteness"), and I didn't need or appreciate Jesus much. Now that I'm close enough to Him to see what holiness really looks like, well, let's just say I love much. In Mark 13, it says, "But Jesus said, 'Let her alone; why are you troubling her? She has done a good and beautiful thing to Me [praiseworthy and noble].'" In Matt 26:10, it reads this way: "But Jesus, fully aware of this, said to them 'Why do you bother the woman? She has done a noble (praiseworthy and beautiful) thing to Me.'"

I couldn't resist putting those two passages in here. The Amplified Bible gives the overtones of the word Jesus used to describe His assessment of the deed. He says it's good, and the word He uses is *kalos.*

Here's the reason I believe the Holy Spirit made sure the stories are there in each Gospel, regardless of which woman it was: Truly I tell you, wherever this good news is preached in the whole world, what this woman has done will be told also, in memory of her. Each woman poured out all her riches to honor Jesus, and He gave each one the honor of being remembered always.

The Second Coming

This one really confuses people because they think there's only one. There are reasons for this mistake, egregious as it is. The information that gives details is in both Testaments and you have to know the whole counsel of God. Sadly, there are scholars, writers, pastors, and teachers who have lumped Christ's returns together based on the most obvious prophecies. In doing so, they have missed some really important distinctions in the appearances. I'm not going to give you all the references, just an overview. This may mess with your preconceptions if you have any. Again, don't take my word for it. The Bereans didn't immediately accept whatever Paul told them. They searched the Scriptures daily to find out for themselves whether what he said was true. Remember, they were Jews and the Scriptures they searched were in the Septuagint—the Greek translation of the *Tanakh*, the Old Testament. At that time, the New Testament was in the process of being written. The Bereans were finding prophecies of Jesus' return in words written hundreds of years before He was born. We have the blessing of additional details provided by prophets, apostles, divine inspiration, and Jesus Himself. So check it out and see what God shows you in your own sweet heart.

Jesus returns twice. The first is the one described in 1 Thessalonians 4:13–18. Here are the salient details. "For the Lord himself shall descend from heaven with a shout, with the voice of the archangel, and with the trump of God: and the dead in Christ shall rise first: Then we which are alive and remain shall be caught up together with them in the clouds, to meet the Lord in the air: and so shall we ever be with the Lord. Wherefore comfort one another with these words."

The event, the catching away (*harpatzo* in Greek) has been ridiculed, some saying the word "rapture" does not appear in the Bible. Well, yes it does, if you're reading the Vulgate, the Latin translation, but the term used isn't the issue. The events are described in several places, and *that's* what matters. Skeptics have also jeered at the image of Christians floating heavenward. Last year I heard of someone releasing a bunch of helium-filled blow up dolls that went merrily into the sky. Pretty silly. I must say the description of the *harpazo* is so far-fetched you would be tempted to believe it's fiction except if you really study the words in their original languages it's startlingly specific and detailed. I recommend Chuck Missler's teaching on it. His is the most grounded presentation I've heard.

Here's my thought on the actual event. The Bible says in the twinkling of an eye we shall be changed and then we'll be caught up in the air. Changed to what? I John 3:2 says "Beloved, now we are children of God; and it has not yet been revealed what we shall be, but we know that when He is revealed, we shall be like Him, for we shall see Him as He is." To me, that means we'll be able to see Him because we'll be the same substance as He is, or maybe in a different dimension. I don't believe there will be thousands of bodies floating up like inflatable dolls. I think, in the time it takes for light to pass into the retina, we'll be transformed and simply disappear from sight.

Notice that Jesus does not come to Earth. We meet Him in the air. I doubt anyone else will hear the trumpet or the shout or the Call. This is for our eyes and ears alone—reserved for those who love His appearing. There are no specified signs or events that signal the approach of this return. It could happen at any time. We are cautioned to keep our lamps full of oil and be diligent in being about our Father's business, attentive to the Beloved Voice, listening for the trump and the upward call. This appearance is associated with imminence. It happens without specified occurrences. On the other hand, there are lots and lots of events that precede Jesus' Second Coming to Earth, when His foot steps on the mountain and the mountain splits. That's the first important distinction.

For this first return, the one where Jesus comes to take His Bride Home, there are many scholars with differing views on how and when it will happen. I'm not pushing any time frame over another. I figure it will happen when it happens and I just want to be ready. However, I want to share a bit of Scripture that makes a case for our establishment in heaven before the Great Tribulation. This is from Revelation 5:10. John is in heaven witnessing the activity in the Throne Room of God. It's not a vision or symbolic; he's watching it happen, using such phrases as "then I saw" or "I heard"—and what he heard was usually pretty loud. The twenty-four elders are casting their crowns at the feet of the Lamb that has just taken the scroll from the hand of the One that is sitting on the throne. And they're singing, "Thou art worthy to take the book, and to open the seals thereof; for thou was slain, and hast redeemed us to God by thy blood out of every kindred, and tongue, and people, and nation, and hast made us unto our God kings and priests: and we shall reign on the earth."

Who are the twenty-four elders? Seems pretty obvious it's the redeemed of the Lord. Of no other group does the Bible say they're kings and priests except Melchizadek, Jesus, and us—the Body of Christ. Simple, right? In the King James version, this passage clearly says "hast redeemed us" and "we shall reign on the earth." No mystery here. Except, in other translations, the pronouns are changed to "them" and "they"—which disconnects the singing elders from the redeemed of the Lamb. Maybe that's just a minor detail to you, but it identifies for me who the elders are, and that the Body of Christ is in heaven before the Lamb starts opening the seals which begin the Great Tribulation on Earth.

The scroll with the seals is the title deed to Earth. How do we know? In biblical times, title deeds were written on the outside and inside. On the outside were the requirements that had to be met by the one intending to take possession of the land. Many times the one wanting to take the land was a kinsman-redeemer (remember Boaz and Ruth? The near-kinsman could purchase Naomi's land, but he also had to marry Ruth). Only a near-kinsman (someone in the family bloodline) could redeem the land. Jesus is our Kinsman-Redeemer. He is of the bloodline of David. He had to be a human being, and He had to pay the price for the land before he could take the title deed and open its seals. Those were the requirements. Jesus met them all.

Why do other versions of the Bible use the other pronouns? I don't know. What I do know is The Blue Letter Bible is available online for free, and you can look up anything in the original languages that you wish, and investigate for yourself whatever mystifies you. As Chuck Missler says, "Don't take my word for it. Look it up yourself and come to your own conclusions." Keeping that in mind, I test everything he says, and I don't always agree with him. By the way, Chuck Missler helped create The Blue Letter Bible.

Here's something else to ponder. When Jesus opens the first seal, this is what John says, "And I saw, and behold a white horse: and he that sat on it had a bow; and a crown was given unto him: and he went forth conquering, and to conquer." (Rev 6:2) Some people think it's Jesus. Why? He's riding on a white horse. All good guys ride white horses, right? Except this one has a bow. Nowhere in Scripture do we ever see Jesus with a bow. Sword, yes. Bow, no. And he's given a crown—designated authority to go out conquering and to conquer. Meanwhile, Jesus is still in heaven. He's not in two places. Maybe the guy on the white horse is a fake good guy. Maybe...The Man of Sin? The Coming World Leader? The Anti-Christ? No way can he be Jesus.

In the Second Coming, the one that people usually think about, preparations start in heaven as described in Revelation 19. First is the Marriage Supper of the Lamb. Then Jesus appears riding on a white horse. His name is revealed as the Word of God, and He doesn't carry a bow. We follow Him on white horses to Earth where He sends angels to gather His elect (people saved during the Tribulation). Lots of events happen before His actual appearance on Earth with more than 1800 prophecies about that Second Coming in the Bible. Quite a few are in Daniel 9, but other prophets also give details. You can't look at only one familiar set of Scriptures. Then there are detailed descriptions of what follow that appearance: He dispatches The Beast, the False Prophet, and sets up His kingdom on Earth for a thousand years—The Millennial Kingdom. Quite a few denominations and Christians think this is allegory, but it makes more sense to me to see it as literal, and it fulfills the promises that have been made throughout the Testaments that there will be a descendant of David on the Throne forever. That Second Coming is described in Matthew 24 and Mark 13 at the private briefing with Peter, James, John, and Andrew on the Mount of Olives. That Kingdom reign follows the Great Tribulation.

That's all I'm going to say about that. For your sakes, you need to know the differences in the two Comings. I think Chuck Missler's teaching on this subject is the most thorough, substantiated with a lot of Scriptures from the whole counsel of God, and detailed as to the differences in the signs and indications and purposes of the appearances. All I want to do here is let you know there are two comings and not to be afraid. One sweet Christian sister told me she is worried she'll be left behind because she doesn't read her Bible enough or go to church enough or pray enough. Really? Is there some tally that measures if you are light enough to float up into the air or too heavy because you're weighed down with insufficient spiritual acts? Sounds like karma to me. In Jesus, there's no karma. It's all about grace and relationship. There is only one qualification: Are you His? If you are, why would He leave you behind? Missler says he thinks when Jesus calls us to come up to meet Him, we will each hear Him calling us by name. I love that thought, and I think it's true. He didn't pay the group rate. He knows every one of us as His beloved individual children. And He knows our name.

I'm ending this chapter with one of my favorite stories from the archives of my life. It symbolizes how I believe God would like us to view the days ahead.

White Water Rafting

I don't like water sports. But my friend needed one more body to fill the boat before he could take his customers down the American River. "I can't swim," I told him.

"You'll have a life vest," he said, "and you'll be perfectly safe. I've done this hundreds of times and I know what I'm doing. Trust me. It'll be fun. You'll be fine."

So I went, but I doubted I'd find it fun. I hate rollercoasters, and shooting white water rapids on the American River wasn't my idea of a good time. But there I was, straddling the Zodiac's inflated rubber side. I had expected to be placed somewhere in the middle of the group, but my friend put me on the right directly in front. I found that very alarming. Then he gave us directions, the meanings of the commands and what we should do when we heard that particular word. Next he pushed off to let us practice in a calm place where the water was smooth. Then off we went, the current catching the Zodiac with surprising power. Oh boy. I was already terrified. Being in front, I could see everything ahead, and I was soon even more terrified as we approached the first rapids. How could we get through? Our captain's voice rang out and all of us paddled accordingly. To my surprise, the boat gracefully skirted the rocks. Well, that wasn't as bad as I thought.

There were more rapids ahead, but they were about the same size and sound as the first ones, and each time we paddled according to directions, we slid around the rocks as neatly as you please.

I was starting to enjoy this when I notice a louder sound ahead. The rapids were bigger and more violent than before. Panic started to rise, but the captain shouted the words and we all moved as one. Neatly the Zodiac swung around the new rapids. That went on as we raced along, the current getting swifter, the rapids bigger, but, surprisingly, I was no longer afraid. The rapids were getting louder and stronger. I could see them coming. To my amazement, I found I had begun to enjoy the ride. Standing in the back of the boat, our captain could see ahead and he knew this river well. I stopped worrying and relaxed. I didn't have to figure out what to do. All I had to do was listen for the captain's voice and follow His commands.

The current carried us swiftly. The rapids were louder and more violent. They were so large and fierce that we could hardly hear anything over the crashing and splashing. Then, unbelievably, the roar increased. Ahead huge black rocks jutted up, resisting the swirling water crashing against the hard wet dark, hurling hissing foam and spray high in the air. I was not afraid. I was thrilled. Our captain shouted commands, we moved as one, the boat glided smoothly around the tumult. Suddenly an enormous wave stood up, a towering wall of pale green glass so high it covered the sky, so still it looked frozen. Through the glassy wall, the sun was setting, a bright orange-golden ball. The transparent green stood motionless, glorious, breathtakingly beautiful. Then, suddenly, it dropped into the river and disappeared.

I wasn't a Christian when I went on the trip down the American River, but after I became one, Jesus reminded me of that time. He told me, as the Captain of my salvation, He knew what was ahead. At each new hazard I would have His vigilant help. He knew the river. He knew the way. He knew what I had to do in order to make it safely around each troubling thing with grace. All I had to do was trust Him, listen to His Voice, and follow His Word. And the End, He promised, would be glorious.

22

These Present Days

Where are we now? Is this just another bump in the road, some horror and chaos that will be over in a few years? In my lifetime, I've never seen so much chaos. Things certainly seem to be unraveling. There's some running amuck going on. Many Christians are asking if this is the End. I'm going to address that in this chapter.

The Olivet Discourse

Not long ago, Jesus told me His *ecclesia*, His Church, was like sheep without a shepherd. I thought He meant they were off wandering on their own, looking for greener pastures and doing their own thing. "All we like sheep have gone astray, each of us going our own separate ways…" But then I read in Matthew 9:36 (AMPC), "When He saw the throngs, He was moved with pity and sympathy for them, because they were bewildered (harassed and distressed and dejected and helpless), like sheep without a shepherd." When I remarked about it to Dan, he said, "Yeah. It means they're easy to pick off and end up somebody's dinner." The sheep are confused and afraid. Scattered from each other and the One who protects and leads them. Why? I think they don't know their life is meant to be extraordinary, supernatural, powerful. They aren't aware of the reality of the war or that they have weapons for it that are mighty through God. I think they don't know how to wield the Word and prayer. But the times we're in, with all the trials and struggles, will be effective in waking everybody up. We have to know the whole counsel of God, and we have to have a strong relationship with its Divine Author.

The disciples asked Jesus when He was coming back and what would be the signs of the end of the age. The first thing He said was, "Take heed that no one deceives you." (Matthew 24:4 NKJV) He described false Christs and false prophets and a lot of deception going on. Since it is the first thing He mentioned, I think it was much on His heart. It makes me think of magicians. They deceive by distraction. Your eye follows the movement of one hand while their other hand is deftly manipulating the item (or, in our case, the data). Where are we now? In the Age of Deception, media and information overload make it easier than ever to fabricate a new truth, a new reality. Who can we trust? I bet you know the answer.

Jesus said, "I am the Way, the Truth, the Life." Since Jesus says He's the Truth, that's good enough for me. I also trust the Bible to be His Word and I know it can be trusted. So let's ask that question again: Where are we now? Let's take a look at what Jesus said. I figure He knows.

There are three accounts of this in the Gospels. Matthew 24 and Mark 13 are very similar, and Luke 21, which has striking differences. Yet, scholars, preachers, commentators, and teachers lump them all together. Why? Because there are words repeated. Don't be deceived, wars and rumors of wars, earthquakes in various places, famines, when you see…flee…, etc. Apparently, people read those words and assume they're minor variations on the same incident.

But wait! Aren't the ones in Matthew and Mark private and at night? Only four disciples are there (Mark specifies which ones). And isn't the one in Luke in the daytime at the temple talking to people in the Court? And though they all say to flee and not go back for anything, in Matthew and Mark, Jesus says, "there will be earthquakes and famines, you will hear of wars and rumors of wars…and then, and then… and then…" In Luke, Jesus says the same group of signs, but says this: "but *before* these things..." See? That's a *huge* difference. Also, the triggers are very different. In Matthew and Mark, Jesus says, "When you see the Abomination of Desolation spoken of by the prophet Daniel, flee..." In Luke, Jesus says when you see Jerusalem being surrounded by armies, flee.

When the Romans besieged Jerusalem at Nero's command, it took awhile for everything to get set up because Nero died. That caused a scrambling for power that delayed the besieging about a year before the city could be completely cut off. I'm certain the delay was helped by interference on the part of the Lord. Then, when everything was in place, the attack began. Josephus reports more than 1,100,000 Jews perished and nearly 100,000 were taken captive. But according to 4th century Christian scholar, Eucebius, not one Christian died. Why not? About thirty-seven years before, Jesus told them ahead of time what to look out for. He was in the Temple in the large outermost area called the Court of the Gentiles because it, as well as a covered area called Solomon's Porch, was frequented by the poor and the sick who were seeking help, along with Gentiles (non-Israelites) and the ritually unclean, who were forbidden, upon pain of death, from entering the interior areas of the Temple.

So Jesus was talking to Gentiles, not His disciples, when He said, "But when you see Jerusalem surrounded by armies, then know *and* understand that its desolation has come near. Then... flee to the mountains..." They listened and watched for the signs, and, when they saw Jerusalem being surrounded, they took off for the hills. Eusebius wrote, "The whole body, however, of the church at Jerusalem, having been commanded by a divine revelation, given to men of approved piety there before the war, removed from the city, and dwelt at a certain town beyond the Jordan, called Pella."

Why am I telling you this? Because it pays to know the voice of God so when He wants to give you instructions you can spread the word and get everyone to safety. It pays to read the Bible *accurately* so you know what Jesus really said. Don't trust your future to the teachings of others, no matter how well-respected they are. Know for yourself what God said, and let Him speak about it directly to your heart.

Early in 2020, COVID-19 suddenly swept across Italy and spread rapidly all around the world, a pandemic began such as has not happened in the lifetime of anyone alive today. The havoc that has ensued has been truly unsettling. It's times like these that the Word of God really shines—light in the darkness, order into chaos, truth in the confusion. In the Bible we can find how superbly God has all things under control. He provides the information we need to understand what's going on and how to deal with it. We can read 2 Timothy and say, "Wow! God said people would be like this." Nothing takes God by surprise. We can see how to put current events into biblical frameworks and implement God's directions for what to do about it. In the following verses, Jesus tells us what we're looking at, and He also says over and over how to respond. So let's go carefully through these significant teachings on End Times that Jesus gave.

Is This The End?

As soon as the pandemic began, people started asking, "Is this the Tribulation?" First, the Great Tribulation, according to Daniel and Jesus, is only three and a half years, not seven, and Anti-Christ (or whatever name you want to call him) has to be in power three and a half years before that. Then he sets up his own abomination of desolation as per the Olivet Discourse of Matthew and Mark, and the real horrors begin. Before that, Jesus said, "Don't be afraid. The end is not yet." It's the beginning of sorrows or, more accurately, the beginning of birth pangs. And He says in each account, "Don't be afraid. These things must come." That's where we are today. We're in the first of the birth pangs. Birth pangs are uncomfortable, to say the least, and they build up to really miserable, but they produce new life. These times of hardships and strange goings on can produce new life in Christ for us if we let Him do something deep and wonderful in our lives. We can learn to trust Him in ways we never have had to before.

As I read the three accounts where Jesus gives signs and predictions of what will be the tenor of the times preceding His Second Coming and the End of all things, I was struck by this one repeated thing:

"And when you hear of wars and insurrections (disturbances, disorder, and confusion), do not become alarmed *and* panic-stricken *and* terrified; for all this must take place first, but the end will not [come] immediately." (Luke 21:8 AMP)

"And when you hear of wars and rumors of wars, do not get alarmed (troubled and frightened); it is necessary [that these things] take place, but the end is not yet. For nation will rise against nation, and kingdom against kingdom. There will be earthquakes in various places; there will be famines *and calamities.* This is but the beginning of [only the first of the birth pangs]." (Mark 13:7, 8)

"And you will hear of wars and rumors of wars; see that you are not frightened *or* troubled, for this must take place, but the end is not yet. For nation will rise against nation, and kingdom against kingdom, and there will be famines and earthquakes in place after place; All this is but the beginning [the early pains] of the birth pangs [of the intolerable anguish]. Then they will hand you over to suffer affliction *and* tribulation and put you to death, and you will be hated by all nations for My name's sake. And then many will be offended *and* repelled *and* will begin to distrust *and* desert [Him Whom they ought to trust and obey] *and* will stumble and fall away and betray one another *and* pursue one another with hatred. And many false prophets will rise up and deceive *and* lead many into error. And the love of the great body of people will grow cold because of the multiplied lawlessness *and* iniquity, But he who endures to the end will be saved." (Matt 24:6-14 AMPC)

Lately God has me reading in Matthew. Early in His ministry, Jesus says, "Do not think that I have come to bring peace upon the earth; I have not come to bring peace, but a sword." (Matt 10:34) Eeek! What happened to Gentle Jesus with a benevolent smile, a lamb in His arms and little children at His feet? This is not End Times stuff He's talking about. He's sending His disciples out, having just given them power and authority to cast out unclean spirits, heal the sick, raise the dead, cleanse lepers, drive out demons, cure all manner of infirmities, and preach the Kingdom of Heaven is at hand. He's telling them He has not come to bring peace but a sword, sharp and severe enough to divide family members from one another? What's *that* about? I was shocked. Then the Holy Spirit said, "The sword is the Word." People will be divided according to how they relate to the Word of God. Is it symbolic, allegorical, moral guidance, Ten Suggestions? According to how seriously we take it, we will be making our choices where to stand. Some will choose to move away. Jesus does not give us room to compromise or blend in. There's a cross in each life. There's a death to ourselves. There's a following that won't be easy, popular, or pleasant. I'm not saying we're to go out and riot. Jesus didn't lead an insurrection against Rome. He said that's not what His Kingdom is about. No, He, Himself was the offense—the righteousness of God, the reality of Authority above any earthly rule. The Light that some hate because they prefer darkness. Bless those who curse you. Do good to those who hate you. Do to others what you want them to do to you. And don't be surprised when they despise you nonetheless. Jesus said we're not better than our

Master. It's the Word of God that causes the offense. It's a bad smell to those on the dark side. Paul says it's the fragrance of Christ to some. To others, it's the stench of death. Even now, before the End, before the Great Tribulation, there is violence happening in our world and in our individual lives. Jesus said in this world we will have tribulation. What does that mean?

To separate the wheat from its covering husk, a hard, thin shell, the grain would be threshed, which meant it would be beaten with a flail. Then it would be thrown up into the air (using a winnowing fork or fan or shovel) and the wind would blow the husks away, but the wheat would fall to the floor and be gathered up. Announcing the coming Messiah, John the Baptist said, "His winnowing fan is in His hand, and He will thoroughly clean out His threshing floor, and gather His wheat into the barn; but He will burn up the chaff with unquenchable fire." (Matt 3:12 NKJV)

Want to guess where we get the word "tribulation"? It's from Latin *tribulare*, "press" "oppress," from *tribulum* "threshing board constructed of sharp points." Jesus said, "In the world you shall have tribulation." The Amplified Bible says "There will be trials, distress, and frustration." But He adds, "Be of good cheer (don't be afraid) I have overcome the world. I've deprived it of power to harm you." (John 16:33) So don't be surprised when it feels like you're being beaten with a flail and tossed around. Jesus, Himself, is going to make sure that good stuff remains behind and all that is empty and useless is done away with forever. That includes in our individual lives. Tribulation makes that separation. It's a good thing.

But back to the Scriptures…

All three accounts contain the same signs. I didn't include them all here, because each one of these very significant teachings is an entire chapter, and you can see for yourself all that Jesus says will happen. Much of it is already happening, and we must remember there are circular fulfillments of everything that is prophesied in the Bible. The Greek mind thinks of prophecy as prediction/fulfillment, while the Hebrew mind thinks in terms of patterns. There are fractals —repeating patterns—all through the Bible, from the smallest detail to the largest overview. It's one integrated message all adding up to the same thing. History, world events, social trends, and seasons of anguish spiral through the years in various forms of fulfillment, and, as the Bible says, it is all written for our instruction.

These repetitions emphasize the inevitability of the events. You may add to that certainty Jesus' assertion that His words will not pass away, but all will come to pass as He said. But what strikes me most in the repetitions is this one thing: see that you are not frightened *or* troubled, for this must take place; do not get alarmed (troubled and frightened); it is necessary [that these things] take place…"

Did you get that? These things *must* take place. It's necessary. It's part of the Plan. It has to happen. God is not surprised by any of this. And He doesn't want us to be either.

He says don't be deceived. Those coming will be pretty flashy, do supernatural things, and be very convincing. Remember, Satan is not ugly. He was one of the smartest and most gifted of the top archangels, and he's made of music. Jesus says to be ready. Don't be thinking the Master is delaying, gone on a long trip and won't be back soon. I keep hearing people saying this: "From time immemorial, they've been saying He'll be back soon. Every generation has said that, and every generation has been wrong. What's the big deal? We're probably going to keep on doing normal life as usual. And, frankly, I don't want to think about End Times. I've got things I still want to do." Then there are those ten virgins. They kept themselves pure, but only five of them made sure their lamps were full of oil. The others ran out, and while they were away looking for vendors for refills, they missed the wedding.

As you know, oil is a symbol of the Holy Spirit, and one of the things in the falling away is the blatant disregard for His existence and the rejection of His presence. Shocking? Indeed. It horrifies me so much I want you to see it again. "And then many will be offended *and* repelled *and* will begin to distrust *and* desert [Him Whom they ought to trust and obey] *and* will stumble and fall away and betray one another *and* pursue one another with hatred. And many false prophets will rise up and deceive *and* lead many into error. And the love of the great body of people will grow cold because of the multiplied lawlessness *and* iniquity." Remember, "iniquity" means "warping" or "twisting," and has to do with replacing God's standard with our own. It's saying our way is right and good and His is null and void.

Us in These Present Days

Many Christian people I know, good, serious, prayer-warriors and all, have been frustrated, angry, depressed, fearful, belligerent, hostile, violent, even wanting to kick some rear ends because of the flagrant disregard for individual freedoms and rights to be ourselves and have our own opinions even if they don't match what others think. And I'm wondering how are we any different from the world (no God present), the flesh (human reasoning, autonomy, and our perceptions), and the devil (Satan—the name, means "accuser")? Where's the oil? Don't be deceived, distracted, disconnected. This is not all that's happening. There's More. God has set us in this time so we can change things—like Daniel in Babylon. We are meant to live in supernatural realms—above natural, above carnal, above flesh.

Jesus said if we say, "Thou Fool!" we are in danger of hell fire. Yet we can be quick to yell at the guy who just drove like a maniac and cut us off, justified in our expressions of rage because he put us in danger. Does that show God's essence and character? Can we see it another way? I remember driving with a friend as he raced to get to the hospital to try to see his father who just had a heart attack. The road was steep and winding and my friend drove very fast, the car screeching around curves, his mind on one thing only: to get there before it was too late.

Maybe when someone drives crazy, we could pray for them. Maybe our children will hear coming out of our mouths the love of God and His concern for each troubled human being instead of words such as, "You idiot!" or "You think you're so important that you have to pass everybody?" When Jesus comes, will we be berating our fellow servants or ourselves? Either way, it's not what Jesus wants us to be doing. He wants us to love one another as He loved us. That means with patience and grace, forgiveness and blessing, not cursing.

It's crazy-making time with regulations, mandates, edicts, and requirements made, then changed, then changed again. Feels like a lot of yanking around. People who are rights-oriented are especially angry now. Jesus is not rights-oriented. He's righteousness-oriented, which is a very different thing. It's hard. It's unnatural. Walking after the Spirit takes supernatural help, but we have the Word and prayer and the Holy Spirit indwelling who reminds us what Jesus said. Love one another as I have loved you. Keep your eyes on Him. This is bigger than you think.

When I asked the Lord how He would have me end this section, He said, "Sing your praises, little ones. Sing your praises as we go forth triumphantly. Come with Me. These are exciting times. Never think of them as fearful times. Do not let your hearts waiver. When your flesh would cry, trust

Me. When your flesh would fear, praise Me. Know this: I'm waiting for you!"

The Real Great Wall

I was climbing the steep stone pavement that angled up to one of the farthest watchtowers that I could see on the length of the Great Wall of China. Most of the crowds of tourists had remained on the lower levels, but God kept urging me to go farther, until at last He instructed me to climb to the watch tower on that extremely high place in the gray stone serpent that lies atop the ridges of impossibly steep mountains in its ambitious attempt to keep out Mongol invaders. It was November. The wind chill was making it debilitatingly cold, but I labored on, step by step, until I got to the small flat interior and looked out the opening at the rest of the wall I expected to see stretching out beyond view. Instead, I saw a rubble of broken pieces. I had forgotten that the part we tourists had been walking on was reconstructed. Beyond the highest watch tower, the wall had not been repaired.

The Lord spoke, "The real Great Wall is not this one. The *real* Great Wall is not this one. The real Great Wall is apparent self-sufficiency." He went on to say that the new Chinese government was only thirty years old, and like humans in their thirties, it was full of energy and hope and vision, but, without God, their strength and power would soon break down, inadequate to keep them safe and secure. "At that time," the Lord said, "they will be open to Jesus." It was 1980. For a very short time, they did become open to Christianity. Pastor Chuck Smith was invited to go teach the pastors there, and the government even invited the leaders of the house churches. Of course, that door has subsequently been sealed shut, and the underground church is suffering persecution most mercilessly. But it is also flourishing

Throughout human history there has been the repeating conflict between trusting God and the decision to operate in autonomy without Him. It has been about obedience or independence, worshiping their Creator or the works of their hands. When the pandemic began, God said He allowed it to dismantle apparent self-sufficiency. That independent spirit is still the real Great Wall, but this is our opportunity to partner with God in restoring communication between Him and the people He created, offering an invitation to friendship with Almighty God and fulfillment of each one's divine purpose in this strange, unprecedented time.

This morning I asked the Lord to help me understand these times and our role in it. He gave me this: "Thus says the Lord Who made [the earth], the Lord Who formed it to establish it—the Lord is His name: Call to Me and I will answer you and show you great and mighty things, hidden, which you do not know (do not distinguish and recognize, have knowledge of and understand)." (Jeremiah 33:2–3 AMP)

In this book, I've told you things about myself you may not have known—things I've thought, ways that I've processed, things God has told me. In words and pictures and stories I've revealed to you things you could not know about me unless I chose to tell you. And it's the same with God. You get a revelation of Him from what He chooses to tell you. In the Bible, in your experiences, in the fingerprints you find around your life, He is always communicating. He's telling you things—about Himself, about yourself, about the circumstances, how to perceive them from His perspective, and deal with and overcome them. In Him, in His Ways, He will show you new things, hidden things that you would have no way of knowing otherwise.

The *Telos*—The Intended End

In the 1980s, I started having visions of the End Times. I'll share with you just one. I saw a sleek, black snake, mouth open wide, its long, needle-sharp fangs curving in half circles of shining stainless steel. It was rushing, propelled swiftly atop a red-roofed train station that looked stationary, but always managed to be under it. The snake sped straight ahead, its mouth open wide. Though I saw nothing, I knew there were interminable horrors perpetrated by the snake as it rushed along unstoppable in the dark. This went on a long time. I wanted to scream and run away. I told the Lord, "I don't want to see anymore." Nothing changed. The snake sped on, mouth open wide, horror mounting until I felt my heart would explode from anguish. I was sure I couldn't bear another second, but the snake went on and on. Then I saw, suspended in the black air directly in the path of the snake, rotating slowly and calmly—even nonchalantly—a cream-colored fan blade. The snake rushed forward directly into the three blades which went unhurried and unconcerned chop, chop, chop. They sliced up the snake all the way to its tail. Then God said, "Evil will go on seemingly unchecked a very long time, and then The End." So I'm not surprised that things are getting worse and worse.

In 2 Timothy 3:3-5, Paul writes, "But understand this, that in the last days dangerous times [of great stress and trouble] will come [difficult days that will be hard to bear]. For people will be lovers of self [narcissistic, self-focused], lovers of money [impelled by greed], boastful, arrogant, revilers, disobedient to parents, ungrateful, unholy *and* profane, [and they will be] unloving [devoid of natural human affection, calloused and inhumane], irreconcilable, malicious gossips, devoid of self-control [intemperate, immoral], brutal, haters of good, traitors, reckless, conceited, lovers of [sensual] pleasure rather than lovers of God, holding to a form of [outward] godliness (religion), although they have denied its power [for their conduct nullifies their claim of faith]." (AMP)

Should we be surprised that some people in these days are violent, hateful, vicious, lawless, haters of God? The Bible said they would be. What surprises me is something I never saw before. Even some who call themselves Christians will be part of that group Paul is warning us about. Maybe they're the tares. I find this part of that Scripture shocking, but there it is: "holding to a form of [outward] godliness (religion), although they have denied its power [for their conduct nullifies their claim of faith]." My friend Debra reminds me not to have unrealistic expectations. The Bible tells us they will be like that. I keep thinking: You can't give what you don't have. I remember what that pastor said about church-going Christians who don't believe the Holy Spirit is real, or the devil either. They deny the power of God, and of God's working through His people. They don't believe the Bible is His supernaturally-authored book, or its accounts are historical, verifiable, or applicable to how we are to live in this present darkness. I'm concerned that they don't even realize how much they're missing—both for themselves and for what they were created to do. The church, not the different denominations or gatherings, but the *ecclesia*, the called-out ones who have taken His name—we're supposed to be a living organism, as connected as members of Christ's body with Him as the Head. Recently when I was talking with the Lord about this, He said His Church is scattered as sheep without a Shepherd, His Body is like a person with Cerebral Palsy whose body does not listen to its Head, and the Bride is blaisé. What ever happened to First Love? We need to be connected. He will tell us how to think through these times in alignment with His heart. Nothing else will sustain us, keep us in perfect peace (with our minds stayed on Him, or cause us to make a difference in the right way—not being overcome by evil, but overcoming evil with good (Romans 12:21)

Is it too hard to live godly in such a perverse and twisted world? I don't think so. We're not living in the time when Nero was lighting his garden parties with torches made of oil-drenched Christians. In the midst of the mess, the Apostle John tells us what God wants us to do, "He who says he abides in Him ought himself also to walk just as He walked." (1 John 2:6 NKJV) We're not talking about having positive thinking or putting a brave face on it; we're talking supernatural enablement, and we have assurance that we can because Jesus told us we would do what He did and more. When we are aligned with God's values, His power can flow through us to do what only He can do.

The same power that raised Christ from the dead is working in us today. Really? Then why is it sometimes so hard to get out of bed? For me, it's a matter of focus. What have I been feeding on? The news? The fears and frustrations of the people around me? Are we tuning up to them or to God? Some frequencies are healing. Some can actually make you sick. It's a good time to find that Secret Place, the place of quiet silence where we can talk to God face to face. It's not all up to us. It's a partnership. But we have to be connected.

Does that mean I think this is The End? I haven't a clue. Nobody knows when that will be—or when our individual end might be. I'm saying the fact that we're alive now means He has something for us to do, and it's a privilege to be contributing our little lives to the history of what's happening—because what we do and say and the way we rear our kids and treat each other—it all matters.

Jesus told His disciples on His last night on Earth, "Peace I leave with you, My peace I give to you; not as the world gives do I give to you. Let not your heart be troubled, neither let it be afraid." (John 14:27 NKJV)

And Peter, writing to the persecuted Church, wrote, "After you have suffered for a little while, the God of all grace [who imparts His blessing and favor], who called you to His own eternal glory in Christ, will Himself complete, confirm, strengthen, and establish you [making you what you ought to be]." (1 Peter 5:10 AMP)

Breathing for Birthing

Birth pangs. That's what Jesus called them. Wars, rumors of wars, famines, plagues… it's all part of the pressures that signal the start of a process that will go on, increasing in intensity, till something new is born. Thinking about that scenario, an old memory came to mind.

I was seven months pregnant. Having heard stories from other women all my life, I was justifiably terrified to face what was coming soon. But a friend had suggested looking into Lamaze, and there I was in a room full of bulging bellies and all of us wives and husbands looking like deer in the headlights.

Over the weeks we learned how to breathe to ride each contraction like a wave instead of fighting it. We learned the three stages of birthing, the kinds of contractions to expect, how they would change, and what to do when they did. Transition was the final and hardest stage. We would have overwhelming urges to push. "Don't!" the instructor warned. And she taught us how to breathe a special way to keep us from hurting ourselves and our babies in that final phase where timing—and waiting—are crucial for a safe and successful delivery. It was all about recognizing the signs, cooperating with each contraction, riding over the pain, and knowing, when things got unbelievably intense, that it meant we were close to the end. "If you do it correctly," she said, "you'll feel pressure, intense pressure to be sure, but not pain."So far, so good. But would it work? We had our doubts. Lamaze was fairly new. Nobody I knew had ever birthed a baby that way.

On the last day, our instructor told us, "I want you to do one last exercise." She instructed us women to do the breathing for Transition while our husbands squeezed one of our ankles as hard as they could. We obeyed. No problem. We all breathed as we had been taught. We knew our stuff. "Okay," our instructor said. "For this last part, I want your husband to do the same thing, but this time I don't want you to do the breathing. Ready? Go!"

Instantly the room was full of screams, unkind words, and accusations. "You squeezed harder!" we snapped. I think each woman wanted sincerely to kick her husband hard in the face. The men looked shocked and apologetic. "No, I didn't. It was the same as last time, or maybe even a little less." The women glared. The men looked bewildered and sorry. I wanted to tell my husband it was okay, but it had hurt so bad! Instead of feeling pressure on my ankle, I had felt blinding, screaming pain. We all did. At first, all of us women were furious with our husbands. Then we realized with a shock what had happened. "It works!" we cried almost with one voice. Then we burst into laughter—and relief. It works! We left that day in peace, knowing we would be able to go through whatever came. We were prepared. I'm sure you already figured out the application. We're in the first of the birth pangs, but we have a Book that tells us the stages, and we have all the tools we need to ride the wave.

Paul wrote this from prison near the end of his life. The Caesar in charge at that time was Nero. Talk about insecurity. That wacko might do anything. He raced around naked in a chariot at night yelling, "You are the light of the world!" Christians were definitely the targets of his madness. And yet Paul wrote this, a statement of total surrender because he accepted his situation as God's choice for him, and not one of us can say that kind of peace cannot be ours in this time of strangeness. Paul is a straight wall in a very crooked world. But if he can, then we can, because God gives the Holy Spirit without measure, in our weakness, His strength is made perfect. The Lord, our God, in the midst of us is Mighty. We can do all things through Christ Who strengthens us.

"Not that I speak from [any personal] need, for I have learned to be content [and self-sufficient through Christ, satisfied to the point where I am not disturbed or uneasy] regardless of my circumstances. I know how to get along and live humbly [in difficult times], and I also know how to enjoy abundance and live in prosperity. In any and every circumstance I have learned the secret [of facing life], whether well-fed or going hungry, whether having an abundance or being in need. I can do all things [which He has called me to do] through Him who strengthens and empowers me [to fulfill His purpose—I am self-sufficient in Christ's sufficiency; I am ready for anything and equal to anything through Him who infuses me with inner strength and confident peace.]" (Phil 4:11-13 AMP)

Earth is in labor. The birth pangs have begun. There is so much fear. But we have the Cross to keep us on course. It reminds us we are not helpless, but we have weapons that are mighty. We have words that change atmospheres and bring the presence of Almighty God. We have instructions, directions, purposes beyond our normal understanding, and we are meant to participate in things that have been planned since before the beginning of time.

I think none of us realizes or takes seriously enough the destiny we have, the part we play in the future of this world. God told me we are here to change what would be without us. Now He is saying it's intricate and much less random than it seems. Walk circumspectly, redeeming the time, making choices based, not on what we see with our eyes and think with our human minds, but on His guidance. More time in His Word, more quiet time sharing our hearts with Him. He is telling me it's much bigger than we think. Our relationship with Him can be much deeper than we have. Our influence on our circles and ultimately upon the world is more profound than we can imagine. Do not take it lightly, and do pay attention. He wants to commune with you as Friend to friend. Jesus said, "As it was in the days of Noah…" This is the time of preparation, and part of that preparation is receiving instructions on what to build.

At the end of JRR Tolkien's *The Hobbit*, Bilbo is surprised to realize the prophecies have come true about the rivers of plenty flowing from a town that was in ruins.

Bilbo says, "Then the prophecies of the old songs have turned out to be true."

To this Gandalf answers, "Surely you don't disbelieve the prophecies because you had a hand in bringing them about yourself? You don't really suppose do you that all your adventures and escape were managed by mere luck just for your sole benefit? You're a very fine person, and I'm very fond of you, but you're only quite a little fellow in a wide world after all."

It has taken me a long time to realize what Tolkien was showing us through his book. There was a big plan and Bilbo was a part of bringing it to pass. All of his adventures and the discoveries, rescues, and escapes contributed to his ability to help bring about the fulfillment of the prophecies. We are small, too, and our little lives seem inconsequential as we struggle through the unfamiliar landscape of these present days. But I keep having this amazing thought that we are participating in the Plan, especially with our prayers. It keeps coming back to me that what we do matters much more than we think, even if it's something spoken in the privacy of our car on our way home on a rainy night. It matters even though you're only quite a little fellow in a wide world after all. Even the smallest person can make a big difference because, behind it all, there is God, and He is mighty.

It makes a difference how we react. It makes a difference what we say. We can show by our words and actions what we're looking at—like me and the fly speck on the window. There's so much more going on behind the glass. There's a war happening where the darkness is increasing exponentially, but there is glory and a fresh, bright revelation of God as well.

Last year the Lord told me, "The darkness and the light will be happening at the same time." It was like two great waves rushing side-by-side, like powerful horses thundering neck and neck. He said, "The darkness will greatly increase, but the light will be brighter, all the moreso in contrast to the darkness." Which one will you believe? To which atmosphere do you want to contribute your energy? Jesus said some things have to happen. They must. It's part of the Plan. It's the gathering together before the sorting out. It's our time to show kindness and speak gratitude that counteracts the fomenting of anxiety and helplessness. God wants to fill our mouths, to inspire, breathe into, to pour His power through us into a frightened, troubled world. He wants to show He is mighty, that He is the only true God, that there is More. He is offering it to everyone. In days of the normal past, they might not have listened. There was no need, no uncertainty. But now He's shaking everything.

When we as the children of God can show there is light in our homes, peace in our lives, and love in our words, perhaps some will see there's a difference in lives lived in the company of Almighty God and want what we have. God wants to show a distinction between the world and His people. And, guess what? We're those people. We get to be the salt of the earth, the light of the world, a song in the night. We get to be part of the fulfillment of what God said would come. Think of it! We get to help it happen. Our love bombs, our prayers, our words of encouragement, our ability to bear up under pressure, our belief in the goodness of God in the midst of a dry and thirsty land. He can make a desert bloom. He can pour water from a rock. Remember Who He is. Remember what He's done. He has conquered the world for us. He's deprived it of power to harm us. We have the armor of God, and the weapons of our warfare are mighty through Him. We overcome by the blood of the Lamb and the word of our testimony, and greater is He that is in us than He that is in the world.

Let us not forget what we've been given. Let us remember the true nature of the battle and not aim our weapons at other people. We wrestle not with flesh and blood. It's a war of multiple dimensions on many fronts with supernatural things going on. We are called for this time. We are built for this time. We are designed for it. And whatever way God has equipped you with your personality and your experiences and your understanding, your heritage, where you live, where you're positioned in time and place—there is something only you can do and no one can do it better. He'll show you. Ask Him.

The Holy Spirit is within us, real, powerful, gracious, wise. He provides everything we need to get to the finish line and bring God glory, even if we're broken or burned or locked up. The Christian life goes far beyond our time on Earth, but while we're here, He gives power to the faint and to them who have no might He increases strength. They that wait upon the Lord shall mount up with wings as eagles. They shall run and not be weary. They shall walk and not faint.

YEA, I AM JESUS—A PROPHECY

"Yea, I am Jesus, the Living One, the One who will fill you till you flow like living streams. I am the One who wants you to know your requests come as a sweet savor. Your requests come to be answered. Your requests come because you have hearts that long for Me. You have hearts that desire to hear Me. You have hearts that will be answered. Your requests shall be answered. Know this: You are the ones. *You* are the ones. If you will walk before Me, if you will know My ways, if you will seek communion in these days, you shall be answered anew. You shall be answered. Yea, I will heal. Even now I am healing. Even now I am healing fully. Believe that which has come. Believe the fullness of it. Take it unto yourself. Accept it. Embrace it. Yea, I tell you, embrace it. Believe. Let your faith run strong. Let your faith run strong. Do not fear to speak forth that which you believe Me for. Speak the word and it will come because I will delight in having answered prayer. I will delight in showing forth My power. Yea, the days are coming when power will be seen once more and it will be My delight to perform it."

Now unto him that is able to do exceeding abundantly above all that we ask or think, according to the power that worketh in us, Unto him be glory in the church by Christ Jesus throughout all ages, world without end. Amen. (Ephesians 3:20-21 KJV)

Acknowledgements

Thank yous to: Carol and Debra for praying me through this process and pulling me out of the ditch when necessary.

Friends and family who contributed their stories to this book.

Cindy and Darda for getting deep into the text and cleaning it up.

Sandy for emailing me Scriptures that often just happened to match what I was writing that day—fingerprints of God.

Hedy, Angel, Fritz, Brownie, Misha, Cherokee, and Mia—assigned to us by God, each with divine purpose and calling.

Resources

Cynthia Leal Massey's story, ***Language of the Heart,*** was published in the May 2000 issue of *Cricket,* pages 14-19.

***

Forging Ahead For God is Darda Burkhart's biography of her father, Percy E. Wills, with some autobiography sprinkled through it. It is available on Amazon, or from its publisher, Trusted Books; a Division of Deep River Books
www.DeepRiverBooks.com

***

Walking In His Way: aligning with the God of the universe
Carolyn Wing Greenlee

How do we keep our balance when everything is shaking around us? How do we see what's going on the way God sees it? And how do we partner with Him in helping bring about His purposes for this momentous time? There are surprising ways to pray, insights that clarify His values in a world that doesn't understand He has infused each life with purpose, significance, gifts, and destiny.

Available on Amazon

***

Carolyn's books on service dogs:

Steady Hedy: Carolyn's descent into blindness and her 28 days of guide dog school with Hedy. It's where she learned your greatest nightmare can become the source of your deepest healing.

A Gift of Puppies: Twelve interviews with puppy raisers and breeder keepers for service dogs.

A Gift of Dogs: Eleven interviews with Carolyn's classmates and one puppy raiser from her training at Guide Dogs for the Blind.

***

Growing Up Guide Pup

Growing Up Guide Pup was founded by Matthew and Amie Chapman. For the last eleven years their charity has featured seasons of puppy raising videos for service dogs, interviews, and education in Service Dog Puppy Raising, etiquette and law. They're the first service dog organization with a mission focused on Public Education Initiatives and helpful solutions for the industry.

GUGP has five operational programs in their lifelong plan. Currently they have been focused on the first program, the Service Dog Litter Project.

Website is https://growingupguidepup.org

"In Every Service Dog Beats the Heart of a Puppy Raiser"

Made in the USA
Las Vegas, NV
02 February 2022

42862468R00193